GETTING USED TO THE QUIET

Getting Used to the Quiet

Immigrant Adolescents' Journey to Belonging in New Brunswick, Canada

STACEY WILSON-FORSBERG

McGill-Queen's University Press

Montreal & Kingston · London · Ithaca

© McGill-Queen's University Press 2012

ISBN 978-0-7735-3999-0 (cloth)
ISBN 978-0-7735-4000-2 (paper)

Legal deposit second quarter 2012
Bibliothèque nationale du Québec

Printed in Canada on acid-free paper that is 100% ancient forest free
(100% post-consumer recycled), processed chlorine free

This book has been published with the help of a grant from the
Canadian Federation for the Humanities and Social Sciences, through
the Aid to Scholarly Publications Program, using funds provided by
the Social Sciences and Humanities Research Council of Canada.

McGill-Queen's University Press acknowledges the support of the
Canada Council for the Arts for our publishing program. We also
acknowledge the financial support of the Government of Canada
through the Canada Book Fund for our publishing activities.

Library and Archives Canada Cataloguing in Publication

Wilson-Forsberg, Stacey, 1972–

    Getting used to the quiet : immigrant adolescents' journey to
belonging in New Brunswick, Canada / Stacey Wilson-Forsberg.

Includes bibliographical references and index.
ISBN 978-0-7735-3999-0 (bound). – ISBN 978-0-7735-4000-2 (pbk.)

    1. Teenage immigrants – New Brunswick – Social conditions.
2. Teenage immigrants – Services for – New Brunswick. 3. Teenage
immigrants – New Brunswick – Interviews. 4. Immigrants – Cultural
assimilation – New Brunswick. I. Title.

HV4013.C2W54 2012   305.23086'912097151   C2012-900171-6

Typeset by Jay Tee Graphics Ltd. in 10.5/13 Sabon

*To my dear friends and families in Fresnillo, Zacatecas
who inspired me to tell this story.*

*A mis queridos amigos y familias en Fresnillo, Zacatecas
quienes me inspiraron para contar esta historia.*

Contents

Acknowledgments

Many people have supported me throughout the process of researching and writing this book. I am especially grateful to Margaret Conrad who supervised my PhD dissertation and gave freely of her time and energy, even after retirement, to make me a better researcher and scholar, and to Donald Desserud, Doug Willms, Fernando Nunes, and Andy Scott for their comments on the original dissertation. I would like to thank Mark Abley at McGill-Queen's University Press who was immensely helpful in shepherding my manuscript through the review, revision, and funding processes, and also Kathryn Simpson for her attention to detail during copyediting and Ryan Van Huijstee for finalizing the book's publication.

Thank you to the people in Fredericton and Florenceville-Bristol who made this research possible by recruiting participants for the study and providing me with valuable information about immigration, the communities, and the schools. And to the young participants, the thirty-three immigrant adolescents who took part in my interviews and focus groups, thank you so much for telling me your stories. I would like to acknowledge the anonymous reviewers at McGill-Queen's University Press whose comments helped make this a much better book. The book has been published with the help of a grant from the Canadian Federation for the Humanities and Social Sciences, through the Aid to Scholarly Publications Program, using funds provided by the Social Sciences and Humanities Research Council of Canada (SSHRC), as well as Wilfrid Laurier University through a Research Office book preparation grant. I am further indebted to SSHRC for funding my research along with the Canadian Research Institute for Social Policy (CRISP-UNB).

Thank you to my parents Doug and Helen Wilson for their continuous encouragement and support. To my family, which expanded by one member as this book was being written, I send my deepest gratitude. Patrik, Rosemarie, and Serlina, your patience, love, and understanding will never be forgotten.

All participants under the age of nineteen whose stories appear in this book have been given pseudonyms to protect their identities, while participants over the age of nineteen have provided permission to use their real names. Permission has been obtained to use all of the interview material that appears in this book.

GETTING USED TO THE QUIET

1

This is Our Home

Origins, Theory, and Method

"It's a good thing you arrived at night," says Lili as she opens the heavy door of the Suburban truck and helps me in.

"Why?" I ask.

"So you won't be able to see anything, of course," she says.

"Oh," I respond.

I recall this scene over and over again as I draw pictures in the thin layer of red dust that is forming on my metal desk. I didn't understand what she meant at the time, but knew it couldn't be good. It did not take long to realize that this town was not the paradise of travel brochures.

The wind blows through the cracked window compromising the warmth of the morning sun. My legs are freezing as I try to no avail to pull my navy knee socks up to meet the frayed edge of my grey skirt. With the tip of my index finger I outline the town's boxy concrete buildings crowned by crimson Coca Cola signs, and its square clay houses left to peel and crumble in the dry desert heat. I think the teacher is lecturing about history. I catch a word here and there, but most I do not understand. In my classes at Fredericton High School I asked a lot of questions, and received more than one detention for talking too much. But here I am silenced. Thirty eager bodies sporting the same school attire surround me, yet I am isolated. At recess my classmates huddle around me, they pass me a warm knitted sweater, and share ham sandwiches and stale cookies from their lunch boxes. They smile and talk to me, showing no sign of patience lost by my broken sentences.

After school I walk home by myself through crowded, grimy streets. Shoe shiners, street vendors, and taxi drivers, all in their allotted spots, nod and say hello. Pig skin bubbles in a caldron of oil, its greasy odour mixing in the air with the aromas of diesel, sewage, and rotten fruit; a cacophonous symphony of ranchero, mariachi, and Casey Casum's American Top Forty resounds from storefront loud speakers. As I walk I am aware that people are watching me. They know who I am and I feel protected and safe.

As an exchange student in Mexico twenty years ago I saw poverty and wealth, and I learned about identity and belonging. I watched, listened, and gradually began to understand the norms and routines of a society unlike my own. And in that messy, ambiguous process of meaning-making that is part of embracing a new language, I learned the expression "*aqui tienes tu casa*," – "this is your home." Economic development and aesthetic challenges notwithstanding, that small community in the arid desert of north central Mexico apparently had the resources to facilitate my inclusion and sense of belonging. Perhaps they knew I was not planning to stay forever. Perhaps I was a novelty, a sun-burned face in a *mestizo* town. But since that positive experience in my adolescence, I have been deeply interested in how citizens in small cities and towns in Canada mobilize to welcome their young immigrants, and how they incorporate these newcomers into initiatives to change their communities for the better.

Immigrants are permanent residents born outside the country where they live. There are three official categories of immigrants in Canada: (1) Economic immigrants, who are independent immigrants and their immediate family members and selected on the basis of a point system. They include skilled labourers, entrepreneurs, and investors, many of whom are now nominated by provinces through provincial nominee agreements with the federal government; (2) Family class immigrants, who are family members sponsored by permanent residents and Canadian citizens; and (3) Refugees, who are admitted to Canada on humanitarian grounds. They include assisted refugees and internally displaced people, as well as refugee claimants. Temporary migrants, including foreign workers and international students, form a fourth category often included in discussions of immigration to Canada. They do not arrive as "immigrants," but once in Canada many of these people apply for permanent resident status.

Immigration policy in Canada is more than simply a process of importing the labour needed for nation-building. It is also an expression of a political idea of who is, or could be, eligible to receive the entitlements of permanent residence and citizenship.[1] It is a highly utilitarian system whereby immigrants who are selected on the basis of educational and occupational skills through a point system are deemed to be more productive than those admitted for family relations or humanitarian considerations.[2] The benchmark of immigrants' integration into Canadian society is often economic – to the extent to which immigrants earn as much as native-born Canadians they are deemed economically well-integrated and productive.[3]

Immigrant adolescents are also by definition permanent residents born outside the country. Adolescence (ages twelve to twenty) is a period of transition in the life course as older children strive to become independently functioning adults, and to meet evolving personal, educational, and career-related needs. It is an awkward time in the life cycle for immigration to occur. While many immigrant adolescents adapt well to Canada and ultimately go on to live comfortable and fulfilled lives, research suggests that the difficulties faced by adolescents in moving to adulthood become compounded by the immigration experience. Immigrant adolescents must adjust to a new culture and, often, a new language, as well as to new surroundings, while simultaneously balancing the contradictory expectations of both family and peers. Their inability to adapt successfully to the norms of society can result in problems at school and can create a greater risk for delinquency and depression.[4] At the same time, these adolescents can be remarkably resilient. Despite high levels of socioeconomic risk factors, immigrant youth generally have better health behaviours and higher academic achievement than their native-born peers.[5]

The Canadian-born children of immigrants are not immigrants themselves, but rather Canadian citizens or what is perhaps erroneously termed "second-generation immigrants." The challenges of fitting in or belonging to a community faced by second-generation adolescents are different from those faced by immigrant adolescents, and hence they are not the focus of this book. Second-generation adolescents still have to struggle with such circumstances as racism and exclusion, despite their often mainstream appearance and behaviour, but unlike their immigrant peers they have experienced migration only indirectly through their parents' struggles.[6] Immigrant adolescents, on the contrary, are purely immigrant. They have spent a significant part of their formative years in another country and have moved to the receiving country as adolescents.[7] These youth form a diverse group. Some are the children of highly educated professional parents who immigrated to Canada by choice or by force; others have parents who are illiterate, low-skilled, and struggling in the lowest paid sectors of the service economy.

From a human capital perspective, investment in adolescents, who will become adults in the near future, deserves special attention. As Canada increasingly relies on immigration to replenish the labour force, the success of immigrant adolescents represents an important ingredient for the country's economic future. Their success is also important from a community development perspective. A growing body of research shows that involvement in the community gives youth the opportunity to help shape local life, while at the same time gaining important protective factors and achieving mastery in social competence, problem solving, autonomy, and sense of purpose.[8] If immigrant adolescents feel accepted as members of a community they may be more likely to meet supportive people, develop social networks, and acquire valuable social skills within the community.[9]

As a researcher, I chose to focus on the integration experiences of immigrant adolescents in New Brunswick for several reasons: (1) There are no published studies that focus specifically on the experiences of this age-group of immigrants in the province and only a handful that look at immigrant adolescents outside of Toronto, Montreal, and Vancouver;[10] (2) Over the years I have become acquainted with immigrant adolescents in Fredericton through volunteer work with the Multicultural Association of Fredericton and the YMCA, and I have observed how challenging their integration into the community can be; (3) While a year abroad as an exchange student at the age of seventeen is a different experience than a new life abroad as a young immigrant, I can nevertheless relate to the emotional journey of adjusting to a new culture and language; and (4) I felt this age group was more likely to lead me to the more informal or intangible social resources that exist in a community. My conversations with immigrants in Fredericton over the years suggested that immigrant adults are focused on economic integration. Naturally, they want to have their foreign educational qualifications and professional credentials recognized, find good jobs, and support their families. Immigrant adolescents tend to stress social integration, such as the need to fit in or belong, the challenge of making friends, and the search for adult role models in a community.

THE WELCOMING COMMUNITY

Researchers pay substantial attention to the role that ethnic networks play in the integration of individual immigrants into society, but they take it for granted that immigrants are settling in cities large enough to attract and accommodate a critical mass of people from the same ethnic background.[11] In the small communities found in New Brunswick and throughout Atlantic Canada, most immigrants and their children still lack substantial pre-existing ethnic networks to support them. The research discussed in this book is based on the assumption that small receiving communities can best fill this void by collectively welcoming and assisting these newcomers. Receiving communities play a critical role in determining whether immigrants will become full participating members of society or whether they will remain on the margins, where they are unable to share the society's resources or contribute to community development to the fullest extent possible.[12] Cultivating relationships with local residents may assist in anchoring immigrants in the new community and forming their identity as part of that community.[13]

Like other provincial population initiatives across Canada, New Brunswick's Population Growth Action Plan emphasizes building "welcoming communities" to integrate immigrants into the social and economic fabric of society.[14] The action plan does not explain what constitutes a welcoming community beyond friendly citizens and the provision of "needs-based" or "client-focused" settlement and integration services. The Immigrant Settlement and Adaptation Program is funded by Citizenship and Immigration Canada and delivered by non-governmental organizations throughout the province.[15] This umbrella program includes Language Instruction for Newcomers to Canada (LINC), which provides language instruction in English or French to all recently arrived immigrants; the Resettlement Assistance program, which provides financial support to government-assisted refugees for up to one year after arrival; and the Host program, whereby volunteers help newcomers to adapt and integrate into Canadian life. In addition, the non-governmental organizations provide translation, health, and social service referrals, and employment-related services (Citizenship and Immigration Canada 2001). Some of them also run summer camps, homework clubs, music classes, youth groups, and other activities for immigrant adolescents. The federal and provincial governments are aware that a welcoming community consists of a whole layer of resources beyond the provision of such formal programs and services; however, that layer is more informal and therefore difficult to describe and measure.

The book borrows the concept of social infrastructure from the literature on adolescent development and community development to describe the relationship being built between immigrant adolescents and the receiving community. *Social infrastructure* consists of community resources and social networks capable of facilitating an individual or group's inclusion and sense of belonging.[16] For adolescents, social infrastructure includes safe places to go to after school, recreational and competency-building activities, and adult connections.[17] *Entrepreneurial social infrastructure* is a community development model that determines which forms of social organization best mobilize collective action in a community, including: acceptance of diversity, inclusiveness, and quality social networks.[18] The book distinguishes between "formal social infrastructure" (community resources such as settlement and integration programs, and education and services received in the school system) and "informal social infrastructure" (engaged citizens, collective action, social capital, and social networks), and pays particular attention to the latter. In their research on community development in rural United States, Jan Flora and colleagues (1991) found that communities that succeeded at community development were those whose social organization was conducive to high levels of social capital, social networks, engaged citizens, and collective action. By changing specific aspects of their social organization, communities that had previously not engaged in development efforts were often able to bring about concrete economic change through community-based activities.

PURPOSE OF THE BOOK

Using an adaptation of the Floras' entrepreneurial social infrastructure model, *Getting Used to the Quiet* looks more closely at the welcoming community in the context of integrating immigrant adolescents in a small city and rural town in New Brunswick where there are no earlier non-European immigrant communities to which the newcomers can affix themselves. I embarked on this research with the orienting idea that a welcoming community is one whose social organization is conducive to high levels of informal social infrastructure. In other words, both the adaptation and integration of immigrant adolescents in a community depend upon the resources or mechanisms in place to engender collective action by the citizens of that community. If citizens can work together to achieve the goal of community development, perhaps they can also work together to create the optimal social conditions for integrating immigrant adolescents.

The purpose of this book is therefore to examine how engaged citizens in New Brunswick set in motion social capital and social networks to create the necessary conditions to support an important aspect of the adaption and integration of immigrant adolescents: sense of belonging. If young immigrants feel they do not have membership in the communities where they reside, this may indicate that these communities lack the social infrastructure to facilitate their adaption and integration, or the communities may have relatively plentiful citizen engagement, social networks, and other social resources, yet somehow fail to connect immigrant adolescents with them.

Adaptation and integration are terms used by cross-cultural psychologist John W. Berry in his ongoing research to answer the practical question: What happens to individuals who have developed in one cultural context, when they attempt to live in a new cultural context (i.e., acculturation)? *Adaptation* in its most general sense refers to changes that take place in individuals or groups in response to environmental demands.[19] Depending on a variety of factors, which will be discussed in the subsequent chapters, adaptation can result in an increased "fit" between the individual and the new cultural context. At this point the individual *assimilates* (i.e., gradually takes on the values, attributes, and social customs of the receiving society to the extent that he or she becomes indistinguishable from the majority population) or the individual *integrates* (i.e., becomes an active member of the receiving community, yet simultaneously maintains a distinct ethnic identity).[20] Integration involves connecting immigrants with their new communities by striving to include them in institutions and activities. Sometimes, however, a fit is not achieved due to *segregation* (i.e., the individual maintains a distinct ethnic identity and refuses – or is refused – active participation in the larger society), or *marginalization* (i.e., there is little possibility or interest in cultural maintenance – often for reasons of enforced cultural loss

– and little interest in having relations with others – often for reasons of exclusion or discrimination).[21]

The immigration literature has generally shown integration to be the most adaptive mode of acculturation, and the most conducive to fostering a sense of belonging and positive ethnic identity.[22] An assumption garnered from much of this literature is that integrated immigrants are more likely to become involved in the receiving community, establish social networks, build social capital and, as a result, stay put. The key to immigrant integration and retention, beyond finding good jobs, is engaged citizens in a "welcoming community." Governments, scholars, practitioners, and entire communities across Canada have embraced these ideas, but to date, there is little empirical evidence to support them.[23]

Although the findings presented throughout this book point to a desire in the two case communities to keep immigrant adolescents and their families there for as long as possible – primarily for economic motives – my objective is not to equate integration and belonging with retention. Qualitative research cannot be used to find that kind of causal effect. Furthermore, with the exception of evidence from the Longitudinal Survey of Immigrants to Canada,[24] which demonstrated that a large majority (87 per cent) of newcomers choose to settle in Canadian cities where relatives or friends already reside, no quantitative study to my knowledge demonstrates a causal relationship between sense of belonging and retention. Undoubtedly immigrants and native residents alike remain in a city or town for a variety of reasons, sense of belonging being only one of them. Instead, *Getting Used to the Quiet* examines how the immigrant adolescents gradually become involved and gain membership in the receiving communities by making connections with peers and adults across groups. The immigrant adolescent participants, in their statements about belonging or not belonging, mention feelings of happiness and optimism (or conversely, loneliness and pessimism), but the data presented in the subsequent chapters support only their involvement in the communities and their ability to build relationships with peers and adults outside of their own small ethnic groups.

The book poses a new set of questions about the immigrant experience as it relates to New Brunswick: How do the actions of engaged citizens of a community factor into immigrant adolescents' sense of belonging? What is the relative weight of formal services and programs for immigrant adolescents compared with the more intangible and informal actions of engaged citizens in a community? In other words, do young immigrants have to be included in formal activities and community structures or is it more important to make them *feel* like they belong in some larger sense? How is social infrastructure for immigrant adolescents affected by socio-demographic characteristics such as class, gender, and race? And, is the social infrastructure the same in an urban and rural setting? I ask these guiding questions in case studies of two communities: Fredericton, the provincial capital of New Brunswick, and Florenceville, a small village in the western part of the province, which as this research began in May 2008, was in the process of amalgamating with the neighbouring village of Bristol to become the town of Florenceville-Bristol. The themes and sub-themes described in the subsequent chapters are based on qualitative data collected over an eleven month period (2008–09) through sustained contact with people in the settings where they normally spend their time.

IMMIGRATION TO NEW BRUNSWICK

The cities and towns of New Brunswick are attractive settings to study the effects of engaged, attentive citizens on young immigrants' sense of belonging to a community because, until recently, these places remained relatively untouched by immigration from countries outside of Europe and the United States. At one time New Brunswick was keenly interested in population growth and had relatively stable flows of immigrants. In the period between 1815 and 1850, for example, its attractive agricultural land and forest industries helped to make New Brunswick "the first destination of emigrants eager to settle in North America."[25] In the early decades after Confederation, New Brunswick attracted domestics, skilled workers, and farm workers from Great Britain, Denmark, Sweden, and other European countries. According to Margaret Conrad and Heather Steel, "despite the uneven record of success, the period between 1867 and 1930 witnessed New Brunswick's most energetic efforts to attract immigration to the province."[26] Those energetic efforts waned following 1930.

Canada's population doubled between 1946 and 1990, and immigrants and their children accounted for much of that growth.[27] Of the more than 3,000,000 immigrants who entered Canada in the two-and-a-half decades following the Second World War, only

28,888 stated that they planned to move to New Brunswick. In 1971 a meagre 14,150 remained in the province.[28] "Caught in a vicious cycle of out-migration and underdevelopment, the province in this period failed to move beyond the blinkered view that immigrants had little to offer other than physical labour," writes Heather Steel in her description of New Brunswick immigration policy from 1945 to 1971. "Not surprisingly New Brunswick attracted a small number of immigrants ... and many of them quickly left the province for better economic opportunities and more generous immigrant adjustment programs elsewhere in Canada."[29] Throughout the 1970s between 1,000 and 2,000 immigrants per year cited New Brunswick as their intended destination (Citizenship and Immigration Canada 1997). In the early 1980s that number decreased to between 600 and 800 annually and it remained at that level until 2006 (Citizenship and Immigration Canada 2007).

Roughly 1.2 million new immigrants formed the greater part of the national population growth outlined in the 2006 Canadian census. Almost 70 per cent of those immigrants settled in Toronto, Montreal, and Vancouver, with Toronto receiving one third of them. Six other metropolitan areas – Calgary, Ottawa-Gatineau, Edmonton, Winnipeg, Hamilton, and London – accounted for 16.6 per cent of all immigrants between 2001 and 2006 (Statistics Canada 2007). In contrast, during that same time period an estimated 13,500 recent immigrants settled in Atlantic Canada, or 1.2 per cent of the immigrants who arrived in Canada (Statistics Canada 2007). The majority of them went to the Halifax metropolitan area. The most common reason immigrants choose to settle in Canada's largest cities (as opposed to the smaller cities and towns of the Atlantic Provinces) according to the Longitudinal Survey of Immigrants to Canada, is to join the social support networks of family and friends (Statistics Canada 2003). These social support networks are also partly responsible for the high levels of secondary migration of immigrants in Atlantic Canada to other parts of the country.

As part of a multifaceted self-sufficiency agenda, the Liberal government of Premier Shawn Graham established the New Brunswick Population Growth Secretariat in 2007 to help reverse population decline and increase the number of people living in the province. At the core of this strategy is the recruitment of 5,000 immigrants annually by 2015 and the retention of 60 per cent of them (Government of New Brunswick 2008). And, indeed, immigration to New

Brunswick has increased since the province put more emphasis on the Provincial Nominee Agreement, which it signed with Ottawa in 1999. This agreement allows New Brunswick to recruit and select prospective immigrants based on provincially designed labour market criteria. In 2006 its annual intake of immigrants doubled from the 600 to 800 of previous years to 1,646. Over half of these newcomers (967) were provincial nominees and their dependents (Citizenship and Immigration Canada 2008).[30] In 2007 the number of immigrants decreased to 1,643, of whom 921 were provincial nominees and their dependents. This number then increased to 1,845 immigrants in 2008, 1,199 of whom were provincial nominees and their dependents. By 2009 there were 1,910 immigrants accepted into New Brunswick, 550 of whom were provincial nominees and their dependents, and in 2010 2,125 immigrants entered the province, 770 of whom were provincial nominees and their dependents. New Brunswick also receives approximately 200 government-sponsored refugees each year (that number has remained more or less the same since 1985), and approximately 1,700 temporary foreign workers and 1,400 foreign students each year.

While all of the Atlantic Provinces now have immigration strategies and provincial nominee agreements in place, settlement in New Brunswick is unique. Newfoundland and Labrador, Nova Scotia, and Prince Edward Island all have one metropolitan centre serving as the destination point for most of their immigrants, but immigrants destined for New Brunswick are dispersed among three cities and at least three small towns. The distribution of immigrants, many of whom are members of visible minority groups, throughout the province ensures that the benefits of immigration are more evenly shared by receiving communities. The lack of a single metropolitan centre, however, divides government-sponsored programs for their settlement and integration into smaller portions resulting in fewer financial resources available in each receiving community. It also divides the social support networks of family and friends found in their own small ethnic communities. As Canada's only official bilingual province, moreover, the protection of francophone language, culture, and identity puts New Brunswick in a unique position with respect to immigration in the Atlantic Provinces. Some researchers and policymakers argue that immigration inadvertently reduces the demographic weight of francophone communities in Canada. To maintain their demographic position, these communities need to attract and retain a percentage of immigrants that corresponds to their own demographic weight. Since approximately 33 per cent of New Brunswickers have French as their mother tongue, then 33 per cent of immigrants admitted to New Brunswick should ideally be francophone.

In short, at some point following the Second World War, a shift in approach to immigration occurred in New Brunswick from widespread opposition to the largely uncritical acceptance of the value of immigration to economic development. This assumption has yet to be supported by empirical evidence in New Brunswick – just as lower corporate taxes have not proven to be the solution to economic growth in the province. As demonstrated in the following chapters, it is clear that immigration works for Florenceville-Bristol, but it is less clear for Fredericton (although there is some evidence to show that international students contribute to the city's education budgets).

Immigrants to New Brunswick now come from, among other source countries, China, South Korea, Egypt, Iran, and Colombia, but their small numbers have thus far resulted in little change to the province's homogeneous ethnic make-up. New Brunswick's level of ethnic, cultural, and linguistic diversity of about 3 per cent of the population remains significantly below the 2006 Census figure of 19.8 per cent for Canada as a whole (Statistics Canada 2007). Therefore, as one of the last provinces in Canada to take a sustained interest in immigration in the post-1945 period, New Brunswick now has the opportunity to create the appropriate community conditions to welcome immigrants from around the world. Quality education and good jobs will bring immigrants to the province, but they do not take the place of culture, community involvement, and sense of belonging. Without those conditions, without that feeling of being at home in the community, relationships between immigrants and established residents will not be cultivated.

SETTINGS AND SAMPLE

Fredericton is changing. One only has to go to the local supermarket on a Saturday afternoon or to the stationary store during the first week back to school in September to see that cultural diversity is much more prominent in the city than it was only two or three years ago. Described by Bruce Hutchison as "the last surviving Home Town in America, uncorrupted and innocent as your grandmother, rocking on her porch chair,"[31] and by the *New York Times* travel columnist Katherine Ashenburg as a refined, charming, sophisticated little city whose "strongly British character has persisted through successive incarnations as a Loyalist settlement, a garrison town, and the capital of an out-of-the-way, traditionally have-not province,"[32] Fredericton is divided into north and south by the curve of the St John River. The north side of Fredericton has traditionally been home to working class and poorer neighbourhoods, with much of the city's infrastructure (and money) located on the south side of the river. The St John River generates a subtle mindset in Fredericton that tends to keep people on their selected side – with north-siders crossing the bridge for work, school, and shopping, and south-siders often finding no reason to venture across the river at all. In recent years, however, new housing developments on the city's north side have swelled, accompanied by a new high school and shopping and recreational facilities, all of which have diminished the north side south side debate. Fredericton had a 2006 population of 50,535 within the city limits, and a census agglomeration of 85,688 (Statistics Canada 2007). Its major employers are the provincial civil service, the retail sector, two universities, the healthcare sector, and a growing number of knowledge-based information technology companies (Statistics Canada 2007).

Historically largely anglophone and racially homogeneous, Fredericton gradually became more bilingual following the passing of the Official Languages Act by the Liberal Government of Premier Louis Robichaud in 1969. Over the years the city has also become more multicultural, particularly during the school year when some 1,000 international university students are in town. Fredericton receives slightly fewer immigrants than the larger city of Moncton and slightly more than Saint John. I chose it as a case study because of the diversity of its immigrant population. I could easily have focused on Moncton or Saint John given their similar immigration levels and numbers of international students. However, when possible, Moncton prioritizes the attraction and retention of francophone immigrants – a test my limited French could not pass during participant interviews – and as a native of Fredericton, I felt I did not know enough about Saint John's socio-historical context to bring justice to a detailed case study. While some of my research findings from Fredericton would be characteristic of any small city in New Brunswick and across Canada, others are unique to Fredericton. Immigrant adolescents in Saint John, for example, would likely tell a substantially different story about their experiences in the community.

Fredericton diverges from the statistical portrait of New Brunswick portrayed by the 2006 census. In 2006 there were nearly 6,000 immigrants in Fredericton. While 3.7 per cent of New Brunswick's population was foreign-born in 2006, the percentage of foreign-born people in Fredericton was 6.9 per cent (Statistics Canada 2009). The immigrants arrive under all three immigration categories, though the majority are now provincial nominees and their dependents. Fredericton also benefits from international students since some of these temporary migrants find full-time employment in the city following graduation from the University of New Brunswick (UNB) or St Thomas University.

The diversity in categories of immigrants arriving in Fredericton has resulted in a more culturally diverse city. Although most immigrants to the province still come from the traditional source areas of the United States and Europe, more immigrants in Fredericton come from China, Latin America, West Africa, the Middle East, and more recently, since the 2006 census, from South Korea (Citizenship and Immigration Canada 2008). At the time of data collection Fredericton was home to approximately 350 immigrant adolescents, according to the New Brunswick Department of Education. My case study of the community involved the participation of twenty of these adolescents: two of them are the adolescent children of economic immigrant parents who were hired by local information technology companies; five are the adolescent children of parents who were given permanent residence through the New Brunswick Provincial Nominee program; ten are the adolescent children of government-sponsored refugees who, having escaped violence and persecution in their home countries, were placed in Fredericton; and three are international students who plan to remain in the province after graduation. Together these teens form a varied group representing a variety of source countries and a variety of cultural, linguistic, and socio-economic backgrounds.

An afternoon sipping coffee while writing notes at the local Tim Hortons donut shop provides a perfect portrait of cultural diversity in the second community studied: Florenceville-Bristol. At four o'clock in the afternoon the coffee shop is busy. Elderly men in denim overalls and work boots sit amongst retired couples. They break conversations to bite into honey crullers and wave an occasional hello to processing plant workers who order their coffee and leave. The women behind the counter chat with the customers as they pour coffee and toast bagels. They are dressed in regulatory beige Tim Hortons shirts and long modest skirts, their heads topped with large netted hair buns. Just after five o'clock a whole new group of customers appear: men and women in stylish dress pants and shirts wearing Global Technology Centre credentials around their necks. The room becomes louder and English conversations are gradually overtaken by Spanish ones.

Florenceville's population increased from 800 to 1,500 when it amalgamated with Bristol in 2008. Florenceville-Bristol is a small rural town tucked into the hills of the Upper St John River Valley. It is one of a series of towns and villages in the potato-farming region of Carleton County. For more than fifty years Florenceville has been home to the headquarters of McCain Foods, Ltd, which was established in 1957 and is the world's largest producer of French fries, as well as a multinational leader in frozen food products. McCain Foods, Ltd is the main employer in the Florenceville-Bristol area. The privately owned corporation employs over 2,000 people in its various farming, manufacturing, and professional support divisions in Florenceville, and 20,000 people in fifty-seven factories around the world. The McCain family name is painted on many public buildings and when the wind is blowing in the right direction the scent of french-fried potatoes fills the air. While McCain Foods, Ltd makes the community economically viable and relatively self-sufficient, it also stratifies much of the population into a tidy hierarchical labour force consisting of owners and managers, international business and information technology professionals, potato researchers, processing plant workers, and long-haul truck drivers, along with well-established farmers who sell potatoes and seeds to the corporation.

I selected Florenceville-Bristol as a case study for a very practical reason: it is the only small rural town in New Brunswick with enough immigrants in the age group I wished to study. The expansion of McCain Foods, Ltd in recent years has attracted immigrants from around the world. In 2006 about 145 immigrants lived in Florenceville and the surrounding areas of Bristol, Centreville, and Bath, and a total of 325 immigrants lived in Carleton County. Approximately 7.5 per cent of residents in Florenceville-Bristol were foreign-born in 2006, and 10 per cent of residents were foreign-born in the county as a whole (Statistics Canada 2009). Most of these immigrants came from India and the United States. Thirty-five of them were temporary residents working mainly as long-haul truck drivers (Statistics Canada 2009). Immigration numbers changed substantially after the census was conducted in May 2006 as McCain Foods, Ltd began to rely on economic (mainly provincially nominated) immigrants to fill highly skilled information technology positions at its Global Technology Centre.[33] Between 2006 and 2009, for example, approximately ten families from Colombia settled in the Florenceville-Bristol area, along with families from Mexico, Moldova, and the Ukraine. The one-industry nature of Florenceville-Bristol gives it unique characteristics, such as better physical infrastructure (a public library and art gallery in such a small town are rare), a longer history of welcoming foreign workers and their families, and more experience with cultural and linguistic diversity. The prominence of a large multi-national corporation in the small community affects the daily lives of the immigrant adolescents, but it does not take away from the community's rurality or the fact that people know one another, depend upon one another, and share many common goals and relationships.

While both Fredericton and Florenceville-Bristol are culturally diverse, the difference between the two communities is that there are no refugees in Florenceville-Bristol. The immigrants, excluding temporary foreign workers, in this small town are a relatively homogeneous group of middle class or aspiring-to-be-middle-class families. Florenceville-Bristol, at the time of data collection, was home to fourteen immigrant adolescents. Thirteen of these teens participated in my research. With the exception of two international students from South Korea, all other eleven participants are the adolescent children of an economically or provincially nominated parent or parents from Colombia, India, Mexico, and Moldova. These teens form a more homogeneous group than their counterparts in Fredericton. Many of them speak a common language – Spanish – and are even from the same city – Medellín, Colombia – and all but the two Korean teens have at least one parent working at the Global Technology Centre.

A total of eighty-five voluntary participants took part in the case studies of Fredericton and Florenceville-Bristol. They were divided into six groups: (1) Immigrant adolescents who had arrived in the communities between 2003 and 2009 (See Appendix Tables 1 and 7);

(2) New Brunswick-born adolescents living in the two communities (Tables 2 and 8); (3) Immigrant adults who had arrived as adolescents from 1989 onward and have stayed in the communities (Tables 3 and 9); (4) Immigrant adults who had arrived as adolescents from 1989 onward and subsequently left the communities (Tables 4 and 10); (5) Members, staff, and volunteers in community organizations who provide services to or are familiar with the immigrant populations in their respective community (Tables 5 and 11); and (6) Residents of the communities who have more informal contact with immigrant adolescents or no contact at all (Tables 6 and 12). The twenty immigrant adolescents in Fredericton consisted of ten boys and ten girls between the ages of twelve and twenty from Belgium, Colombia, Congo, Guatemala, Iran, Indonesia, Liberia, the Netherlands, Sierra Leone, South Korea, Taiwan, Venezuela, and Vietnam, and the thirteen immigrant adolescents in Florenceville-Bristol consisted of five boys and eight girls between the ages of thirteen and twenty from Colombia, India, Mexico, Moldova, and South Korea.

Because immigrants and community organization members were not available in sufficient numbers to be meaningful under random sampling techniques, participants were identified through purposive sampling and invited to take part in the case studies. Purposive sampling does not aim to produce a statistically representative sample of a population, or to draw statistical inference. Rather, it ensures that individuals displaying certain attributes such as ethnicity, mother tongue, age, gender, race, immigrant classification, and socioeconomic status are included in the case study.[34] The problem with purposive sampling is that the types of people who are available and willing to participate in the study may be different from other members of the population who cannot be located, and this might introduce a source of bias. For example, immigrant adolescent participants in Fredericton were found and recruited through the schools, universities, religious centres (primarily churches, but also the Fredericton community Mosque), and the Multicultural Association. It is possible that at the time of data collection there were immigrants between the ages of twelve and twenty residing in the city who were not in school, university, or church, and who did not participate in multicultural association activities.[35]

The exceptions to the purposive sampling technique were the immigrant adolescents in Florenceville-Bristol – since their numbers were so small I invited all fourteen immigrant adolescents residing in the

Florenceville-Bristol area to participate in the research (one was not available to be interviewed) – and the local residents in Florenceville-Bristol, who were selected randomly. Despite small numbers, there is a wide range of immigrants in the two case communities and this is the representation I sought to achieve when selecting my participants. Overall, I see my sample as neither tightly controlled, nor scientific, but rather, as a thoughtful and purposive process. My aim for the research, moreover, has not been to generalize findings from this sample to the wider population of immigrant adolescents in this province or across Canada. Any generalizations of the research findings are made to theory rather than to people.

In Fredericton the recruitment of adult participants was relatively straightforward. No one refused to be interviewed and some of the community organization members spent an entire morning or afternoon with me. The purposive sampling technique in Fredericton caused a snowball effect among community organization members and local residents, with each interview resulting in a new list of potential participants. The process of identifying potential adolescent participants, inviting them to participate in the study, distributing disposable cameras, receiving parental and individual informed consent, and scheduling an interview or focus group took a great deal of time in Fredericton (eight months in all). I recruited over half of the twenty volunteer participants at religious centres, the University of New Brunswick, and the Multicultural Association. In the fall of 2008 I received permission from the local school district to conduct my research in the two high schools and four middle schools in Fredericton.[36] I went to the schools several times, introduced myself to the students, and distributed disposable cameras and consent forms, but in the end only one student came forth to participate. History teachers at Leo Hayes High School took an interest in my research during the winter semester of 2009. At that time, I discovered that the key to recruiting adolescent participants is working with the teachers and arranging to interview the students during class time. I recruited four immigrant adolescent participants at Leo Hayes High School and six New Brunswick-born adolescents.

The recruitment of participants was much faster and smoother in Florenceville-Bristol. McCain Foods, Ltd, the Multicultural Association of Carleton County (MACC), Carleton North High School, and Florenceville Middle School all agreed to participate in the research before I ever entered the community. The Director of Human

Resources at the McCain Global Technology Centre and his international recruiter contacted all immigrant employees with children in the age group I wished to study. With the majority of parents aware of the research, I proceeded to meet with the principals and Guidance Counsellors at the schools, who in turn introduced me to all of the immigrant adolescents and arranged interviews with them. I returned one week later to the schools and interviewed thirteen of the fourteen immigrant adolescents over a four-day period. With no immigrant adults meeting the condition of having arrived in the community as adolescents and remaining there, I was able to identify, recruit, and interview over the phone two immigrant adults who were attending universities outside of the province. All community organization members in Florenceville-Bristol were invited to participate in the study, and local residents were selected randomly in public locales.

THE DATA

Interviews with participants to elicit their views and opinions were my primary research method in each community. A total of sixty-five interviews were conducted in Fredericton and Florenceville-Bristol. All were semi-structured, with the questions open-ended and flexible enough to allow respondents to elaborate on points of interest. Participants were asked broad, open-ended questions related to their involvement in the community, programs and services available for immigrant adolescents, adult role models, knowing one's neighbours, making friends, the acceptance of cultural diversity in the community, and whether the community feels like home. Specific questions, probes, and transition messages varied according to each group.

In addition to the sixty-five interviewees, ten New Brunswick-born adolescents also participated in focus groups at the schools. Throughout the focus groups I asked the teens many of the questions designed for their immigrant peers. Asking the same questions allowed me to determine whether or not the experiences and feelings expressed by immigrant adolescents are unique to them or shared by all adolescents. Discussions amongst the New Brunswick-born participants also gave me an idea of how they feel about their immigrant peers, including whether they have formed friendships with them and if and how they are helping their immigrant peers to settle into the schools and communities. The focus group method was further used with ten immigrant adolescents in Fredericton, most of whom had recently arrived as government-sponsored refugees from Africa and South America. While the questions were identical to those asked in semi-structured interviews with immigrant adolescents, I used a variety of techniques to elicit responses, including brain storming sessions and word association games such as "A welcoming community makes me think of ..." and "my ideal community would look like this ..." By stepping back from the role of researcher and acting more as a moderator of the discussions, I gave the teens the opportunity to interact with one another and share ideas.

To complement this verbal data I observed the immigrant adolescent participants as they took part in extracurricular activities in school (Florenceville-Bristol) and at the Multicultural Association (Fredericton), paying particular attention to their interactions with each other and with their New Brunswick-born peers. I also gave the teens disposable cameras and asked them to take photographs of places in their community where they feel most comfortable. Using the photographs as a prop during interview sessions allowed me to prompt discussion by having the participant describe the context of each photograph. The teens were able to take me through the content in the photographs and this helped me to see their own spaces in the community more clearly, as well as their social relationships within those spaces.

All of the participants contributed valuable insights to the research. The passion and candour of the community organization members resulted in long, detailed interview transcripts, while the community residents provided fewer, but thoughtful, remarks on a subject that many of them admitted knowing little about. The immigrant adults who arrived in Fredericton and Florenceville-Bristol when they were young gave me an idea of how community resources and community acceptance have evolved over time. It is the immigrant adolescents, however, who are the central focus of this research. In the course of my investigation I met Abo from Sierra Leone, who aspires to be a famous actor; Caroline from Belgium who has read the *Harry Potter* series in three languages; Musi from the Congo who is notorious for his powerful kicks on the soccer field; Eric from South Korea who hopes to continue singing while at medical school; Heena from India who danced her way to pageant success; and Ale from Colombia who loves the saxophone and fears the yellow school bus that she had "only ever seen in movies."[37] These are but a few examples of the youth who I had the pleasure to speak with. *Getting Used to the Quiet* tells their story and the story of the social infrastructure being built around them.

SOCIAL INFRASTRUCTURE

Leo R. Chavez writes that "in addition to the factors typically used to explain the settlement of immigrants, imagining oneself as part of a local community also has a powerful influence."[38] *Sense of community* or *sense of belonging to a community* is a feeling that citizens have of belonging in a group, and the shared faith that their needs will be met by the commitment to be together.[39] The absence of sense of community has been found to engender feelings of alienation, isolation, and loneliness,[40] while a strong sense of community has been linked to a range of positive outcomes including improved well-being, empowerment, sense of efficacy, life satisfaction, and happiness.[41]

Sense of community has the same relevance for adolescents' well-being as for adults, with the primary predictor of sense of community for adolescents being the number of people from whom they receive support.[42] Adolescents who have a strong sense of belonging to their communities and supportive, varied social networks, who feel safe and can trust those around them, have been found to have pro-social development, reduced criminal behaviour, improved academic performance, and higher retention rates at school.[43] The literature also suggests a strong relationship between belonging to a school community and academic motivation, participation, and achievement.[44] Students who experience a sense of belonging and peer acceptance in school are more likely to enjoy school, to be engaged academically, to participate in school activities, and to persist toward graduation and university.[45]

A substantial body of research supports the notion that, for children and for adolescents in particular, community context matters,[46] and local communities have assets that can be mobilized to support adolescent belonging, identity, and development.[47] The underpinnings of much of this work come from Richard Jessor and Shirley L. Jessor's theoretical writing on problem behaviour and psychosocial development in adolescents, and Urie Bronfenbrenner's ecology of human development (Bronfenbrenner 1979, 2005). Both theories focus on the relevant dimensions of the larger social environment and acknowledge that children do not develop in isolation, but in relation to their family, home, school, community, and society. Since adolescents typically spend a good deal of time away from their homes in the neighbourhood and wider community, explanations of community influences based on peers, role models, schools, and other neighbourhood-based resources would appear to be more relevant for them than for younger children.[48] Bronfenbrenner defined *development* as lasting and continuous change in the way a person perceives and deals with the environment.[49] For Bronfenbrenner, a stable environment is especially important to healthful development throughout childhood and adolescence. *Migration*, in contrast, defined as the geographical relocation of people, is a destabilizing condition for children who must learn to cope not only with the stresses of growing up, but also of moving. Migration is a type of ecological transition that involves change in the social, cultural, and physical environment of the child.[50]

The programmed aspects of community social infrastructure for adolescents include the quality and content of education received in the school system, as well as the kinds of services – recreational and educational – that are available to youth within the community at large. Structured activities during non-school hours, for example, do more than fill idle time and keep adolescents out of trouble. As Jodie L. Roth and Jeanne Brooks-Gunn describe, "youth development programs foster positive development by providing opportunities for youth to nurture their interests and talents, practice new skills, and gain a sense of personal or group recognition."[51] When optimally designed, these activities place strong emphasis on continuity and predictability;[52] they allow adolescents to draw on positive role models, encouragement, support, and advice;[53] and they provide a strong sense of membership, commitment, explicit rules and responsibilities, and expectations for adolescents' success.[54]

Social infrastructure for immigrant adolescents is in place in the formal sense in Fredericton, and though under-funded and at times overwhelmed, this infrastructure continues to develop and mature. Studies show that religious practice acts as a protective influence allowing first generation immigrant youth to maintain higher levels of well-being than their native-born peers of similar demographic and family backgrounds.[55] In accordance with this literature, churches and other religious centres are an important social support for the immigrant adolescents who participated in the case study of Fredericton, with over half of them stating that they are Christian and attend church, or that the church has welcomed their families. Religion plays a big role in the lives of many Fredericton residents. The city and surrounding rural areas have over 125 churches, including several Anglican, Roman Catholic, and Protestant churches of assorted denominations. Three of the Central and South American boys say they occasionally attend Mass at St Dunstan's Roman Catholic Church, the West African teens spoke enthusiastically about their involvement in Sunset Drive Pentecostal Church, and the three girls from East Asia are very active in the activities of the Meeting Place and the Brunswick Street Baptist Church. Some of Fredericton's churches are associated with specific Christian ethnic communities. The First Wesleyan Church, for example, lends the building to the Korean community on Sunday afternoons, where members hold their own service with a Korean pastor; St Dunstan's Church has a large Central American congregation; and several Chinese and Korean families attend Brunswick Street Baptist Church. The latter is also known for its volunteer efforts to resettle refugees in the city. Wilmont United Church works at the national level to promote the involvement of diverse cultures in the United Church of Canada and the Meeting Place reaches out to international students, holding a Sunday morning service on the UNB campus.

Fredericton also has a Synagogue, Hindu Temple, Mosque, Shambhala Buddhist Centre, and a Baha'i Faith Centre. Two of the immigrant adolescents who participated in the case study are Muslim. One attends the Fredericton Mosque and says she is "somewhat active" in the local Islamic Association, while the other, despite being Muslim, prefers to attend Wilmont United Church with his neighbours. Ethno-cultural associations such as the Chinese Cultural Association, the Korean Association, and the Islamic Association offer language and music classes to this age group, in some cases combined with lessons on religion; they also involve the teens in organizing community events, and in public outreach activities. Within the wider community, youth activities such as dance and basketball at the local YMCA appeal to some of the immigrant adolescents, and four of the participants attended a Boys and Girls Club when they were younger. For the most part though, the formal programs for immigrant adolescents revolve around the schools and the Multicultural Association of Fredericton.

Formed in 1974, the Multicultural Association of Fredericton (MCAF) plays a vital role in settling and integrating immigrants into the community. The association delivers a suite of Citizenship and Immigration Canada-funded settlement programs, which are designed to assist immigrants with their integration into Canadian life. MCAF is also responsible for public outreach in that it seeks to foster, through educational workshops, publications, and multicultural events, an understanding between New Brunswick-born residents in the community, settled immigrants, and recently arrived immigrants. The association, which is overseen by a board of directors, currently employs ten full-time and twenty part-time staff. It also recruits, trains, and manages several volunteers who through the Host program help immigrants to overcome the stress of moving to a new country by providing moral support, directing them to available services, helping them practice English, and including them in social events and professional networks. Some of the volunteers who speak French are paired with immigrants from French-speaking countries, but MCAF's overall programming is conducted in English (see http://www.mcaf.nb.ca/).

Along with Citizenship and Immigration Canada, MCAF's programs are funded by federal and provincial government departments and by private and community foundation grants.[56] Youth programming is relatively new to MCAF, and only recently has it received a stable funding base. The MCAF youth group gives immigrant adolescents aged twelve to twenty a safe environment in which to socialize and enjoy activities while fostering self-esteem and leadership skills. The group meets on Saturday afternoons for "Youth Blast" which combines fun recreational activities with educational events to promote cultural diversity in the community. Music classes were recently introduced as part of the youth programming, as well as a homework club with volunteer tutors. At one point MCAF had its own soccer team and the youth committee is now working on a program to introduce immigrant adolescents to winter sports.

Schools in Fredericton also play a critical role in making immigrant adolescents feel welcome in the community. Fredericton High School receives the majority of immigrant adolescents in grades 9–12 though their numbers are also increasing at Leo Hayes High School. Younger immigrant adolescents attend four middle schools in the city, and those who wish to complete their schooling in French attend École Sainte Anne. Of the twenty immigrant adolescents who participated in the case study during the 2008–09 school year, five attended Fredericton High School, four attended Leo Hayes High School, two attended Devon Middle School, one attended Albert Street Middle School, and six were at École Sainte Anne.

Fredericton High School has a guidance counsellor who is responsible for "newcomer students" (the term used by the Department of Education to describe both immigrant and international students), and a full-time tutor who helps the teens adjust socially, culturally, and academically to their new school community. The school also shares an "English as an Additional Language" (EAL) teacher with Leo Hayes High School. At the high school level, newcomer students who speak little or no English are placed in an EAL classroom for part of the day (two periods) until they become comfortable enough with the language to move into the academic curriculum in mainstream classrooms. In response to the increasing numbers of immigrant and international students, Fredericton High School introduced an orientation week for newcomer students in September 2009, and has a full-time settlement worker on staff through a collaborative effort with MCAF and the Citizenship Immigration Canada Settlement Workers in the Schools (SWIS) program. The four middle schools also share EAL teachers and some have youth host or "buddy" systems in place that match locally born students with newcomer students.

École Sainte Anne has a full-time settlement worker who oversees the integration of newcomer students into the school community. The settlement worker works closely with MCAF and with the newcomer students' parents in order to understand their current situations at home, their educational backgrounds, and basic cultural aspects of their lives. École Sainte Anne does not place newcomer students in a separate "French as an Additional Language" classroom. The school relies on tutors and resource teachers to enable the students to gradually learn the language. In the classroom, websites are given to the newcomer students to assist them with basic French terms so that they are not lost for the whole class. School administrators and teachers believe that the newcomer students who arrive with little or no fluency in French will slowly adapt to the language by being immersed in the mainstream classrooms and in the school corridors. École Sainte Anne also pairs newcomer students with responsible local students to accompany them between classes. My case study included three older immigrant adolescents who study at UNB. With a long history of attracting international students to its various faculties, UNB is equipped with a full-time international student advisor who works closely with the students as they complete their degrees. A wide array of clubs and associations for international students further smooth their integration into the university community.

Florenceville-Bristol is too small to be able to support programs and services targeted specifically at immigrant adolescents, or even at local adolescents. Outside of the schools, that appear to keep students busy during school hours and in an extracurricular capacity, most organized activities for this age group involve a half-hour commute to the larger town of Woodstock. Although the Multicultural Association of Carleton County in Florenceville-Bristol does not offer youth programming, it nevertheless serves as a valuable social resource for the adolescents, if only indirectly. McCain Foods, Ltd can also be considered a social resource for immigrant adolescents, along with local churches.

The Multicultural Association of Carleton County (MACC) was formed in 2003 by immigrant employees at McCain Foods, Ltd with the initial mandate of facilitating contact and communication between newcomers of different cultural backgrounds and established residents of Florenceville-Bristol. In 2008 MACC began delivering the standard Citizenship and Immigration Canada-funded suite of settlement programs to immigrants, which includes basic levels of English language instruction, employment counselling, finding accommodations and family doctors, and placing children in the education system. The organization is governed by a board of directors and is staffed by five full-time employees. It recently initiated a volunteer Host program in the community and is now in the process of hiring a volunteer coordinator (www.maccnb.ca).

Given its small size and limited budget, MACC targets programming primarily toward the spouses (mainly wives) of foreign-born Global Technology Centre employees and foreign-born long-haul truck drivers who work in the Florenceville-Bristol area.[57] The Host program, for example, involves women in the community spending time with immigrant women, including them in recreational activities, and tutoring them in English. While most of its funding is dedicated to settlement programs,[58] MACC continues to emphasize its original mandate of facilitating contact and inter-group interaction. The organization has what I consider to be an informal side, that shows in its efforts to offer social activities to the citizens of Florenceville-Bristol including Spanish classes, ethnic and Canadian cooking classes, and salsa dancing lessons. Two of the immigrant adolescents I spoke with described MACC as a fun place to hang out, one immigrant adolescent volunteers there, and the immigrant adults I interviewed described MACC as an important part of their lives when they were younger. The immigrant adolescents also receive indirect benefits from MACC through its support of their families, especially their mothers.

Prior to the establishment of MACC, the town's main employer, McCain Foods, Ltd provided basic settlement services and English language training to the employees it recruited from around the world. The company still delivers ongoing English language training and professional development through online courses, as well as social activities to immigrant employees, but has passed other settlement-related services to MACC. It would not be a stretch to argue that in Florenceville-Bristol MACC seeks to take care of immigrant women, McCain Foods, Ltd takes care of immigrant men, and the schools take care of immigrant children and adolescents. But beyond the provision of any particular service, McCain Foods, Ltd, and especially its Global Technology Centre, is a social support for immigrant adolescents and their families because it has adopted an organizational culture that accepts and promotes cultural diversity. The managers of McCain Foods, Ltd recognize that cultural diversity contributes to their bottom line by making it easier to attract and retain good employees, lowering costs by developing skills in-house (and some would argue by keeping salaries low), and developing a "multicultural" reputation that helps attract even more foreign talent. This organizational culture appears to be transmitted through McCain's many employees to Florenceville-Bristol and its social institutions, and it plays a big role in the overall attitude of the community toward immigrants.

As in Fredericton, local churches in Florenceville-Bristol provide an important social support for the immigrant adolescents and their families. There are ten churches in Florenceville-Bristol, as well as a life-size wooden replica of Noah's Ark (according to the dimensions given in the Old Testament), that houses a privately owned Evangelical bible school. The Baptist Church is deeply rooted in the Upper St John River Valley of New Brunswick, and with four separate congregations in Florenceville-Bristol it is regarded as the most welcoming of immigrants. The Baptist mandate is to search out new people and make a point to include new people in its church family, regardless of whether these newcomers are from other countries, other provinces, or from next door. According to the staff of MACC, two Colombian women recently attended a Sunday service at Florenceville Baptist Church. They were so impressed with the warm welcome they received that they returned the next week. When the service began the two women were astonished to see the scripture translated into Spanish and projected on an overhead for them to follow. On another occasion, one of the Colombians arrived with very few possessions. The Baptist Church was notified and the congregation organized a house-warming gathering, providing the newcomer with enough for her apartment to be comfortable.

Most of the Latin American immigrants settling in Florenceville-Bristol are Roman Catholic. The Roman Catholic Church is not a recruiter church like the Baptist Church, but the newcomers who find their way to the church are made part of the congregation and are supported as such. Immigrants are included in all the Catholic activities, and are treated like members of the family. The Catholic faith is a very strong factor in Latin culture, and this warm approach ensures a continued Catholic presence in the immigrants' lives. All but one of the immigrant adolescents I interviewed for the case study referred to themselves as Christian, and most attend church with their families. For some of them, their involvement in church is no more than following their parents to Sunday service, but for others, church involvement provides social support through youth groups and broader involvement in church projects. The only non-Christian adolescent is from India. She travels to Fredericton once a month with her family to visit the Hindu Temple. Diverging from these stories, three of the older immigrant adolescents voiced surprise at how religious and conservative the residents of Florenceville-Bristol are, and spoke of feeling excluded because everyone belongs to a church but them.

Beyond a doubt, the primary source of social support, or the biggest piece of formal social infrastructure, for immigrant adolescents in Florenceville-Bristol is school. All thirteen of the adolescents who were interviewed for this research referred to school as "their community." School is the focal point of the Florenceville-Bristol data. At the time of data collection three of the immigrant adolescents attended grade 8 at Florenceville Middle School and the others were in grades 9–12 at Carleton North High School. Neither the middle school nor the high school has formal programs in place for new-comer students. There are no Guidance Counsellors who specialize in issues particular to international students, no in-school settlement workers, no youth buddy system, and no EAL classrooms. The immigrant adolescents are placed in mainstream classes with their peers and teaching assistants, leaving the classes only for short periods of English language tutoring with resource teachers. In some cases parents decide to enter their adolescent children a year behind their peers so that they will have more time to grasp the academic material in English. Spanish-speakers have also occasionally been brought into the schools to interpret and translate for those immigrant adolescents and parents from Latin America. In short, the immigrant adolescents are treated no differently than their New Brunswick-born peers, and for the most part, any social support offered by the schools falls more into the category of informal social infrastructure, as will be noted in the remaining chapters.

Formal programs are a crucial component of social infrastructure, but as good as these programs are they are not fully capable of offering the kinds of supports, opportunities, and relationships that young people need. "Young people do not grow up in programs, but in families, schools, and neighbourhoods," write Roth and Brooks-Gunn.[59] Richard Lerner and Peter Benson contend that strengthening social infrastructure in a community is less a responsibility of programs implemented and managed by professionals, and more a mobilization of public will and capacity.[60] In other words, social infrastructure has a side that is more informal, less tangible, and more difficult to measure and document. It is these more informal aspects of social infrastructure in a community that appear to relate Bronfenbrenner's ecology of human development theory to theories of civic engagement and social capital.

NVivo 8 was used to organize and analyze my collected interview transcripts, field notes, journals, and photographs. The qualitative research software allowed the data to be easily coded and coded passages could be retrieved and inspected again, with options of recoding and combining codes. Coding is the process of bringing together passages in the interview transcript that seem to exemplify an idea or concept. It is a way of abstracting from the source data to build a greater understanding of the forces at play. Each passage is read carefully to identify what is going on and each of these components is recorded as a separate code. At a first level of interpretation, this type of coding allows the researcher to view each component independently, giving a recontextualized perspective on each concept or topic.[61] At a second level of interpretation, slicing data into component parts opens up analytical possibilities through the recombination of component passages. Actions might be viewed in association with contexts, or issues with responses, to see the pattern of which ones are linked (because they were coded together on the same passage)[62] In my analysis, data collected from each participant were constantly compared to the other participants, and towards the end of the study the findings from each case community were compared and contrasted. As interviews progressed, a hierarchy of themes and sub-themes began emerging from a core category and eventually, the themes began to merge together into pairs, sets, and relationships. Five themes are discussed in the subsequent chapters: Making Contact; Public Awareness; Social Capital and Social Networks; Citizen Engagement; and Sense of Belonging. These themes, and related sub-themes and codes, represent the layers of social resources that exist in Fredericton and Florenceville-Bristol for the adaptation and integration of immigrant adolescents. Together they form the communities' informal social infrastructure. Although many of them are the same in the two case communities, on the whole, the Florenceville-Bristol data tell an entirely different story about the town's informal social infrastructure.

2

Reaching Out and Pulling Us In
Making Contact

Addressing immigrant adolescents' sense of belonging to a community does not necessarily involve looking at the needs of the immigrant adolescents or at the needs of the receiving community; rather, it involves close consideration of the interactions taking place and the social dynamics occurring within the larger receiving society. It also requires a focus on the degree to which institutions are open or closed to immigrants, since social interactions are supported and even created by the structure of institutions such as schools, churches, local governments, and corporations.[1] The dominant culture determines the character of these institutions, as well as the norms and values of the receiving society. Immigrants may preserve their institutions and culture to greater or lesser degrees, and they may also influence the character of the dominant institutions to greater or lesser degrees.[2] Where interaction is fluid and cultural and linguistic boundaries are transcended, at least some of the newcomers and established members of the community come to see themselves in new ways.

In his often-cited book *The Symbolic Construction of Community* (1985) Anthony P. Cohen maintains that in small communities children learn and practice how to be social, becoming part of the system that ensures that things are done in acceptable ways. Especially important are attitudes and values relating to trust and reciprocity, because they enable community members to treat each other as fellow citizens, rather than as strangers or as potential enemies. Some scholars contend that trust and reciprocity prosper in closed, homogenous communities where informal norms and sanctions are particularly strong, i.e. the *similarity-attraction hypothesis*.[3] These communities are thought to be more cohesive in that residents are more likely to become engaged in common objectives.[4] Therefore in the literature on immigration and multiculturalism it is often assumed that the more diverse a community, the less inclined its members will be to develop close ties with their fellow community members.[5]

Research evidence from the settler societies of Canada, the United States, and Australia nevertheless suggests that, with increased contact between people of most cultural backgrounds, existing stereotypes start to break down and a more trustful relationship becomes possible, i.e. the *contact hypothesis*.[6] The contact hypothesis[7] proposes that several conditions are necessary in order for intergroup contact to be successful in reducing prejudice and enhancing tolerance. In Gordon Allport's original (1954) formulation, these necessary conditions included: (1) That positive contact be supported by authority figures as well as social and cultural norms (but voluntariness among participants is important); (2) That participants be of equal status within the situation; (3) That cooperative interdependence exist among participants across groups; and (4) That individualized contact have the potential for friendships across groups. In addition, Stuart W. Cook (1985) emphasized that: (5) The interaction must encourage behaviour that disconfirms stereotypes that the groups hold of each other.[8] Following this hypothesis, the first step to building relationships between native citizens of Fredericton and Florenceville-Bristol and immigrant adolescents is to make contact. To be accepting of diversity and open to change, citizens of these communities need to be given the opportunity, or actively seek that opportunity to meet and get to know immigrants, just as the immigrants need to meet and get to know local residents. Increased interaction would make the *other* group less threatening and more familiar.

FREDERICTION

In Fredericton that first step toward getting to know one another appears, by most accounts, to be missing. Immigrants and local residents do not know each other. A number of reasons for this lack of personal contact were given by the various categories of participants. All pointed to obstacles to meeting one another rather than an unwillingness to meet.

Our Paths Don't Cross

Local residents and immigrant adolescents in Fredericton are not avoiding one another; they merely are not given the opportunity to meet on a daily basis because their paths do not cross. Jason Slattery, a local resident participant who has little daily contact with immigrant adults and no contact with immigrant adolescents, contends that people in Fredericton are not making contact with immigrants because the frenzied pace of work and family keep them too busy to reach out and meet the newcomers. Fredericton is a small city with short commute times, but people are still busy:

> I don't mean to be ambivalent about new immigrants, but I'm not given the opportunity to meet them on a daily basis ... [pause] ... I guess they are kind of out of sight out of mind for many people who are so busy working, studying, and taking care of their children that they don't have time to look around and notice that Fredericton is becoming more diverse. And unless they are adolescents themselves, or the parents of adolescents, they aren't going to go out of their way to meet the immigrant adolescents in the community. (Jason Slattery, 28 November 2008)

All of the non-European immigrant adolescent and adult participants describe the culture of New Brunswick as too "family-oriented." These participants argued that people tend not to socialize outside of their tight kin and friendship networks, a claim that is consistent with themes Baukje Miedema and Nancy Nason-Clark (1989) documented in their study of immigrant women in Fredericton. Residents come home from work and school and spend the rest of the evening inside their homes with their families. In effect, the same strong social ties that bring benefits to the members of these tight networks commonly enable them to bar others from access. "People stay in their houses a lot. Maybe their families are big and they don't need friends," says Martine (Martine, 28 February 2009). The adolescents who are from densely populated European cities, however, describe the local culture as similar to their own cultures, but remark that Fredericton's open spaces "allow people more space to breathe and to choose whether to make contact or keep to themselves" (Caroline, 1 April 2009). Local residents and community organization members characterize Fredericton as a "cliquish" town, where those not born there "come from away" no matter the length of time they have resided in the community. Godfrey Baldacchino (2006) noted similar concerns in his study of immigrants on Prince Edward Island. When sharing their stories about moving to the island, respondents cited the solid homogeneity and non-multiculturalism, informal communication channels, and robust kin and friendship networks as providing a strong sense of identity and resilience to the island society. This, they claim, is very welcoming to visitors and tourists, but at the same time, is very difficult to penetrate by those who "come from away" and stay longer than the visitors and tourists do.[9]

Many of the immigrant adolescent participants think the cold weather keeps people inside their houses. The winter months are difficult for the immigrant adolescents, not only because the cold is brisk and insufferable or because the sidewalks are slushy and slippery, but also because residents of Fredericton stay inside their houses even more than usual, "doing their own thing" with their doors closed and curtains drawn. Fajar, an international student from Indonesia, describes these circumstances as "troubling":

> In Jakarta I lived with my family in a large housing block and we had lots of friends there. We would often pool our food together for a big dinner or we would be outside a lot of the time chatting. And when people moved into that block we would always welcome them. We would go to their houses and introduce ourselves ...Yeah, our door was always open and people were always at our house. Here it is different because it is cold most of the time and it gets dark early. People keep their doors and windows closed and they just don't go outside much. Maybe that's it; they just can't go outside much. For six months of the year there are no signs of life here and I find that really troubling. (Fajar, 19 November 2008)

Christmas in Fredericton is a particularly lonely time for those immigrant adolescents who come from Latin America where the holiday is celebrated outside in the open air with lots of people:

> Christmas is quiet here. I think that is when we miss home the most. In Latin America Christmas is a huge celebration with like,

a thousand family members gathered together outside. We eat
mountains of food, set off firecrackers, and make lots of noise,
and we dance all night to loud music [laughing]. But here it is
so quiet. The city is empty. People stay in their houses with their
families for a whole week it seems. (Luis, 14 February 2009)

Lastly, some of the participants argue that other than the Saturday farmer's market there is no common space where all of the cultures in Fredericton can come together to meet and get to know one
another. For local resident Kevin Clark, this comes down to organizing community-wide events:

The market works so well for people to mix. People from all
over the world sell things, there is an entrepreneurial spirit, and
just the social aspect of seeing different faces is so important in
a place like Fredericton. But the market is only on Saturdays. We
need more opportunities to meet each other. I just don't think
that that opportunity is there right now ... I guess at a municipal
government level it does help if we could organize events where
immigrants and local people can meet each other and learn
about each other. If any of these events exist now, I don't know
about them. (Kevin Clark, 2 June 2009)

Others, like George Feenstra, contend that the common space is
there in abundance and it is welcoming, but immigrant adolescents
are not taking advantage of what the city has to offer: "There is a lot
of mingling in Fredericton's public spaces, especially in its abundant
green spaces; I would encourage young immigrants to just be out
and about meeting as many people as they can" (George Feenstra,
29 August 2008).

Immigrant adolescents may not be mixing with local residents in
the city's many public spaces, but they are found in those spaces.
One of the first questions I asked the immigrant adolescent participants, was "where do you like to hang out in the community?" The
participants not only answered my question, but they took photographs of their favourite places to supplement their answers. Almost
without exception, all of the boys took photographs of Fredericton's
soccer fields, followed by photographs of downtown spaces such as
Officer's Square, and green spaces such as parks. In the following
quotation Lucus describes his photograph of O'Dell Park:

It is amazing to have such a big jungle in the middle of a city. There are trails there where you can go hiking and walking. We did gym class there in grade 9. There are also places where you can get together to cook dinner and have a picnic. The city is surrounded by forests and when you fly in that is all you can see. I would rather be here in the trees than in a large city full of buildings. The other thing I find so amazing in the trees are all of the little animals, like squirrels. I love the squirrels; they are so cute. (Lucus, 25 August 2008)

The girls, in contrast, took photographs of the Public Library, the two high school libraries, and the Harriet Irving library (UNB), followed by photographs of their homes. Because making high grades in school is important to all of the immigrant girls I interviewed, the library is a natural place for them to spend their time. They are also avid readers. Caroline, for example, who arrived two years ago from Belgium, has a self-proclaimed "huge obsession with *Harry Potter* books." She has read the series five times in Dutch and French, and is now attempting to read them in English. The library provides a space for the girls to feel confident and to focus on what matters to them (and their parents) – a quality education followed by good career opportunities. When they are not in the library they tend to stay at home. Home is where their hearts are and no one put this better than Mai:

We love to sit in our backyard and sometimes we just sit there in the backyard and chat. We didn't have a backyard in Taiwan. There wasn't enough space and here the air is very fresh. I also like to be in the kitchen. I love to cook and bake with my mom. We share the cookies, and drink coffee and chat. I didn't drink coffee until I came here and now I really love it. (Mai, 10 December 2008)

Some of the boys and girls also took photographs of MCAF, churches, schools, and the shopping mall. Overall, these visual images of the everyday worlds of immigrant adolescents in Fredericton tell a story that participants themselves believe best represents their environment. The images enabled me as a researcher to look at their world through their eyes, an important issue for those who conduct research on the experiences of marginalized groups.[10]

It is worth noting here that not all immigrant adolescents will have equal access to Fredericton's public spaces. Immigrant adolescents whose families arrived as refugees or as economic and family class immigrants of low socioeconomic status are not evenly dispersed in neighbourhoods throughout the city.[11] Rather, due to a shortage of low-income and public housing, they are located together in two or three low rental apartment complexes in the north-side neighbourhood of Devon. They are also dependent on public transportation. Therefore, outside of school, the only public spaces to make contact with these teens are on the city's limited bus route. The immigrant adolescents I interviewed are often left out of Sunday afternoon picnics, soccer games, and other recreational activities on the south side of the St John River because there is no bus service on Sunday. They are also left out of "their own" youth activities at MCAF because the MCAF staff can only provide them with limited transportation.

Do You See Me?

"I see you" is a quotation by George Feenstra. It was spoken early in the data collection process and stayed with me as the interviews progressed. The exact quotation is:

> I've been doing everything in my power to make some kind of face contact with immigrant people just to see what happens. And that traces to a South African man I met in Vancouver. He spoke of a greeting they have in Africa, which translates from Zulu as "I see you." And the response would be "thank you for seeing me ..." So I make a tremendous effort to see all the people who I meet along the way. (George Feenstra, 29 August 2008)

George Feenstra was the only participant to utter these words as a statement of optimism. For the immigrant adolescent participants, the words formed the more pessimistic question "do you see me?" The sub-theme reflects a feeling that citizens of Fredericton have toward immigrants that appears to range from indifference (i.e. a lack of any interest or concern) to, at best, ambivalence (i.e. attitudes containing both positive and negative elements).[12] "The thing that is most difficult or unwelcoming about the cultural mix here is not as overt as someone yelling at you telling you to get out of their city, but rather more subtle in that most local community members don't notice you are here at all," says the International Student Advisor at UNB. (International Student Advisor UNB, 17 October 2008)

Immigrant adolescents want to be noticed, not because they are different, but because they are normal teens with the same needs as any other teen in Fredericton. As Feena, a recent arrival from the Netherlands, put it "I guess I would have to say that a welcoming community is one where as an outsider you are treated the same as everybody else; where you don't feel like everybody is looking at you funny because you are not from there" (Feena, 31 March 2009). Most of the immigrant adolescent participants feel ignored and at times invisible at school and in the wider community. The EAL teacher at Fredericton and Leo Hayes High School, speaks with deep conviction about this situation:

> A welcoming community would be when a young immigrant walks through the door people will approach him or her and say "you are new, where are you from? What's going on? Hey come eat lunch with us." Right now this scenario just doesn't happen. That you are acknowledged is so important ... Yes friendship with depth is important, but for me that acknowledgement has to be there first. I watch the kids walking down the hallway and nobody even looks at them. Initially, all I want for my kids is for somebody to acknowledge that they are walking beside you. You don't have to go and hug them, just please don't ignore them. (EAL Teacher, 11 February 2009)

The immigrant adolescents want their peers to reach out and pull them into their groups and activities. Every one of the immigrant adolescent participants described how difficult it is to get to know people in Fredericton and to become involved in the community. They see the flurry of activity around them, but do not understand how to take part in it: "We need to feel included in activities," says Luis. "How can I explain? Well, for example, if there is a group of kids playing soccer and I am watching them they will call out to me 'hey are you new here? Would you like to come and play with us?' A welcoming community would reach out and pull us in" (Luis, 14 February 2009). As Lucus demonstrates, personality type plays into this argument with extroverted, confident teens able to make that initial effort to make contact with peers and make friends relatively quickly, and introverted, shy teens less able to reach out and make that contact:

When I came to high school I was told that the kids would be very friendly and that they would talk to me, they would say "Hey how are you?" and invite me to hang out with them. But that is not the way it is at all [laughing]. So I thought "Okay what do I do now?" because I was shy and my English wasn't good enough to talk to them. So after a while, I decided that I should go and introduce myself to people because if I don't I will be alone." (Lucus, 28 August 2008)

The thirteen immigrant adolescent participants who are involved in MCAF youth activities proposed the introduction of a youth host program in the community, whereby local and newcomer youth are purposefully paired up, perhaps according to age and mutual interests. The local adolescent could then show the immigrant adolescent around the community and introduce him or her to more people. The arranged relationship with the local teen would, according to Pablo, "help us to not get lost and show us the right ways to do things here, like the right way to behave" (Pablo, 28 February 2009). Abo elaborates on this point adding that he would like to have a friend who can help him to learn positive behaviour:

When you come here you don't know how to behave so you take the same behaviour you had back home and that might not be right here. I think it is important that people our age are at school or in the community to tell us what we should do and what we shouldn't do. When I got here I didn't know how to behave and how to stay out of trouble. Things were different in Sierra Leone and Senegal. In the refugee camps I had to fight to survive. Here someone needs to give us advice, and good advice not bad advice. (Abo, 28 February 2009)

Youth host programs operate in Fredericton schools with varying levels of success. École Sainte Anne has had some success pairing local and newcomer students at the middle and high school levels. Fredericton High School tried the initiative, but was unable to encourage local students to participate beyond the handful of socially conscious teens who would have become friends with the newcomers without the host program in place. The guidance counsellor at Fredericton High School who specializes in the school experience of newcomer students, argues, moreover, that the expectations the immigrant adolescents have of their local peers are simply too high and misplaced in our culture:

> The immigrant adolescents are generally satisfied with life in Fredericton, but I don't think that they are as satisfied that they have incorporated into the school as well as they could. I think their expectations are too high. Perhaps they expect that the local kids at school will reach out to them and say "Come on over and give me a hug big guy." And that just doesn't happen here. It is just not how our culture works. So they end up disappointed and then the adjustment process takes that much longer. (Guidance Counsellor, 26 November 2008)

Mateo, an especially astute adolescent from Colombia, was the only other participant in Fredericton to pick up on the topic of culture. He equates his inability to meet people in the community with a somewhat cold and apathetic local culture:

> People here are friendly. There is no question about that. They say hello, they smile, and they seem nice. But, gosh, should I say this? [pause] There is something very superficial about their friendliness. Something is missing. I can't express what that something is. There is no word in English. I'll say it in Spanish ... gosh, I am forgetting my Spanish, oh yes the expression is "*El calor humano* [human warmth]." It is not something you see or something you express, it is something you feel. And here I don't feel it. (Mateo, 28 October 2008)

"Do you see me?" appears to have two codes attached to it. The first involves the question of who is responsible for integrating immigrants in the community, and the second focuses on the limits of politeness and political consciousness when acknowledging cultural diversity in the community.

LEVEL OF RESPONSIBILITY
The perceived indifference or ambivalence toward immigrant adolescents may be the result of citizens of Fredericton taking for granted

formal programs and services for immigrants or overestimating the quantity of programs that actually exist in the community. Unlike new immigrant-receiving communities in the United States where local government institutions are not guided by a national integration policy and, hence, are uncertain of the role they should play with new immigrant populations, a national settlement and integration policy is in effect in most of Canada. However, because Fredericton is the provincial capital of New Brunswick, the divisions of responsibility between the municipal and provincial governments, on the one hand, and civil society on the other are often blurred. One teacher at Leo Hayes High School explains that Fredericton has such a good system in place for taking care of immigrant adolescents that there is no need for the wider community to reach out and build relationships with them. He lists services for immigrants that are targeted only at specific groups of immigrants, such as resettlement services for refugees, or programs that no longer exist in Fredericton, such as the Welcome Wagon:

I think immigrant adolescents are integrating just fine into this community. There seems to be a lot of programs out there to help the adolescents and their families settle in, like the Multicultural Association settlement programs, the Welcome Wagon that gives gift baskets and orientation packages to newcomers, the newcomers club, and the buddy systems in the schools. I imagine all of those programs are helpful. I am sure there are plenty of groups who help people settle in and make immigrants more comfortable. Those are organized things at the government level and not really up to the community in general. I haven't heard that we are unwelcoming. (Teacher, 1 January 2009)

Jason Slattery, in contrast, notes that relationships are formed at the grassroots community level and have little or nothing to do with formal programming:

Well, I think that relationships have to be formed at the ground level, which means that people in general need to embrace the concept and be open to change. I don't think that any level of government can have much role in making a community a welcoming one. I don't think government sponsoring specific organizations to welcome newcomers plays a huge role either. None of this would be as effective as people in the community willing to be friendly, to make contact with, and willing to interact with immigrants on a daily basis. That would be the key to success I would think. If I went to another country and was trying to figure things out and fit in, it wouldn't be the government I would be dealing with it would be the people of that country. So I don't think we have done a great job reaching out to these young immigrants to date, but it is important. (Jason Slattery, 28 November 2008)

THE LIMITS OF POLITENESS

These attitudes may also result from attempts, by the citizens of Fredericton, to be polite and non-intrusive in the lives of immigrants in order to give them the chance to blend into the community. However, the citizens have become so polite and non-intrusive that they have crossed over the line of politeness or political consciousness to the point of ignoring immigrants altogether. This is a contentious issue in the New Brunswick Population Growth Secretariat, where it has been discussed with respect to the development of a mass media campaign aimed at raising awareness about the benefits of immigration and cultural diversity. Well-meaning government officials, some of whom are immigrants themselves, think it is wrong to draw attention to immigrants as being "different" or to "other" them, even if those differences are being celebrated by a community. Teachers also question how much attention is too much when adolescents want nothing more than to blend in with their peers at school:

> Sometimes teachers want to make a big deal about a student being from a different culture. They welcome that student by attempting to celebrate that culture and certainly they mean well by this. When I want to be welcoming I try not to draw attention to that and it is not because I don't want to know about that student's culture but because I want the student to feel a part of the immediate culture of where they are now ... Adolescents don't want to stick out. But I've seen things done that were like that where the school would hold an assembly or they would talk about where the child comes from and the moment they do that they unintentionally segregate that child or community of children even more. (Philip Sexsmith, 8 January 2009)

The same argument holds for additional language classrooms, which may unintentionally serve to segregate immigrant adolescents and inadvertently perpetuate the identity of "otherness" that is imposed on them.[13]

It takes four to seven years to become sufficiently fluent in an additional language for academic learning.[14] Without adequate support, immigrant children and youth fall further and further behind academically, and are substantially less likely to participate in school activities or to connect with local peers. While providing newcomer students with "sheltered" instruction in special classrooms, English as an Additional Language (EAL) programs often separate the immigrant adolescents from their English-speaking peers for part of or the entire day. As will be noted in chapter 4, peers sustain and support the development of significant social competencies in youth, including tangibly supporting academic engagement by clarifying readings or lectures and helping one another in completing homework assignments.[15] But because immigrant adolescents often are segregated in EAL classrooms, they have limited access to a network of peers beyond their immediate immigrant group or across immigrant groups. Recent studies by Carola Suárez-Orozco and colleagues (2008; 2010) in the United States reveal that, in many cases, immigrant youth have almost no meaningful contact with English-speaking peers. More than one third of the immigrant students reported that they had little opportunity to interact with peers who were not from their country of origin, which clearly contributed to their linguistic isolation.

Do You Hear Me?

Continuing the theme of indifference and ambivalence, the immigrant adolescent participants also emphasized being heard or listened to by local residents. Like many adolescents, immigrant adolescents *often* complain that adults do not listen to them or accept their opinions. The widely held view of adolescence as a tumultuous time of raging hormones and rejection of adult values may lead adults to believe that they know better. The immigrant adolescents claim they are not listened to, but they tend to focus more on being immigrants than on their adolescent angst. They have stories to tell. They want to talk about where they are from. I could see their eyes light up when I expressed interest in the details of their lives. Some of the participants wanted to talk about the positive aspects of their countries of origin, and of the adventures and joys, the trials and tribulations of adjusting to life in Fredericton. Others wanted me, as a researcher, to make people aware of the sad truths of the world, of their struggles and sometimes the sheer horror of their previous existence. Many of the immigrant adolescent participants note that people in Fredericton live in their own little worlds and do not take the time to listen to their stories:

> I would say, [pause] oh my goodness ... a welcoming commun-
> ity is where they accept you for who you are and they are willing
> and eager to listen to your story. A lot of people just don't; all of
> us, some of us, or most of us don't really care to listen to new-
> comers' stories. That happens. It would be hard for local people
> to get to know a stranger, and to be really close to a stranger,
> and especially a stranger from across the world who knows little
> English. (Van Anh, 5 November 2008)

Citizens of Fredericton often assume that if immigrants are visible minorities then they do not speak English. This imagined language barrier makes them even less prepared to strike up a conversation with the teens. "Here they all assumed that I didn't speak English so they kept their distance from me. Hey, I would have preferred being asked crazy questions over being completely ignored," says Gaby. "It wasn't until they figured out that I spoke fluent English that they started talking to me at all" (Gaby, 14 February 2009). Immigrant adults looking back on their adolescence in Fredericton were more likely to consider personality as a factor. Andrew, for example, notes that shyness does not get us anywhere. Immigrants and local residents simply need to develop enough confidence to speak with one another:

> I used to be quiet, but in the refugee camp I became bold. I had
> to find my voice and speak loudly because if I didn't talk I didn't
> survive. I was the only child in my family. I was used to having
> everything done for me and having adults speak for me. At the
> refugee camp I had to come out of my shell. So I had no prob-
> lem speaking to people in Fredericton ... People in Fredericton
> need to come out of their shell and get over the fear of talking to
> strangers. Who is a stranger? Go and talk to someone you don't
> know and you will learn so much. You don't need to spend all
> your time with that person, just a few minutes. Go home and
> tell your family "I spoke to someone new today." People here

are formal and shy. That really needs to change if we are all going to take this ride toward diversity together. (Andrew, 12 July 2008)

"Do you hear me?" appears to have one code attached to it, which touches on the challenge of learning a new language and how local residents handle that language barrier.

THE LANGUAGE BARRIER

Participants spent an enormous amount of time talking about the challenge of learning English. Immigrants and local residents overwhelmingly cited language acquisition and communication barriers as the greatest challenge to settling into Fredericton. All categories of participants talked about it, and all understood how difficult learning a second or an additional language is. Language skills affect adolescents' abilities to detect social nuances in the school setting and are also highly predictive of academic success.[16] The ability to perform well on multiple-choice tests, to extract meaning from written text, and to argue a point both orally and in writing are essential skills for high levels of academic achievement. Language proficiency also affects the degree to which adolescents feel connected to what goes on in their classes, a key determining factor in academic performance.[17]

Only six of the twenty immigrant adolescents spoke English before immigrating to New Brunswick. One of the adolescents is a native Spanish-speaker from Venezuela, who arrived in Fredericton via North Carolina where she learned English. She is now at École Sainte Anne learning French. Five of the adolescents are from English-speaking Liberia and Sierra Leone. The two adolescents from Sierra Leone are siblings who also speak French because they spent time in a refugee camp in French-speaking Senegal. The remaining fourteen immigrant adolescents spoke little or no English when they arrived in Fredericton. Two of them are from French-speaking Congo, and one from Dutch- and French-speaking Belgium. Although the francophone adolescents go to French school, they have also had to acquire English outside of school, since Fredericton is predominantly an anglophone community. Four of the adolescents are Spanish-speakers from Guatemala and Colombia; the two Iranian adolescents speak Farsi, and the final five speak Mandarin Chinese, Dutch, Korean, Vietnamese, and Indonesian.

Those participants who came from English-speaking countries or from countries where English is widely used were still confronted with a language barrier upon arrival in Fredericton because of the "different" way they spoke the language. When I asked the participants from Liberia and Sierra Leone what language they speak at home they answered "broken" English and "bad" English; and Feena's English training in the Netherlands did not seem to help her in Fredericton:

> We learn English at school in the Netherlands, but it is British English and mainly grammar. I was not used to having conversations in English. I could answer only basic questions. Soon after we arrived I was on the school bus. The kids on the bus asked me "where are you from?" I understood that and answered "Holland." Then they asked me more questions and I didn't understand a word! [laughing] So I said "talk to my sister." She was standing behind me and could speak more English than me [laughing]. Grammar is only part of a language. I learned it and I remember it, but if you don't use the language a bunch of verbs aren't going to do you any good. So I had to learn English. I was put in school and everyone was speaking English. I couldn't keep going to my brother and sister at lunch time and ask them to translate for me. (Feena, 31 March 2009)

Six participants (immigrant and non-immigrant) referred to the local residents as being in a hurry all the time and becoming impatient when trying to understand an immigrant's "broken" English. In some cases the individual's English is not broken at all, but merely accented. Jason Slattery sums this issue up as follows:

> Aah, I can't say for everybody, but if it were me and I was moving to this city, if I didn't speak the language then I would find it very difficult. Our society is built on a very frenzied level, our patience is low, and we are not necessarily willing to take the five or ten extra minutes to listen to someone try to communicate in a broken second language. My experience is that we are not really willing to do that. And the worst part is, that individual may speak the language, but even the slightest accent seems to grind at our patience. (Jason Slattery, 28 November 2008)

Language learning is an anxiety-provoking experience for many students.[18] Richard Clément and Richard Gardner refer to *additional-language confidence* as the subjective feeling of being able to cope adequately with situations involving the use of an additional language.[19] The immigrant adolescents think that their "poor" English isolates them from their peers. Heo, for example, remarks that when peers hear her trying to speak English "it scares them away" (Heo, 31 January 2009), and Mateo feels as if he missed his window of opportunity to meet people because he could not communicate properly in English when he first arrived in the city:

My first few months in Fredericton were the worst experience I had ever been through. Settling in was really awful. I spoke English when I arrived. I listened to a lot of English in Colombia, but I was not involved in many English conversations. I didn't realize that it would be so different here; that it would be such a shock. I got confused in conversations, my tongue would get caught, and my ideas would get lost. I couldn't express myself and that made me feel inadequate and isolated. I had a hard time meeting people, and even as my English improved I couldn't seem to meet people. I think they kept assuming that my English was still poor even though it had improved. It was too late to attempt to make friends with them at that point so I gave up. (Mateo, 28 November 2008)

The feeling of isolation resulting from the language barrier also affects how the immigrant adolescent participants perceive themselves. The adolescents remarked that they felt "stupid" and "inadequate" when speaking and writing English, that people couldn't see they were intelligent individuals because they could not get their point across. Mai, for example, states that not being able to express her thoughts in English made her feel like she was "less of a person," and she describes her frustration at not letting people know that she really is "a smart person" (Mai, 10 December 2008). Many of these teens were top students in their home countries; many of them were deeply involved in their communities in their home countries; and many of them left a lot of friends behind. The immigrant adolescents become very impatient with themselves when they cannot learn English in a few months and pull their grades back up to their home country levels. As one immigrant adult puts it, "of course you want to learn it in a month or two so you can meet people, make friends, and get on with your life in this new place. But learning a new language doesn't work that way at all; it is a long, frustrating, lonely, and painful process" (Alfonso, 30 December 2008).

Not surprisingly, language and communication barriers are also associated with boredom. How can a student find school interesting if he or she does not understand the content being taught or the conversations taking place in and outside the classroom? Upon asking the immigrant adolescent participants to describe their classrooms, several of them referred to the number of ceiling tiles above them in their home room, and the various shapes of stains on the walls and carpets. The other interesting twist on this topic is how the language barrier affects the immigrant adolescents' career choices. Two of the Asian girls I interviewed are excelling at math and science in high school and plan to enter the nursing program at UNB. Yet, neither girl actually likes math and science, the subjects are merely easier to understand in English:

> Actually in Korea I wasn't good at science or math and I didn't much like those classes. I was very good at social studies and history. And even though English is so hard, I actually was good in my English class in Korea because I like to read literature. But here I don't understand social studies and subjects like that at all because the language makes it very difficult for me. But I do understand math because it is numbers and we already did that math in Korea two years ago. So now I am good in math, but I don't actually like math. I understand chemistry too. So the subjects I like changed when I came here. (Heo, 31 January 2009)

Fortunately, acquiring English (and in six cases both English and French) as an additional language is a hurdle that the immigrant adolescent participants have overcome, or are well on their way to overcoming. Most of them will go on to not only learn the language, but ultimately to master that language. At this point Fredericton as a community begins to look a whole lot better and the immigrant adolescents regard language acquisition as an accomplishment to be proud of. "Once you learn English you can do more things for yourself," says Musi (Musi, 1 August 2008).

FLORENCEVILLE-BRISTOL

The small setting of Florenceville-Bristol with its single main street and handful of businesses provides ample opportunity for daily interpersonal interaction between residents. Contact is so important and inevitable in this setting that the theme anchors the remaining themes and sub-themes associated with the community. All of the participants in the case study of Florenceville-Bristol stated that local residents and immigrants have no choice but to make contact with each other in this community with a small population, one main employer, and so few places to go. Whether this contact goes beyond a casual "hello," and whether all sectors of the population actually take pleasure in it will be discussed in greater detail here. What is clear in the data is that the immigrant adolescents are noticed and they are listened to, and if there are any subtle or obvious bad feelings about the recruitment of immigrants to the community, the adolescents are unaware of them.

All Paths Lead to the Same Destination

Whether it is the bank, public library, grocery store, or pizza parlour, all paths in Florenceville-Bristol lead to the same destination. It would be difficult to go anywhere without running into friends and acquaintances. Florenceville-Bristol is largely a one-industry town with many adults employed by the various divisions of McCain Foods, Ltd, and a few more employed by the schools and in the small service sector. The pace of life for families is slower, with short commute times, no traffic, and more time to be "out and about." As such, all of the local residents I interviewed could not only describe meeting immigrants in the community, but could also detail how relationships with them developed. For Katherine Sheriff, a local resident who works at the town's only hotel, initial contact with immigrant families has resulted in close friendships:

> I socialize a lot with the immigrants in Florenceville-Bristol. I now have a good friend from India and another from Cuba. I invite them and other newcomers to dinner at my home and they do the same for me ... I was recently at a barbecue at the home of the family from Moldova, and dinner at the home of a family

from the Ukraine. This was shortly after the two families arrived
... It is not only people who work at McCain Foods who arrive
from different countries; there are also a lot of truck drivers here
from Russia and Romania. They are here on short contracts and
rent rooms in the same building where I live. I also play volley-
ball with a lot of them at the open gym at one of the churches.
(Katherine Sheriff, 2 April 2009)

Katherine went on to stress how important it is for people to get out
of their houses and socialize so as not to feel the isolation of a small
rural community. She described the "traditional farm families" in the
Florenceville-Bristol area as being more likely to stay in their homes
and less likely to make contact with immigrants.

Unlike their peers in Fredericton, the immigrant adolescents in
Florenceville-Bristol do not describe local residents as "keeping to
themselves." On the contrary, the local residents are regarded as
friendly and accommodating. The immigrant adolescents did, however, emphasize how few local residents actually *are* in the community. All fourteen adolescents come from big (and in the cases of
Mexico City, New Delhi, and Seoul, enormous) urban centres. So
even though they see people on a daily basis, the population of the
town is so small they often feel lonely. Jorge, for example, arrived
from Medellín, Colombia three years ago at the time of our interview. From his flawless English and passion for snowmobiles, one
would never know he was not born in New Brunswick, but even he
finds the low population density difficult to adjust to:

Getting used to the quiet has been very difficult. It is so quiet
here. I am used to a very big city with lots of city noises. I don't
necessarily miss the city noises but I miss the music. [pause ...
sigh] There was always music playing in Colombia. Christmas
time in Colombia was never quiet. There was always music and
dancing and huge crowds of people. Getting used to the empty
spaces and not having people around has been kind of lonely.
(Jorge, 1 April 2009)

Monica, who is also from Medellín, notes that there are fewer
people around, but also more time to spend together as a family. "I
like how close families are here," she says. "Supper is a very special
meal where the whole family sits down and eats together. That is a

really nice tradition in Florenceville that my family has adopted. In Colombia we never ate a meal together as a family; we were all too busy" (Monica, 1 April 2009).

The adolescents do not equate winter with loneliness and increased isolation, although some of them are astonished at how many people actually do leave their houses in the winter:

> People in Florenceville-Bristol go outside even when it is snowing. The first snow storm after we came here I thought everything would just stop. I was really afraid to go outside. I thought it was dangerous. But everyone went to work and to school like there was no snow at all. They just dressed in warm clothes and went out! [laughing] The stores are still full of people. The only difference is, when they meet they stop and talk more about the weather. That surprised me. And when it gets dark early people still keep on going. I thought we would all stay home and go to sleep. (Ana Lucia, 1 April 2009)

The winter season is celebrated in Florenceville-Bristol, with both MACC and McCain Food, Ltd regularly organizing recreational activities such as ice skating, curling, and downhill tubing for the newcomers. The immigrant adolescents describe their lives in the community as full of outdoor adventures all year round. When they are not in school the teens are playing in the snow, riding bicycles on public trails, swimming in the public pool, and playing a variety of sports. They spent a substantial amount of interview time talking about feeling safe, secure, and free in Florenceville-Bristol. For example, though still suffering from culture shock, Claudia from Mexico City relishes her new-found freedom:

> It is so small. When we drove from Fredericton to Florenceville I just couldn't believe it. It was trees and fields and no people here. It is just so small here. It was really a shock for my whole family ... [pause]. But it is safe. I can go out and walk around even in the dark and nothing will happen to me. I know that. I couldn't walk around in the dark in Mexico because somebody could kidnap me. Even if I was allowed to be out in the dark I wouldn't do it because I know something will happen to me. Here I am free to do what I want. There is no traffic and there is more time here. Time in Mexico City moves so much faster; faster than

the traffic! [laughing] I really like the summer here. It is very
pretty and the air is fresh. The sky is blue and there is no smog.
(Claudia, 1 April 2009)

Less than half of the immigrant adolescent participants took
photographs of their favourite places in Florenceville-Bristol to complement their interviews. The few photographs I received are nevertheless consistent with the verbal data. Both the boys and the girls
presented images of their schools, followed by natural settings such
as the tubing hill (it was a cold spring at this time), trails, and the
board walk along the St John River, as well as their bicycles, and
in two cases their snowmobiles. The girls also took several photographs of themselves with their friends, and photographs of their
bedrooms. With the exception of the latter photographs of friends
and bedrooms, there appeared to be no marked differences between
the photographs taken by boys and those taken by girls.

I See You

Life in small communities has often been compared to life inside a
fishbowl, where nothing is hidden and everyone knows everything
about everyone else.[20] Overlapping social networks bring community
members together as neighbours, sharing resources and potentially
having contact on a regular basis.[21] Along with this sharing comes
the increased probability of shared information as well as knowledge of others. Newcomers do not go unnoticed in Florenceville-
Bristol. For the immigrant adolescents being seen is not necessarily
a bad thing, especially if it is their abilities and talents being recognized rather than their differences. When interviewed, the staff and
students in the two schools had no problem describing the personality and strengths of each immigrant adolescent. By way of illustration, three of the newcomer teens are exceptionally musical. Even
before they learned English, staff and students were able to recognize their musical talents and tap into them. Ale, who plays the
piano, clarinet, and saxophone, was recruited by the school band
soon after she arrived and was also invited to play the background
music for the Carleton North High School graduation prom; Eric, a
singer, dancer, and athlete, has earned the nickname "South Korea's
Justin Timberlake" from local peers who hold him in high esteem;

and Stefan didn't even realize he had a talent until it was pointed out
to him by the Settlement Program Coordinator at MACC only two
days after he arrived from Moldova:

> I was driving back to Florenceville with Stefan and his little sis-
> ter in the back seat. And he had this pop bottle, and the things
> he could do with that bottle; it sounded like there was a percus-
> sion band in the back seat, I'll tell you! I quizzed him, and no he
> wasn't interested in sports. He was interested in drama and mak-
> ing movies, but music not so much. But when I told the music
> teacher at the school about that pop bottle, he said "oh we have
> got to get him in here." So Stefan joined the school band as well.
> (Rita Ebbett-McIntosh, 2 April 2009)

The immigrant adolescents say that they have been included in
groups and activities at school, and even more so once they learned
enough English to be able to communicate. They also spend time at
the homes of their New Brunswick-born friends and they reciprocate
with invitations to their houses. Stefan, for example, invites local
friends to a monthly horror movie night at his house; Ale organ-
izes study groups at her house, and one local adolescent, Melanie,
who participated in my focus group at Carleton North High School,
describes her first dinner invitation to the home of a friend from
Colombia as follows:

> One day one of the girls from Colombia invited me to stay for
> dinner at her house. They had this rice dish and it had coconut
> in it, and I am allergic to coconut. I broke out in hives almost
> instantly, all over my body. Her parents were really embarrassed.
> They didn't know what to do and they were afraid to send me
> home with hives all over me. But we remained friends and I am
> at her house all the time, but they don't feed me coconut any-
> more. (Melanie, 3 March 2009)

"I see you" is associated with two codes: "Our Responsibility"
highlights the small-town characteristic of people looking out for
the youngest members of the community, and "A Healthy Curiosity"
takes a more detailed look at local and immigrant adolescents making contact in the schools.

OUR RESPONSIBILITY

Robert Sampson, Stephen Raudenbush, and Felton Earls (1997) hypothesized that collective efficiency, defined as social cohesion among neighbours combined with their willingness to intervene on behalf of the common good, is linked to reduced violence. With respect to the younger members of a community, collective efficiency is a "construct that relates to the shared expectations and mutual engagement by adults in the active support and social control of children and adolescents."[22] Collective efficiency is rooted in James Coleman's discussion of social capital as a source of social control, which will be further discussed in chapter 4. Coleman lamented the disappearance of informal family structures and tight community networks that produced this social control, and he called for formal institutions to take their place.[23] These theoretical constructs came to mind as the immigrant adolescents and adults described being "watched" or "looked out for" by local residents in Florenceville-Bristol. Again, the immigrant adolescents appear to be treated no differently than local adolescents. There are no formal programs targeted at this age group, and outside of school, few organized activities to keep them busy or out of trouble. The citizens of Florenceville-Bristol do not appear to take it for granted that adolescents are being looked after, and seem to take it upon themselves to keep an eye on them. Below, fourteen year-old Monica tells a story about her experience with collective efficiency:

> Everyone kind of watches out for us here; they know what we are up to, which is okay as long as we are behaving ourselves. Once I was playing with rocks outside on my street and this guy called the police on me. I was just throwing rocks at a tree and he went and called the police. [laughing] Umm ... okay, so it wasn't a tree it was a window, but still I got in trouble because my parents found out almost instantly [laughing]. I was just doing it because I was bored. (Monica, 1 April 2009)

For the remainder of the immigrant adolescents who participated in the case study, being watched by local residents and not "disappearing into the background" adds to their sense of security. Adwoa, an immigrant adult from Ghana, has mixed feelings about her adolescent years in Florenceville, but describes vigilant neighbours as "bringing about a sense of closeness and security you won't find in more populated centres" (Adwoa, 18 May 2009). And according to Eric: "Here everybody knows everybody else. They know who I am and they really take care of me; when I get into trouble they help me" (Eric, 1 April 2009). My focus group with New Brunswick-born adolescents revealed that they, too, keep an eye on their immigrant peers. Ashley, for example, recalled a moment when she scolded her newcomer classmate for her inappropriate winter footwear: "There was this big snow bank at the middle school last year and I saw Claudia sliding down the side of it wearing these little shoes that only covered half of her feet. I yelled at her to get down before she froze her feet off. I showed her my winter boots, pointed to them and said "boots. You need boots!" (Ashley, 3 March 2009).

A HEALTHY SENSE OF CURIOSITY

Although the immigrant adolescents are treated the same as New Brunswick-born adolescents, they nonetheless stand out as newcomers, and local residents are curious about where they come from and why they are in the community. "We were really the first family to arrive in Florenceville from Colombia," says Vanessa. "People were very curious about where we came from and why we were here. After three years they still are very curious about us and like to learn about us" (Vanessa, 1 April 2009).

That healthy sense of curiosity is particularly obvious in the schools, and it may be one of the reasons why the schools have managed to create such a welcoming environment for the newcomers. Almost all of the adolescent participants (both local and immigrant) describe this sense of curiosity in their schools. Heena, a grade 12 student from India, notes that her classmates "were just really nice to me all the time. They were very curious about me and asked me a lot of questions. Some of the questions were silly, but at least they wanted to learn about me" (Heena, 1 April 2009). And, looking back on his time at Florenceville Middle School, Shreyans, who now attends university in Ottawa says:

I enjoyed school and I had a lot of friends. When I arrived at the middle school the kids were very curious about me. They were so interested in learning about India. I remember my first day the weather was bad so we had recess in the gym. A whole group of kids circled around me and asked me a bunch of questions. It was a little disconcerting but they meant well. They all

introduced themselves and we became good friends. That curiosity and interest continued for the four years I was in Florenceville. (Shreyans, 6 May 2009)

Adolescents in Florenceville-Bristol are not endowed naturally
with an overactive sense of curiosity; rather, this curiosity has been
instilled in them by their teachers and by school administrators.
As will be noted in chapter 3, the students at Carleton North High
School and Florenceville Middle School appear to be more aware
of the world than their counterparts in Fredericton. Learning about
the source countries of their immigrant peers has been incorporated
into the academic curriculum. Sometimes, if they receive advance
warning of new students coming from abroad, the teachers will prepare the local students for their arrival through the use of geography
books, online articles, and audiovisual materials. Curiosity is further
peaked by the introduction of food. Dianne Lord, a guidance counsellor at Carleton North High School, describes below the intercultural contact that frequently happens in the cafeteria through the
sharing of lunches:

> They say there are three ways to deal with diversity, you can
> either shun it, tolerate it, or you can embrace it, and I really think
> here that the students go out of their way to embrace diversity.
> They are very curious about other countries and the teachers
> make every effort to have their students learn as much as they
> can about the immigrant students. I have seen the local students
> in the cafeteria trying food that one of the immigrant students
> brought for lunch; perhaps something particularly spicy they
> have never tried before. Or vice versa – I think of fiddleheads. I
> can remember when we brought fiddleheads in for the girls from
> Colombia to try. They thought "oh my we are going to eat those
> ferns?" So it is the same thing. It is all about the food; our society
> is all about food. (Dianne Lord, 14 April 2009)

This curiosity about new food also occurs amongst the adults at the
Global Technology Centre where the local IT workers have apparently developed a taste for Heena's mother's "Monday Samosas"
and Vanessa and Stefanie's mother's "Pay day Empanadas."
    Two of the immigrant adolescents from Latin America are not as
convinced as the other eleven about the friendliness and curiosity

shown by their peers at school. Both Claudia and Ale pick up on the same dichotomy – of the cold, apathetic Canadian culture versus the warm, embracing Latin culture – that Mateo mentioned in the Fredericton case study.[24] Ale contends, for example, that friendliness and curiosity do not go deep enough in Florenceville-Bristol:

> Language can be fixed in time as you gradually learn English. It was the culture that was different. I don't find the culture here to be particularly welcoming. It lacks a certain warmth. It is, well, it is a cold culture. Here the kids might make one initial attempt to say hello and introduce themselves, but when they notice that the new kid speaks little English, they give up and walk away. After that they don't pay any attention at all to the new kid in the class. The culture is just so different that way. I think that Latin people are very warm. We like physical contact with people. One meter apart is just too much. We have to be right in your face [laughing]. We kiss and hug a lot [laughing]. (Ale, 1 April 2009)

I Hear You

The immigrant adolescents did not spend a lot of interview time describing their lives prior to immigrating to Florenceville-Bristol. Discussion of their home countries really only came up when making comparisons with their new lives in rural New Brunswick. They did not mention local residents not wanting to listen to their stories; on the contrary, the local residents seem to want to learn as much as possible about the adolescents. In the Florenceville-Bristol case study the sub-theme "I Hear You" largely revolves around its associated code "Overcoming the Language Barrier." The code focuses on the mental and emotional challenges of learning an additional language, and on the efforts made by the schools to overcome that language barrier.

OVERCOMING THE LANGUAGE BARRIER

Consistent with the Fredericton data, learning English and overcoming the barrier to communication are critical components of the Florenceville-Bristol case study. All of the participants discussed the challenges related to learning English. Of the fourteen immigrant adolescents residing in the community, only two spoke fluent English when they arrived and none spoke French. Heena grew up speaking both English and Hindi in her native India and Stefan took intensive English classes at his school and passed the Test of English as a Foreign Language (TOEFL) before leaving Moldova. The two boys from South Korea, Eric and Alex, spoke no English when they arrived in Florenceville-Bristol and the rest of the immigrant adolescents are native Spanish-speakers from Colombia and Mexico, who arrived with limited English capabilities.

Naturally, communication challenges are associated with loneliness, boredom, frustration, and sheer exhaustion. In this respect the adolescents' stories are no different from their immigrant peers in Fredericton or from the findings in the academic literature. The following quotation from Eric is especially revealing of the loneliness brought on by not being able to speak or be understood:

> My first year here was very difficult. I didn't speak any English at all so I couldn't communicate with my guardians. I didn't have friends in school. I mean they were very nice to me, they tried to talk to me at first but I couldn't speak back so I think after a while they just gave up. So I felt alone here and really out of place. I missed Korea a lot and I was sad. So that was the worst part. (Eric, 1 April 2009)

Ale elaborates on why learning English is such a "big headache" stating that "I had to train my ear to understand English eight hours a day. I was so exhausted and so frustrated that I couldn't speak. I love to talk. I am not a quiet person. The whole experience was just horrible" (Ale, 1 April 2009).

That frustration was also evinced by their local peers who would attempt to communicate with the newcomers, then lose patience and give up. "The kids were friendly enough. They came to me to introduce themselves and ask me questions," says Andrés. "I just sat there and tried to listen as all of them came and talked to me. Eventually, though, I think the kids got frustrated that I couldn't communicate and they stopped talking to me. When I learned more English we became friends (Andrés, 1 April 2009). Conversely, when the Spanish-speaking immigrant adolescents attempted to use the smatterings of English they had learned in their home countries, their local peers did not understand, and once again became frustrated and gave up:

My first year here was horrible actually. The first challenge I encountered was the school bus [laughing]. I had never seen a yellow school bus before, just in the movies. So I got on to the bus and I didn't know where to sit and everybody was looking at me. And I tried to talk to them. I thought I spoke some English, but they didn't understand what I was saying. The kids in school were friendly enough and they tried to introduce themselves to me, and talk to me, but when they didn't understand what I was saying they walked away. (Ale, 1 April 2009)

At this point the immigrant adolescents stopped all attempts to speak English and stayed with the other Spanish-speaking teens until their English improved.

Like their peers in Fredericton, the immigrant adolescents in Florenceville-Bristol expressed tremendous pride in having ultimately overcome the language barrier. When asked about their proudest moment since arriving in the community they all responded that their grades have improved as their English language proficiency progressed. "I learned English and I am very proud of that," says Andrés. "Even my reading and writing is better in English and I do better in school now as well" (Andrés, 1 April 2009). Doing well in school and making their parents proud mean a great deal to these teens. Becoming fluent in English allows for the further reward of close relationships with New Brunswick-born classmates. Ale has even begun dating a local boy in her class. She was one of only three immigrant adolescents in the two case studies to discuss the issue of dating. While I was curious to know if the immigrant girls and boys were establishing romantic relationships with local peers, peers within their own immigrant groups, or across immigrant groups, dating and sex were not topics the teens were comfortable discussing, nor were they necessary for my research objectives.

The data reveal that the big difference between the two case studies is not the process of learning an additional language, but rather the effort that has been made, by both the immigrant adolescents and the staff and students in the schools, to overcome the language barrier. There is a sense of comfort in numbers at the schools. The two South Korean students could very well have clustered together to speak Korean all the time, and there is now a critical mass of Spanish-speaking students at the high school who could have stuck together and never learned English. But this did not happen. The immigrant adolescents are close friends. They clearly relied on one another initially to adjust to their new schools, and the teachers even encouraged this by putting them in the same classes. Yet, a huge effort was gradually made on their part to leave that ethnic and linguistic comfort zone so that they could make friends with local peers and learn English more rapidly. Jorge, for example, says he spends far more time practicing martial arts and riding snowmobiles with his New Brunswick-born friends than he does with his Colombian counterparts and, despite residing in the same house, Eric and Alex have made a pact to not speak Korean with each other.

The staff and students in the two schools have also endeavoured to overcome the language barrier, though it is important to note that having a majority of newcomer students speaking the same language (Spanish) makes it easier for the schools to cope. The lack of a separate EAL classroom where newcomer students can be placed until they can manage the academic curriculum in English means that teachers have had no choice but to figure out how to communicate with them. They have had to improvise, be creative, use available technology such as online translators, and even learn some Spanish and Korean themselves. Due to increasing interest on the part of staff and students to learn Spanish, Florenceville Middle School is now looking into the possibility of offering Spanish as part of its curriculum. Vanessa, at Carleton North High School, noted that some of the local students made this effort as well:

> At first we only talked a little bit and well, I guess we communicated by pointing at things and playing charades [laughing] but then we became best friends and things have stayed that way. Kids would help me with my homework and explain things with simple words when I didn't understand something in class. One girl bought a little electronic translator so that she could communicate with me and I thought that was very nice. (Vanessa, 1 April 2009)

The interview transcripts retrieved from the local adolescents also make reference to communication attempts, and as amusing as they are, their words are genuine:

> They are such nice people and we tried so hard to talk to them even when they didn't speak any English. It was hilarious when

we all tried to communicate at first. We all would smile and
point and we would play charades and make signs with our
hands and faces. When that didn't work we tried dictionar-
ies. Sometimes I will write the word down in English for them
to look at, and well, [pause] that doesn't help much but I try.
(Brandon, 3 March 2009)

And, according to Ashley, if all else fails there is always *Sesame
Street*: "I used to watch Sesame Street so that I could learn the Spanish word of the day and come to school and say it [laughing]. Most
of the time I would forget it by the time I got to school though.
I didn't watch the whole show just the Spanish word of the day
[laughing] (Ashley, 3 March 2009).

The Florenceville Baptist Church's efforts to translate biblical
scriptures into Spanish for Spanish-speaking newcomers has been
a welcome gesture; in the context of the larger community. MACC's
initiative to have immigrants from Colombia offer Spanish classes
to local residents is also a good one. As noted at the local Tim Hortons, Spanish conversations are now heard with greater frequency
in Florenceville-Bristol. A public outcry against a foreign language
encroaching on their town could have been made (and perhaps it
is being made by a minority of residents), yet instead the residents
of Florenceville-Bristol chose to take the initiative to learn the language. Katherine Sheriff sums up this project as follows:

Recently the Multicultural Association began to reach out a lot
more to the local community. They involve the local community in events and now the immigrants are trying to give back.
There is a husband and wife here from Colombia; she gives Salsa
dancing lessons, and he gives Spanish Classes. These activities
are always full. Some of the local people want to learn Spanish
so that they can better communicate with the Colombians and
Cubans coming in. I take the Spanish classes myself. I am not
very good at it, but I try. (Katherine Sheriff, 1 April 2009)

CONCLUSION

The integration of immigrant adolescents into a community begins
with the context of reception they encounter on arrival. Context
of reception, and particularly how the established residents of the
receiving society perceive and categorize the young newcomers, may

affect their ability to make connections and become involved in the community. This chapter examined the everyday interactions that are gradually taking place between the immigrant adolescents and established residents in the two case communities. Clearly, in order to make the kind of contact required to build fruitful relationships, the citizens of Fredericton and Florenceville-Bristol would have to be aware that the immigrant adolescents are actually in the communities, which brings the book to the second theme of public awareness.

3

Where Are We From? Why Are We Here?

Public Awareness

The small but growing body of academic literature on immigrants in New Brunswick generally describes the province as home to small, close-knit, deeply rooted, coherent communities lacking experience with ethnic, cultural, and linguistic diversity. This literature also indicates that New Brunswick lacks the resources to ensure that immigrants become part of those communities. Overall, this writing sheds light on the New Brunswick communities' deficit of knowledge, and in some cases, lack of acceptance of newcomers.[1] For New Brunswick to welcome the immigrant families it attracts, residents of communities throughout the province need to take the time to meet these immigrants, learn about their experiences, and help them establish local connections, both professionally and socially. The more people know who these newcomers are, where they are from, and why they are here, the better the chances that this will happen.

As noted in the previous chapter, contact hypothesis suggests that when individuals of two cultural groups come into positive, personal, and cooperative contact with each other, they will get to know each other, thereby reducing or eliminating prejudices. Conversely, the similarity-attraction hypothesis states that when one perceives another to be similar to oneself in relation to various characteristics (for instance attitudes and values), this will be positively evaluated.[2] Social identity theory and integrated threat theory are two additional theories which offer explanations for why people do not appreciate cultural differences.

Social identity theory[3] asserts that group membership creates in-group categorization and enhancement in ways that favour the in-group at the expense of the out-group. Henri Tajfel and John C.

Turner (1986) showed that the mere act of individuals categorizing themselves as group members was sufficient to lead them to display in-group favouritism. According to social identity theory individuals seek to achieve positive self-esteem by positively differentiating some valued quality of the in-group from a comparison out-group. Ethnocentrism is here assumed to be an inevitable consequence of social identification.

Integrated threat theory[4] is a branch of conflict theory, which generally views society as comprised of opposing groups controlling resources and attempting to maintain their advantaged position. Integrated threat theory breaks perceived threats into three specific types: realistic threats include perceived threats to the welfare of the group and its members; symbolic threats are associated with values, beliefs, and attitudes and are perceived to undermine the worldview of the group; and negative stereotypes contain elements of threat in that they lead to anticipation of negative events and interactions.[5] As Marlene Mulder and Harvey Krahn point out, "immigrants pose a [realistic] threat to Canadian-born workers who believe that they will face increased labour market competition. They might also be concerned that because immigrants would accept jobs that others will not take, increased immigration will lead to worsening labour conditions and lower wages."[6]

FREDERICTON

In the Fredericton data one of the most obvious themes is the general lack of public awareness about immigration and cultural diversity. Citizens of Fredericton seem to be aware of New Brunswick's immigration goals and population growth targets, but they are generally not knowledgeable about who is in the community now, where they are from, and why they are here. It is widely held in literature on acculturation that more public awareness leads to more accepting attitudes toward immigrants because people learn to think more positively about them. Undoubtedly many citizens of Fredericton are ambivalent about immigrants, but ambivalence can quickly turn into negativity if the ambivalent respondent is primed with negative information.[7] Therefore collecting and publicizing information, gathered through research, about why immigrants are here and how they benefit receiving communities would provide people with the tools to question and deflate any exaggerated claims and

misinformed critiques.[8] Public awareness has at least two layers to
it, represented by two sub-themes: (1) "Cultural Stereotypes and
Racism," and (2) "We Are New at This."

Cultural Stereotypes and Racism

For immigrant adolescent participants in Fredericton a lack of public awareness is expressed through cultural stereotypes, and, at
times, racist comments from peers and adults. Over the years Canadians have, perhaps unconsciously, regarded immigrants as potential threats. We have adopted many cultural stereotypes of how
immigrants are, how they should be, and how they should adapt
and fit into our culture. Regardless of the immigration category
under which they arrived in a community, immigrants are often seen
as migrants from Third World countries looking for a better life in
Canada, or as refugees escaping poverty, war, or other adverse circumstances in their countries. Saskia Sassen notes that "the general
public believes that the decision on whether to take in immigrants
is a primarily humanitarian matter; we admit immigrants by choice
and out of generosity, not because we have any economic motive or
political responsibility to do so."[9]

All of the non-European immigrant adolescents I interviewed in
Fredericton complained that their peers know about only the negative aspects of their countries or regions of origin. Cultural stereotypes and mass media images of malnourished, dying African
children, Colombian cocaine cartels, and Middle Eastern suicide
bombings are often the only means Fredericton youth have of understanding the world, and of grasping what they believe is the reality
of these young immigrants:

> They ask if I came because something is wrong over there. I
> spend so much time trying to tell them about the good things in
> my country. They just think about the bad things. The first thing
> they ask is "Why are you here?" and they automatically think
> that because I am from Iran that there is a war there. The news
> reports about our countries only when terrible things happen so
> that is all the people in Fredericton know about us ... So the local
> kids ask us about wars and they walk away. They don't give us
> the chance to tell them more about ourselves or to let them know
> that we are more like them than they think. I feel like they want

the quick and dirty information and that's it. They walk away with it. (Jasmine, 14 February 2009)

Whether right or wrong, these perceptions lead to a lot of "silly" questions from curious peers. The questions are usually genuine and innocent, and the immigrant adolescent participants regard them more as annoying than malicious. As such, they handle the questions in different ways depending on their age, personality, and other individual-level characteristics. Twelve year-old Kito, for example, is bothered by his peers' lack of knowledge about his native Africa; he takes "question period" as yet another chance to show off the youthful sense of humour that has made him popular at middle school:

> People ask me a lot of questions and I get tired of it so sometimes when they ask me where I am from I just tell them I was born in Canada. Then they ask "Where do your parents come from?" and I say "I don't know." [laughing] And other times they hear me and my brother speaking in Swahili and they ask "What is that language?" and I tell them "It's French. I learned it at École Sainte Anne, didn't you learn it? You must have missed that class" [laughing]. (Kito, 14 February 2009)

Jaime, on the other hand, arrived in Fredericton in grade 6. At the age of seventeen he has grown accustomed to curious peers and takes their questions as an opportunity to educate them about his reality:

> When the local kids ask me questions I answer them. Even if the questions are silly or bad, I know I have to answer their questions because that educates them. I don't mind and you kind of have to keep a sense of humour about it all. I'm from Colombia so you can only imagine some of the crazy questions I get [laughing]. After all, when does the news or the movies ever have anything nice to say about Colombia? (Jaime, 14 February 2009)

The immigrant adolescent participants acknowledge that cultural stereotypes demonstrate a lack of understanding and a healthy sense of curiosity rather than maliciousness on the part of their peers, but some participants, especially the members of visible minority groups, note that questions and jokes can go too far. Mateo, for example, says: "I can tell when people are joking you know. Friends ask me if I know how to process cocaine, and I know they are joking and I joke about it as well. I'm okay with that. But some people say these things too much and I know they are not kidding. There is something more behind it" (Mateo, 28 October 2008). And Luis clearly knows the difference between innocent and mean comments:

> What has always bothered me, not so much in middle school, but in high school, are the racist comments. They are not so much racist or negative towards you, but towards one race like Hispanics or blacks. I know those comments are not innocent and that makes me feel so uncomfortable. It bothers me so much. I feel like saying something, but when it is a whole group of kids saying it I just keep quiet. It is better to just keep quiet and stay out of trouble. (Luis, 14 February 2009)

"White," "Black," Hispanic," and "Oriental" are ambiguous and inconsistent racial categories that are nevertheless ingrained in North American society. It is widely accepted in the social sciences that these are not objective, scientific, biological categories, but rather represent notions that developed historically. They have no biological significance beyond the meaning attributed to them by the members of society.[10] Some authors also refer to a "new racism" or "cultural racism" in Canada.[11] This form of racism has shifted from a focus on crude ideas of biological inferiority and superiority to a language of race that excludes by using the symbolic concepts of national culture and identity.[12] According to Peter Li: "With the growth of non-white immigrants in Canada in recent decades, the term *immigrants* has increasingly assumed a folk meaning that associates it with newcomers from a different racial and cultural background ... Thus, the immigration question becomes a *de facto* question about non-white newcomers, and about the racial and cultural tension such immigrants are presumed to have brought to Canada."[13] The preference of one so-called race over another is a subtle yet unfortunate feature of New Brunswick society. This province, like the rest of Canada, favoured the settlement of European immigrants until the 1960s. As Margaret Conrad points out "although the Immigration Act [of 1912] in theory welcomed most able-bodied newcomers, New Brunswickers made no effort to hide their preference for British and Scandinavian settlers."[14] While efforts are now made to hide the preference for European immigrants, my data demonstrate that Eurocentrism apparently still exists. In a largely white city, fair-skinned, blue-eyed immigrant adolescents from Northern Europe are going to have an easier adjustment and a more obvious welcome than their black peers from Africa or Hispanic peers from Latin America.

Abo has had great difficulty getting along with his classmates since he arrived in Fredericton from Sierra Leone. He too has experienced the name-calling by white peers that Cynthia Baker and colleagues (2001) describe in their study of acts of racism toward visible minority adolescents in New Brunswick. Also similar to the study was the fact that authority figures in Abo's schools consistently discounted the importance of the racial slurs, seeing name-calling as something all children do and all children have to put up with. Several researchers in Canada, the United States, and the European Union have suggested that racism is a salient interference in immigrant adolescents' friendship development with local-born peers.[15] Abo admits that he has reacted to persistent bullying the only way he knows how – with violence. As a result he has been suspended from school several times and shuffled back and forth from one school to another:

> They wanted to fight and I didn't want to fight. After the experience I had back home in Sierra Leone I just didn't want to fight anymore. I was tired of fighting all the time for everything I needed or wanted and I told them that. But they called me "nigger" again and again and I just couldn't take it anymore. You know, one time this buddy called me nigger in class and I stood up, pulled him from his desk, and punched him right in front of the teacher. The teacher heard him call me nigger, said nothing, and had me suspended anyway. (Abo, 28 February 2009)

Callie's initial reaction to racist comments from peers was to throw punches as well, but she learned quickly that the behaviour is not acceptable:

> I don't fight with people anymore, but it is really hard not to. They call me racist names all the time and try to take advantage of me. I tried to ignore them but they wouldn't stop calling me names so one day I did hit one of the girls in the school and I got into trouble. I don't do that anymore. When this happens, and it happens all the time, the first thing that comes to mind is to hit

them, but I know that isn't the best way to deal with mean kids. So I try to put their words out of my head and think about something else. I think ignoring them is the best way of handling it. (Callie, 28 February 2009)

Callie goes on to describe that she perceives racism as a constant feeling of exclusion at school. "I felt welcome enough in school, but I seriously wonder if it was the first time the kids at my school had ever seen a black person. They looked at me like I was some kind of alien." And Auma, who like Abo and Callie is also from West Africa, points out that, "at my school if you are white people will hang out with you. The white kids are popular, they have friends and they get good grades. But if you are the black one it is really tough to get friends or to be good at anything" (Auma, 28 February 2009).

The New Brunswick-born adolescents who participated in focus groups at one of the Fredericton high schools describe a "welcoming school community" as being free of racism, bullying, and victimization; they could not (or would not) specify an incident when bullying had occurred or racist comments were made toward their immigrant peers. Of the six immigrant adults who participated in the case study, two told stories of perceived racism toward them when they were adolescents in the city, but then recanted the stories, referring to them as "misunderstandings." Xenia notes, for example, that "perhaps I was treated differently in a way because I am Latina with darker skin and hair, but I know now that is not racism. A lot of people in Fredericton have never lived or travelled anywhere else; when they meet someone who doesn't look like them or is from another culture they are not sure how to handle that situation" (Xenia, 24 November 2008). And Alfonso says that what he thought was racism was actually the culture shock and language barrier he was initially faced with:

There were some bad feelings in the work place where I thought I felt a little bit of racism. It was not obvious and it could have been because I was in a state of mind where I felt confused and out of place. In reality, [pause] looking back, [pause] I mean, [pause] I don't think it was racism I felt, but rather the people I worked with were busy and they didn't have the patience to try and understand me while I was learning English. (Alfonso, 30 December 2008)

As a researcher, I cannot refute the racial name-calling by white peers in Fredericton; however, it remains unclear to me whether the exclusion described by the black teens has less to do with their race and more to do with their family's low socioeconomic status. It would be interesting to discern whether the adolescent children of black university professors in Fredericton encounter the same racism at school. Whether associated with race or socioeconomic status, it is nevertheless evident that the non-white refugee adolescents of low socioeconomic status (who make up about half of the population sample in the Fredericton case study) are not making contact with their white, middle class peers as relative equals.

It could be said that "kids will be kids," and they will simply outgrow the kind of bad behaviour brought on by a lack of knowledge about the world. The three older immigrant adolescent participants who are enrolled at UNB, for example, did not mention cultural stereotyping or racism on the part of peers, despite their racial or ethnic minority status. Nonetheless the general acceptance these immigrants found in the university community probably has as much to do with the multicultural campus as the maturity levels of the students. If cultural diversity is lacking in New Brunswick, it is much more apparent on the campuses of UNB and St Thomas University. "University students are more likely to have positive interactions with people from different ethnic backgrounds, and race relations are generally regarded as good on campus" (International Student Advisor, 7 November 2008). Yet, racism is undoubtedly a deeply ingrained response among some New Brunswickers. Indeed, cultural stereotypes and racism become far more serious when adults are involved.

Pablo, a thirteen year-old participant from Colombia recalled his first day at a Fredericton middle school when the homeroom teacher introduced him to the class, pointed to Mexico on the map and told the class to ask their new classmate questions about Mexico so that they could learn about the country. From that day on Pablo was referred to as the "Mexican kid" on the school grounds or, much to his dismay, as the "dirty Mexican" (Pablo, 28 February 2009). While the immigrant adolescent participants in Fredericton generally spoke very highly of their teachers, there are a few teachers who are described as "well meaning," but who "just can't get the whole cultural diversity thing right" (Abo, 28 February 2009). Two of the grade 11 girls noted that they have had to prove to their teachers that they are smart and capable by getting high grades in math and science. Heo from South Korea is determined to demonstrate to her teacher that her "poor English" does not make her a student with special needs, and Jasmine, from Iran, that the scarf covering her head does not make her "a less evolved woman" (Heo, 31 January 2009; Jasmine, 14 February 2009).

During interviews, community organization participants emphasized the lack of awareness in Fredericton around immigration in general and the challenges facing immigrant adolescents in particular. They maintain that the immigrant adolescents are probably welcome in the community, but the local people do not understand their situation very well:

> I think that we could do better as a community. I think that people don't really know that so many immigrants are here. They are just not on most people's radars. They don't really understand the plight of newcomers. They don't understand how hard it is to settle in and integrate into the community. And I think the only people who really "get it" are those who have left the community and perhaps experienced that adjustment for themselves. They have seen it for themselves how hard it is and tend to reach out to newcomers and embrace diversity in the community ... Unfortunately those people are few and far between. I think most people would walk down the street, see a couple of Korean kids, smile at them perhaps, and then they would be out of their minds completely just a couple of minutes later. (Guidance Counsellor, 26 November 2008)

The community organization participants noted that many people in Fredericton have not travelled outside of Canada or even outside of New Brunswick. "They do not realize that there are other ways to do things, that our way is not the only way," says Brian Carty (Brian Carty, 13 January 2009). And as emphasized above, it is only a small group of people (both adolescents and adults) who are likely to be engaged with immigrant adolescents. These individuals are accustomed to cultural and linguistic diversity and cast a much wider net around their perceived self-identity. More often than not, such engaged individuals have themselves travelled, or lived in another part of the world, or are immigrants or the children of immigrants.

Sheer numbers of immigrants will influence opportunities for contact. With more immigrants settling in Fredericton, there is a greater sense of urgency to set up programs, introduce interventions, and make a general effort to get to know them. As immigrant families continue to move into neighbourhoods around Fredericton, and as they become more culturally and politically involved in the community, public awareness will gradually increase and more relationships will form between newcomers and established residents. Former Member of Parliament Andy Scott believes that we are slowly heading in the right direction on the immigration front. Perhaps accepting immigrants is merely a question of time, knowledge, and a generational shift:

> Certainly if you interview my older kids who are twenty-two and twenty-four, they would be surprised that you would even bother to ask these questions. They went to a fairly multicultural school and even here in Fredericton they spent their adolescence with kids from all over the world. So their sense of all of this is very different, and that is a good thing. There is not even a tiny little piece of them that wouldn't see a massive increase in visible minorities or non-European immigration as a wonderful thing for this community. Whereas, well probably not my generation, but for my parents' generation that would have been something that would have troubled them; again not for malicious reasons, but for lack of knowledge. The numbers of people who have passports increase quite dramatically from one generation to the next. The more aware people are of the world around them, the more open they are to diversity. (Andy Scott, 18 December 2008)

All of the community organization and local resident participants agreed that a social marketing campaign is needed to dispel myths and stereotypes and inform people of the benefits that immigrants bring to their community. Over half of those participants want to see a multicultural curriculum taught and practiced in all New Brunswick schools, though it remains to be seen what such a curriculum might look like and how it would be presented:

> We need to work on teaching about immigration and diversity in the schools. Not all of them know a lot about immigrants

and teachers are very important to youth. Youth look up to teachers. Whatever they say the youth take it seriously. So what if the teachers have their facts wrong? What if the teachers tell their students that all immigrants are refugees, that all ethnic and racial minorities are immigrants, or that all ethnic and racial minorities don't speak English and need to be placed in an EAL class? What then? (Jeremías Tecu, 25 September 2008)

Kimberley Graham, who runs a program for immigrant women at the Fredericton public library, and George Feenstra, a United Church minister, argue that building awareness about immigration and cultural diversity should begin in the local churches since biases against immigrants are borne out of the churches in some instances. As Kimberley points out:

The churches in Fredericton would be good spaces to educate people about the benefits of immigration for the community. However, it all depends on the church. I think the Anglican and United Church do a wonderful job on this topic, but there is also a big Evangelical community here ... You can never have an open-minded discussion with an Evangelical group. When I look for volunteers in the community to work with immigrants I stay away from certain church groups because people need to be non-judgmental and non-prescriptive and some of these church groups never fit this bill. I tend to look for people from altruistic backgrounds like social development and education because they are more comfortable working with diverse groups of people. (Kimberley Graham, 7 October 2008)

While it is not entirely clear which churches are defined as "Evangelical," there is an element of fundamentalism within some churches in Fredericton, and perhaps even more so in churches in Florenceville-Bristol. Fundamentalism implies a return to the fundamentals of faith in the context of modernization of most other religious sectors.[16] Some Fundamentalist churches in New Brunswick follow social gospel teachings, calling on Christians to change society on behalf of the poor, marginalized, and powerless. Others adhere to socially conservative values and to the bible. The latter churches generally are not open to homosexuality, and they do not accept debate and challenge to their ideology. Cultural and racial diversity are often not tolerated by these churches, and they believe that things are better left unchanged.

We are New at This

The local resident participants may not be aware of who is in Fredericton now or where they are from, but they do know about the New Brunswick population growth strategy and realize that immigration to the city is going to increase. These residents are unsure of what to do with the immigrants once they arrive. "If we are not doing a good job welcoming newcomers it is because we are new at this," they argue. Most of the local residents I interviewed, the same participants who admitted to knowing little about immigration and cultural diversity, describe Fredericton as open to diverse cultures and opinions, but "a bit late off the mark" compared with the rest of Canada when it comes to welcoming immigrants. Some local resident participants questioned their responsibility toward immigrants in the community, while others appear to be awaiting directions from the provincial government as to how to welcome the newcomers. One participant requested advice about how to integrate immigrant adolescents into the community:

> I think if community members were told ways to make these kids feel like they belong here we would try our best to do those things. Like I said, people here are well meaning. If we aren't doing a good job welcoming immigrants it is because no one has told us how to go about doing that. We don't give a lot of thought to it I guess. If the government, the provincial government, or maybe the city government could tell us what we could do better we would do it. (Tracey Pyne, 26 December, 2008)

Fredericton's schools are microcosms of cultural diversity in the wider community. One official in school district eighteen remarked that, while the Population Growth Secretariat has been working hard to achieve a target number of immigrants to New Brunswick, the Department of Education has been completely unprepared for the immigration wave it has been experiencing over the past two years. According to the official, there has been no defined approach to accommodating students coming into the schools from non-English speaking countries:

Everybody, each school, each district is working on it helter-skelter. We have no curriculum; we have no defined resources to work with; we have no defined framework for the delivery of services. So when students arrive from different countries the teachers say "well what am I supposed to do with them?" They are at a loss because they have not been trained to accommodate different cultural groups and different languages. In high school, for example, teachers focus so much more on their subject areas. The Korean students, who have been coming in large numbers, they are high flyer academic achievers, but they are still learning English. They are coming into university preparation classrooms. Anyone who can't keep up with the class becomes a deterrent for the teachers because they are held accountable for the performance of students and they are not used to slowing down and accommodating kids. (School District Eighteen Official, 15 January 2009)

The school district official does point out, however, that circumstances are changing for the better because many of these adolescents, the Korean population especially, "have a work ethic that is tantamount to anything you could find around here." These teens have been achieving at very high levels despite the fact that they are studying in English, and "their achievement has kind of tempered some of the concerns of the teachers" (School District Eighteen Official, 15 January 2009). At Fredericton High School, the guidance counsellor specializing in newcomer students and the EAL teacher have been the primary support providers for immigrant adolescents in the school. The guidance counsellor notes that the topic of including and integrating immigrant students is at the forefront of discussions now. "Teachers are realizing that they need to talk about this because they want to be the best that they can be and the school community wants to be the best that it can be as well. For a long time the topic was out of sight out of mind, but it is in our faces now and we know we have to work on it" (Guidance Counsellor, 26 November 2008).

FLORENCEVILLE-BRISTOL

In Florenceville-Bristol, making daily contact with immigrants at work, school, and in public spaces has resulted in a general public awareness that immigrants reside in the community, and that the majority of them are from Spanish-speaking countries. According to the people who participated in the case study, most residents of Florenceville-Bristol accept the immigrants and embrace the cultural diversity they bring. The local resident and community organization participants expressed satisfaction at how far the community has come over the last few years with respect to putting prejudices aside and welcoming immigrants. Nevertheless, while praising the efforts made by the community all participants in this case study, except for the immigrant adolescents, made mention of sectors of the population who do not accept the change that immigrants represent. This theme of public awareness is therefore divided into two opposite sub-themes: (1) "We Are Getting Better at This" demonstrates the pride that Florenceville-Bristol residents, and especially staff and students in the schools, have for their efforts to welcome and include immigrants; and (2) "Immigrants Take Our Jobs" focuses on those sectors of the population who believe that economic gain for newcomers means economic loss for them.

We Are Getting Better at This

Immigrant adolescents in Florenceville-Bristol did not discuss cultural stereotypes as described by their Fredericton counterparts and they largely regard "silly questions" about their home countries as positive expressions of interest. The only individual to mention cultural stereotypes and racist name-calling was Adwoa, an adult and the only participant of African descent:

The most difficult part of settling in the area was overcoming the stereotypes and misconceptions about who I was and the place I'd come from. Then finding a sense of belonging in a place where no one looked like me or had a similar background ... bad [things] did happen. During the first week at my new school, for example, I was approached by a classmate who punched me and told me to "wipe that dirt off my face" (in reference to my dark complexion). Florenceville is changing but still has a long way to go. Many people are born there and never stray far from the area. This lack of exposure can lead to narrow thinking and the ignorance that breeds intolerance. Generally the people are very friendly but would benefit from a broadening of perspective. (Adwoa, 18 May 2009)

Incidents of racism were not mentioned at all by the adolescent participants, though it is important to note here that in the social construction of race almost all of the teens from Colombia and Mexico in this case study would be considered "white"; only those from India and South Korea would be viewed as members of a visible minority group. And yet, I found it curious that local residents still associate the immigrants in Florenceville-Bristol with being "non-white." As one local resident put it "we are white and considered rich and they are darker and give up a lot to come to this country; therefore we need to do everything we can as a community to help them adapt to their new surroundings" (Local Resident, 2 April 2009). Approximately 70 per cent of the population of Medellín, Colombia, from which many of the teens originate, are ethnically European, and Mexico City is a cosmopolitan metropolis that does not necessarily represent the country's *mestizo* roots. It therefore appears that the friendly, hospitable citizens of Florenceville-Bristol are still unconsciously positioning white, Anglo-Canadians in the centre of their cultural map and the minority cultures on the periphery.

Although the most recent wave of immigrants arrived in Florenceville-Bristol between 2006 and 2009, the recruitment of immigrants to the community by McCain Foods, Ltd began in the mid-1980s. At that time the newcomers came primarily from Cuba and India. The local resident and community organization participants therefore maintain that over the years they have gained valuable experience welcoming immigrants. "We have come a long way you know," says Katherine Sheriff. "Once the initial shock wore off that so many immigrants were settling here, and once we became more secure about our own identity as a community, we came a long way; we are more open-minded now" (Katherine Sheriff, 1 April 2009). Similarly, Teresa Rogers notes that "at first the local people didn't know the newcomers; then over time they became very curious about them. Now, I guess you could say they treat them as any other new person in town (Teresa Rogers, 1 April 2009).

The schools were initially unprepared to include children and adolescents who did not speak English, but as mentioned in the previous chapter, they too "got the hang of it" over time. But again, the welcoming environment in the schools appears to have less to do with formal policies and curricula and more to do with informal endeavours to communicate and build relationships. In response to being asked how they feel about immigrant adolescents in the community, Ashley noted that "at school we don't even think about it. They are just like everybody else and everybody is friends with them. They are nice kids. We are always excited when kids come in from different countries. They are friends with everybody you know, even people you wouldn't think they would be friends with; we are like marble cake we all mix together" (Ashley, 3 March 2009).

The schools not only teach students about the world, they also seem to embrace every opportunity to celebrate cultural diversity and include the larger community in the festivities:

> Once these children arrived in order to introduce them to the community we held *Christmas Around the World* that first year so that each of them could present how they celebrated Christmas to the community. So that was kind of fun. We also held a couple of cultural nights for parents where the newcomer parents could bring their favourite food and get to know the other parents. I find people in Florenceville are very eager to try different ethnic foods ... Our school is about to celebrate a cultural diversity week in May, so that is another way we welcome them, by planning these types of events. (Calvin Brymer, 14 April 2009)

In addition to welcoming young immigrants, over the last twenty years, Carleton North High School has satisfied its interest in international education by sending local adolescents abroad and receiving exchange students through Rotary International. The schools also receive the children of parents who come from around the world to reside at the Falls Brook Sustainable Living Centre, which is located in the rural outskirts of Florenceville-Bristol. According to its website (http://www.fallsbrookcentre.ca), the Falls Brook Centre is "a sustainable community demonstration and training centre that promotes exemplary sustainable practices in agriculture and forestry." The Centre is active at the policy level with environmental non-governmental organizations and other partners on the national and international stage.

Immigrants Take Our Jobs

The overwhelmingly positive stories told by local adults and adolescents in Florenceville-Bristol diverge with an unwelcoming attitude
shown by some of the more established residents in the community. Douglas L. Palmer (1991) observed that Canadians were less
positive toward immigrants when unemployment rates were high.
Unemployment fosters the belief that immigrants will take away
jobs, despite the fact that Palmer found no evidence of native
Canadians losing jobs when immigration increased. Indeed many
researchers have noted that opposition to immigration rises during
periods of recession.[17] Economic insecurity and competition for a
smaller number of jobs may manifest themselves in racial prejudice
and restrictionist preferences in immigration policy. Whether or not
fears that immigrant labour could supplant native workers are well
founded is a subject of considerable dispute in academic journals.[18]
Education has often been associated with liberal attitudes on racial
policies and acceptance of immigrants.[19] Education is also related
to economic position, such that better educated people tend to earn
more money and are generally less threatened by economic down-
turn than the less educated.[20]

Unlike Fredericton's service-based economy, the population of
Florenceville-Bristol is predominantly employed in the working
class or "blue collar" divisions of food processing and manufacturing at McCain Foods, Ltd. Community organization participants in
the case study stressed that there are individuals in town who think
that immigrants are taking their jobs away and decreasing wages,
but that is not the case. "The positions that the newcomers are hired
for are very specialized," says Rita Ebbett-McIntosh, Settlement
Program coordinator at MACC. "Before McCain Foods and MACC
advertise internationally we advertise nationally, provincially, and
locally with no luck, but the old myth that immigrants are coming into the community and taking people's jobs is still there" (Rita
Ebbett-McIntosh, 15 April 2009). For Charlotte Evans who grew up
in Florenceville, the belief that more immigrants mean fewer local
jobs is difficult to dispel:

It is hard for me to answer your questions with an open mind,
as I grew up near McCain Foods. My father made his living

there for thirty-five years along with most of the people's families I attended school with ... When McCain's started bringing in immigrants it started getting harder to get a "good" job there. The locals would be hired for the labour jobs at the plant, but more often the office jobs would be filled by immigrants ... [pause] ... I have grown to accept diversity, but growing up it was also taught to me that immigrants coming to McCain Foods was not a good thing for the community. Immigrants threaten our livelihood. I don't believe this now, but I know some of these jobs are being given to immigrants because they are willing to work for less money. So I guess if we were to better welcome immigrant adolescents we would have to start by not seeing their families as taking anything away from us. (Charlotte Evans, 9 May 2009)

Cheaper internet and information technology, including the digitization and codification of information in the era of globalization, allow many tasks to be separated from the main activity of the business undertaken by McCain Foods, Ltd. The international recruiter for McCain Foods, Ltd, notes that "the elimination of twenty-five office positions by the company when it outsourced accounting functions offshore to India in 2008 served to strengthen distrust of foreigners in the community, even though the corporate restructuring had nothing to do with the newcomers" (International Recruiter, 1 April 2009).

A second employment-related issue involves the traditional farm families and their collective memories of how things used to be. Two of the local resident participants described the potato farmers in the area as "willing to tolerate immigrants until they voice opinions on issues they know little about." In Carleton County, for example, students are given time off from school in early fall to pick potatoes. The farmers claim they still rely on this extra help during the potato harvest and feel threatened by growing public opinion that the break should end. One local resident described the issue as follows:

When it comes to the potato break it seems that newcomer opinions just aren't welcome. For people who didn't grow up with the break and don't quite get why the farmers need the kids to help harvest the potatoes, well the farmers don't like those people very much. They argue that "you are new here;

you didn't grow up here; you don't understand why the potato
break is important so how can you possibly have an opinion?"
Constantly in the school this is a big bone of contention because
many parents don't like to have their children go back to school
early in the summer and then you have the farmers saying: "We
need the kids." And the farmers do need the kids because on the
family farm they [the kids] are old enough to drive the farming machinery and there are still all kinds of jobs to be done.
And well, someone has to look after the little ones while mom is
working on the harvester. And boy, you go to some of the meetings about potato break and they don't take well to outsiders
having an opinion. (Local resident, 2 April 2009)

Other participants strayed away from the economic arguments,
alluding instead to a generational shift in the community. According to these participants the old timers, who generally do not accept
immigrants, are being replaced by a younger generation who are
more aware of the benefits of cultural diversity. Still others think
that the Evangelical Baptist and Pentecostal churches in what is
known as the "Carleton County Bible Belt" shun cultural diversity,
but they would not elaborate on the reasoning behind this belief.
The same fundamentalism mentioned in the Fredericton case study
is present in Florenceville-Bristol; the small size of the community
magnifies the fundamentalist sentiment that much more. According
to Alex Himelfarb, "one-industry towns in Canada are characterized by an accentuated sectarianism; the small community that has
one church shared by all denominations is indeed rare." Himelfarb
goes on to state that "the large number of churches, each serving
a different denomination is a concrete indication of the deep religious cleavage in most of these communities."[21] It is possible that a
religious division exists in Florenceville-Bristol with respect to the
acceptance of modern liberal thought, and the pursuit of the changes
that immigration brings. However, the immigrant adolescents seem
to be largely unaware of any negative feelings that these differences
in opinion may cause.

CONCLUSION

Many of the participants in the two case studies expressed optimism that a heightened awareness of the challenges faced by young

immigrants, and the contributions they make to Fredericton and Florenceville-Bristol, might encourage local residents to get to know them better and to take an interest in their lives. Engaged citizens connect the adolescents with social networks that can be effectively mobilized into the social capital that facilitates their involvement and membership in the two receiving communities.

4

Reaching Our Potential

Social Capital and Social Networks

Jeremy Boissevain maintains that personal access to many valued resources and opportunities in society occurs through the messy business of commanding, negotiating, and managing diverse social relationships, that is, by way of social networks.[1] Social networks are analogous to social freeways, allowing people to move about the complex mainstream social landscape quickly and efficiently. Following this metaphor, a fundamental dimension of social inequality in society is that some of us are able to use these freeways, while others are not. The most prominent feature of Boissevain's framework is the notion of social capital, which is broadly conceptualized as "the network of associations, activities, or relations that bind people together as a community via certain norms and psychological connections, notably trust, [and] which are essential for civil society and productive of future collective action or goods, in the manner of other forms of capital."[2]

Pierre Bourdieu and James Coleman are most commonly recognized in the academic literature for introducing fundamental conceptions of social capital to the study of social phenomena. Pierre Bourdieu focused on the benefits accruing to individuals by virtue of participation in groups, and on the deliberate construction of social networks for the purpose of creating this resource called social capital.[3] Bourdieu emphasized the reproduction of power and privilege that accompanies the inequitable distribution and utility of social capital across social classes.[4] He argued that people's social capital is determined by the size of their relationship network, the sum of its cumulated resources (both cultural and economic), and how successfully people can set these resources in motion.[5] James Coleman defined social capital by its function as "a variety of entities with two elements in common: they all consist of some aspect of social structures and they facilitate certain actions of actors within the structure."[6] Coleman included in this definition some of the mechanisms that generate social capital (such as reciprocity expectations and group enforcement of norms); the consequences of its possession (such as privileged access to information and social control); and the appropriate social organization that provide the context for both sources and effects to materialize.[7]

Both Bourdieu and Coleman stressed the intangible character of social capital relative to other forms of capital. Whereas economic capital is in people's bank accounts and human capital is inside their heads, social capital inheres in the structure of their relationships.[8] To possess social capital individuals must be related to others, and it is those others, not themselves, who are the actual source of their advantage. Both sociologists, Bourdieu and Coleman agreed that social capital resides in forms of social organization that produce something of value for the individuals involved.[9] Bourdieu and Coleman were especially interested in how social capital operates to facilitate the creation of human capital in children and youth. Their influential interpretations have commonly been used to study the benefits of social capital on school-related outcomes.[10] In the period of adolescence, social capital largely refers to the social support inherent within an adolescent's family (Bourdieu referred to this within-family social capital as "cultural capital") but also through membership in interpersonal networks outside their immediate family.

For immigrant adolescents, developing social capital means accessing and building connections to individuals who might help them to better fit into their new community and achieve their goals as new Canadians.[11] Such connections are important for negotiating the move to a new school and adjusting to a new community, culture, and language. It is not known in the literature whether these young immigrants have access to more or less social capital.[12] Grace Kao argues that immigrant youth have less access to social capital, but they reap greater rewards from the little they have compared to native-born youth.[13] Minority and immigrant youth tend to come from lower socioeconomic status households than do their white native-born counterparts. This tendency would lead researchers to expect lower levels of social capital, yet membership in an ethnic group or a tightly knit immigrant community may reap social capital rewards of its own.[14]

Based on the immigrant adolescents' accounts of life in Fredericton and Florenceville-Bristol, it is clear that the distinction that Robert Putnam (2000) developed between bonding and bridging social capital is also important. Bonding social capital refers to inward-looking relationships and networks of trust and reciprocity that reinforce ties within such groups as families and ethnic communities; bridging social capital is concerned with outward-looking connections amongst heterogeneous groups of friends and acquaintances. Both bonding and bridging social capital are important, but it has been argued that bonding social capital permits people to "get by," while bridging social capital enables people to "get ahead." Prior to Putnam's discussion of bridging social capital, Mark S. Granovetter (1973) coined the term "strength of weak ties" to refer to the power of indirect influences, outside the immediate circle of the family and close friends, to serve as an informal employment referral system. This theory assumes that open heterogeneous social networks would facilitate the process of immigrant integration because these kinds of networks would allow more ties to the cultural majority than the established, close-knit co-ethnic networks of the immigrant community.[15]

FREDERICTON

In Fredericton immigrant adolescents described family members as providing crucial forms of emotional support. The teens have also become bound together in their own social network by virtue of being immigrants, but as a group they demonstrate very little of the kind of social capital that would bridge them with New Brunswick-born peers and other established residents in the community.

Family Ties and Ethnic Networks

The importance of family ties, hard work, and optimism about the future appear to be values shared by all of the immigrant adolescents who participated in the case study of Fredericton. Whether from Latin America, Africa, Asia, or Europe, these teens come from cultures where the family system is an integral part of daily life. Of the twenty immigrant adolescents interviewed in the city, eleven live in two parent families and five live in single parent families, with the mother. In the latter families, the fathers were killed or left behind in political violence; the fathers remained in the home country to work or they returned to the home country to work when no jobs were available in New Brunswick; or the mothers immigrated with their children to start a new life in Fredericton following marital break-up. In addition to these families, one participant lives with his older sister, and the three university students who participated in the case study live on their own in residence. All of the immigrant adolescent participants have siblings either in Fredericton or in their home countries.

The immigrant adolescents go to family members for advice, usually mothers, but also fathers and older siblings. All are intensely proud of their parents or parent and are aware of the sacrifices made on their behalf. Callie was one of many participants to elaborate on her relationship with a parent:

My mom is the most important person to me. She works very hard to take care of us and I really look up to her ... A happy time for me was when I went to the Fredericton Exhibition for the first time. My mom wasn't working yet so she went with us and we spent the whole afternoon together. It was good family time together. We had fun and we felt safe. That is the good part about Fredericton, you can go out and spend time together as a family and feel safe. My mom has two jobs now so we don't spend as much time together anymore. (Callie, 14 February 2009)

When asked about their proudest moment or biggest accomplishment since arriving in Fredericton, almost all of the immigrant adolescent participants referred to making their parents proud rather than themselves. For the university students, receiving scholarships and holding part-time jobs make them proud because they are no longer "financial burdens" on their parents. Fajar, for example, remarks that "I can pay my own tuition. I get jobs here and there and I work during the summer. So I could pay my tuition this term and that has helped my parents a lot" (Fajar, 19 November 2008). Mateo says that his parents needed to use all their savings to keep him in university. "I now have a student loan, but want to make high grades and get scholarships so I won't be a drain on my parents anymore," and Van Anh emphasizes that "I have been independent for so long and I feel good about being on my own and making decisions on my own, and I help my family out because I don't have to use their money; I have scholarships, bursaries, and part-time jobs to support myself" (Van Anh, 5 November 2008). For the younger adolescents, doing well in school and learning English make their parents happy, and this in turn fills them with enormous pride. Mai touches on this topic when discussing her relationship with her parents:

My mom is really happy when we talk about our day at school, when we share things with her. My mom says life isn't easy here, but for us we just do our best to study as much as we can and do well so my mom thinks it was a good decision to come here. We spend a lot of money to live here and my mother does so much for us. My dad too; he is a good dad and he works hard in Taiwan to keep us here. So I just want my parents to be proud of me and not have to worry about me. When we first arrived in Fredericton and we were getting used to being here I got an eating disorder. I am also proud that I overcame my eating disorder because my family doesn't have to worry about me anymore. I put my family through a lot during that time. (Mai, 10 December 2008)

These findings are supported by Andrew J. Fuligni (1997; 2001) who noted that immigrant adolescents' motivation to do well in school is partially fuelled by a sense of obligation to repay their parents for the sacrifices the parents made to come to North America, and by a desire to obtain well-paying jobs and to help support their families in the future. Immigrant parents often use the rhetoric of sacrificing their lives in their country of origin and accepting limited opportunities in the receiving society so that their children can benefit from freedom and socioeconomic mobility.[16] Research further suggests that immigrant families compensate for the absence of outside social networks and bridging social capital in the receiving society by emphasizing social capital in the form of familial support, a support that includes preserving the cultural orientations of the home country[17] and a strong sense of familial obligation.[18]

While the immigrant adolescents in Fredericton talk about integration largely in the context of finding their way around and making friends in the community, they also spend a significant amount of time worrying about their parents. About half of the participants' parents have not found jobs in Fredericton resulting in deteriorating household finances:

> The community would be more welcoming if there were more ways to learn English and to learn the things you need to know to get a job. If parents could get a job right away there would be less worry. You know it is hard for us to start school in September when we don't have all the school stuff we need. Maybe the government could give money to families to buy school stuff and we could pay [it] back later. (Pablo, 28 February 2009)

Pablo's family has government sponsored refugee status, but some of the children of economic immigrants also expressed concern that their parents are still unemployed. In some cases the parents arrive in the city as provincial nominees with the intention of starting their own business, but the business plan is delayed or does not work out. The economic insecurity of these families corresponds with evidence from the National Longitudinal Study of Children and Youth (NLSCY) showing that more than 30 per cent of all immigrant children in Canada live in families whose total income falls below the poverty line.[19] Abdolmohammed Kazemipur and Shiva Halli also found that immigrants in Canada are consistently overrepresented among the poor and that, among immigrants poverty rates are higher for members of visible minority groups, who are mostly recent immigrants.[20]

The immigrant adolescents worry about their parents and, reflecting the literature on immigrant children and youth, they also "parent their parents." Alejandro Portes points out that the children of immigrants are often forced to become their "parents' parents" as their knowledge of the new language and culture races ahead of the adults. "This generational role reversal," argues Portes, "undercuts parental authority to control youth as they enter an increasingly complex society marked by the ready availability of counter-cultural models."[21] Other scholars refer to this phenomenon as "cultural brokering" or "language brokering."[22] These activities may involve translating documents sent home by a local school, arranging for medical appointments, answering the telephone, or simply explaining to parents what their native-speaking friends are talking about. Mai is learning to drive because her mother is too afraid to drive the car in the winter; Heo interprets English conversations for her parents and accompanies them to medical appointments, bank appointments, and parent-teacher meetings. The teens also teach their parents about local social and cultural norms. Martine for example, tried to save her mother the embarrassment of wearing excessive perfume in public places:

> One day my mom stepped on to the bus and the bus driver, who was a woman, told her she was wearing too much perfume and couldn't come on the bus. Can you believe that, too much perfume? So she didn't know that people here don't wear perfume and when the bus driver told her that her perfume was too strong she felt really bad. My mom doesn't understand that people are allergic to perfume. So I had to explain that to her. I think maybe allergies are a Canadian thing. (Martine, 28 February 2009)

For the immigrant adults, parenting their parents is a memorable part of their adolescent years in Fredericton, with many of them stating that they were the ones in charge and their parents were the dependants. Carlos describes this situation as follows:

> Settling into Fredericton was empowering, but at the same time it was scary. The whole immigration process certainly pushed me to the edge, but it also allowed me to perform at my highest level. I was fourteen years old when we arrived in Fredericton and I had the best English in my family. That put me in the driver's seat at a very young age. I had to translate for my mother, make important decisions and ensure that everything went smoothly. My family depended on me to settle in and integrate into the community. (Carlos, 25 May 2009)

Unlike family ties, adolescent participants did not spend a great deal of time discussing the role of ethnic networks in their integration into Fredericton. Local resident participants mentioned ethnic networks, assuming they would be an important aspect of the immigrant adolescents' lives. Community organization participants continuously grouped the immigrant adolescents into their corresponding ethnic group – the Latin Americans, the Africans, the

Koreans, the Europeans – when discussing their lives in Fredericton,
and the immigrant adults described how important Fredericton's
recent, small ethnic communities and ethnic mentors were to them
in their youth.

Certainly it can be garnered from the literature that ethnic networks would be a significant factor in the integration of immigrant adolescents. James Coleman argued that emotionally intense,
bounded networks among parents and other adults surrounding
children enable these adults to "establish norms and reinforce each
other's sanctioning of the children."[23] Following this line of thinking,
scholars have posited that children from some immigrant groups are
successful in school because they come from families and communities with close, emotionally intense bonded networks that transmit
certain values, beliefs, and expectations.[24] For example, Min Zhou
and Carl Bankston's study of how Vietnamese American students
have maintained a high level of achievement found that children and
youth who are more highly integrated into their ethnic group are
likely to follow the forms of behaviour prescribed by the group, such
as studying or working hard, and to avoid the forms of behaviour
proscribed by the group.[25] Yet, immigrant adolescents in Fredericton only mentioned ethnic networks with reference to their Korean
peers, who according to them, "stay together all the time speaking
Korean and don't want to make other friends." There are small, relatively recent ethnic communities in Fredericton (the biggest are Chinese, Korean, Latin American, and Muslim) and while the parents of
the immigrant adolescents often rely on the bonding social capital
made available to them by these networks, the adolescents I interviewed are more likely to rely on the bonding social capital provided
by other immigrant adolescents from a variety of different ethno-
cultural backgrounds than to stay in their own ethnic groups.

It is only natural that immigrant adolescents will seek out and
befriend other immigrant adolescents, because despite being from
different countries and cultural backgrounds, and speaking different
languages, these teens have the experiences of migration and adaptation in common. I noticed a warm relationship among the adolescents who participated in the focus groups at MCAF, and all the
immigrant adolescents referred to a friend from another country.
The EAL teacher describes the relationships that develop between
students in her classroom:

The kids in my EAL class become very close. Some days I cry because by the end of the term some of these kids are best buddies. So you have the Korean girl with the Romanian girl over here and they sit with the African girl at lunch and the other day I was listening to the kids as they were trying to plan to go swimming together. The Colombian girl is with the Korean girl and the other Korean girl and they are planning what they are going to do on the weekend. It is really wonderful. Here they feel comfortable speaking with their broken English because the other person's English is broken as well. (EAL Teacher, 11 February 2009)

Neighbours and the Kindness of Strangers

"Good neighbours" are words the local resident participants used to portray Fredericton as a community. According to them, the ability to know one's neighbours and to rely on one's neighbours is characteristic of life in Fredericton. For immigrant adolescents, however, knowing one's neighbours appears to be a factor of the neighbourhood where one lives. Christopher Jencks and Susan Mayer (1990) developed several theoretical ways in which neighbourhoods might influence the development of children and adolescents. Contagion theories are based on the power of peer behaviours, including imitation and pressure, to influence other children to exhibit problem behaviours; theories of collective socialization suggest that adult members of the community act as role models, monitoring and influencing children who are not their own. These theories would predict that living among affluent neighbours would encourage child competence, achievement in school, and avoidance of problem behaviours.[26] Jeanne Brooks-Gunn and colleagues (1993) found reasonably powerful neighbourhood effects – particularly the presence of affluent neighbours – on childhood intelligence quotients (IQs), teenage pregnancies, and drop-out rates, even after differences in socioeconomic and family characteristics were adjusted for.[27] In Fredericton, like most cities, where one lives is at least in part determined by one's socioeconomic status.

For immigrants, socioeconomic status is often related to the immigration category under which they arrive in Canada. Armed with occupational skills or ample financial resources, economic immigrants tend to purchase houses in middle class, family oriented neighbourhoods. According to the school district eighteen official I interviewed, Korean parents conduct extensive research on schools in Fredericton when they arrive in the city. To ensure their children learn English, the parents choose schools that do not have large numbers of Korean students already enrolled in them. They then purchase a house in a neighbourhood near that school (School District 18 Official, 15 January 2009). Government sponsored refugees may also be educated professionals, but they arrive in Fredericton with little money and few, if any, personal belongings. Such refugees receive federal social assistance for one year. Canada is also one of only a few countries that require refugees to repay the government for their airfare within one year after arrival. Often refugees are simply unable to afford these costs on top of living expenses. While they are able to choose which neighbourhood to live in, their choices are limited by a shortage of low-income housing. As mentioned in chapter 2, a substantial number of refugees from Africa and Latin America reside in apartment complexes located in a single north-side Fredericton neighbourhood. Research has demonstrated that clustering low-income families in high-poverty neighbourhoods can lead to their social and economic isolation, which compromises children's chances of eventual self-sufficiency.[28]

The participants I interviewed from Belgium and the Netherlands could not say enough good things about their neighbours in the rural suburb of Douglas. According to Feena, "when we moved into our house in Douglas people kept knocking on our door and giving us cookies and apple pies. They would knock and say 'Hi, I am your neighbour. Have some pie' and we were not used to that at all. They are all very nice. Some of the neighbours even cook entire meals for us and we are a huge family." (Feena, 31 March 2009). And Lucus' elderly neighbours in the established Fredericton neighbourhood known as "the hill" advise him, take him to concerts and museums, and pass their evenings chatting with him in their garden. In contrast, participants from Colombia, Congo, Liberia, and Sierra Leone who live in low-rental apartment complexes in Devon have either not met their neighbours at all, or have had unpleasant encounters with them. With the exception of a neighbour in Devon named Chantelle – mentioned by Auma – who invites the teens to her house to do crafts and play board games, the only other "neighbours" consist of a group of Jehovah Witnesses who frequent the apartment complexes. As Mark reported, "at the apartment we met some church people who brought us to church. That's fine but I wanted to meet my neighbours" (Mark, 28 February 2009).

Fredericton is also home to strangers who are kind to immigrants. The immigrant adolescents describe strangers as friendly and helpful when they are lost and in need of directions. Abo and Auma described a city bus driver who has been kind to them: "There is one bus driver though. He is like us [black] and kind of old. He is so nice to us. When we don't have the proper fare he lets us ride the bus for free. He makes us feel welcome in Fredericton" (Abo and Auma, 28 February 2009). It was an immigrant adult participant, however, who told the most delightful stories of experiences with strangers when he was younger. Andrew rarely went hungry: "People were always leaving food at my door. At Christmas people who I didn't even know came to my door with food. For over a month I was eating this food that people kept leaving for me. I saved a lot of money that month." When Andrew first arrived in Fredericton he was buying shoes at the local Wal-Mart, and he met a cashier named Becky: "She asked if me if I just arrived and ended up taking me and my family to her place for dinner. She has been a close friend ever since." He also received support from strangers to help him bring his mother from Sierra Leone: "People would leave cheques in plain white envelopes. They would simply write 'for Andrew's mother.' Sometime they would contact me through the registrar at the university and say 'Andrew you don't know me, but what can I do to help bring your mother here?' There are really good people in Fredericton" (Andrew, 12 July 2008).

Friends

Immigrant adolescents in this case study reported that they first and foremost draw upon their friends to help them cope with the move to Fredericton. Networks of peers help them to become familiar with school, find their way around, learn the unwritten rules and practices of a new culture, and become confident and settled. Their responses are consistent with the literature on adolescent development, which suggests that peer relationships represent a vital segment of adolescents' social support system. For immigrant adolescents, membership within peer social networks appears to provide the resources necessary to foster developmental gains and school achievement.

These positive outcomes occur in spite of the many stressors associated with their acculturation, and with segregated and economically marginalized schools and neighbourhood environments.[29]

Friends often influence immigrant adolescents' school performance even more significantly than they do local adolescents because immigrant parents, in some cases, do not possess the educational background to have access to the institutional knowledge needed to succeed in school and prepare for university. They can therefore serve as a source of bridging social capital by providing access to important social networks, as well as providing a critical orientation toward values.[30] However, this requires that the immigrant adolescents have friends with the requisite social capital to share. The reality is that immigrant adolescents' opportunities to come into contact with and befriend local-born peers are often limited. The process of making friends with the New Brunswick-born adolescents has been difficult for most of the immigrant adolescents in Fredericton, and for those participants who are recent arrivals, that process is still far from complete. Regarding the difficulty of making friends, Martine opines "Making friends? Well out of a scale of one to a million I would say a million" (Martine, 14 February 2009). The EAL teacher also sums the situation up nicely with a single comment: "Last Friday one of the girls walked up to me and said 'Mrs. D. I want a friend.' And my heart just broke for her" (EAL Teacher, 11 February 2009).

Part of the difficulty of making friends goes back to the immigrant adolescents and local adolescents not making that initial contact, or not making the effort to get to know one another. As Van Anh points out, "When you come here as a teenager people your age already have their circle of friends and it is very hard to fit into a group; to break through those circles. You can make friends with them but not really good friends because they already have those friends from their childhood" (Van Anh, 5 November 2008). For adolescents, friendships develop at school. On this topic Feena notes that: "Leaving my friends behind in Holland, coming to a new school where I didn't know anyone, trying to make contact with people without any English. That was very hard. Most of the time they are friendly, but these kids have been together since elementary school and it is hard to get to know them." She also notes that the system of switching classes according to the subject rather than staying in a homeroom for the duration of the day makes meeting people that much more difficult: "In Holland we stay with our friends in the same class all day and the teachers come to us. Here the bell rings and we switch classes and each class has a new group of people. I was so surprised about that. The bell rang and I didn't know what to do. I thought 'Oh no, now I have to make contact with a whole new group of kids!'" (Feena, 31 March 2009)

School is especially relevant to the development of peer relationships because it is the most important societal institution adolescents have to commit themselves to.[31] Schools cater to their friendship needs and serve as important daily settings in which adolescents can build up their networks through reciprocal social relations. They provide teens with opportunities to gain information, observe, and imitate their peers. This, in turn, buttresses the development of social competence in the classroom, self-esteem, and identity,[32] and it fosters academic engagement and achievement.[33] Yet, all too often local adolescents are ambivalent to the presence of immigrant students. In a 2000 study by the Canadian Council on Social Development, immigrant youth participants described school as the focal point of their lives. The majority indicated that their first year in Canada was difficult, and that school was often traumatic; these immigrant youth described school as a place where they felt homesick and socially isolated.[34] Orientation to school was described as "being thrust into a sink or swim situation – having to learn the language and make friends quickly."[35]

The other difficulty has to do with finding common ground and making contact on an equal footing. Some of the immigrant adolescent participants claim that they are just too different from their local peers, that they have different cultural or socioeconomic backgrounds, that they look different, or speak another language, and perhaps most importantly, the immigrant participants emphasize that they have different beliefs and values than their local peers. Callie equates her inability to make friends with her race:

I meet people at school but a friend, a real friend who has the same interests as I do and is from my background, or at least understands my background, it is impossible. I don't mean to be racist, but really I'm the *only* black kid. I feel very different. Sometimes I walk into a room full of white kids and I wonder how I should act. I want to fit in but I also want to be myself. So I find it easier to make friends with people of my colour and from my background. I try to approach kids at school but I feel like my English is no good or it sounds mixed up and I just look different than they do. (Callie, 28 February 2009)

Feena has been able to make friends with the local adolescents in her school, in spite of her standards and values being so different than the local girls, but she prefers to stay with an exchange student from Germany who she feels she has more in common with:

When I came here I made friends, but they really aren't the kind of girls I am used to. We are quite different. So then I met an exchange student from Germany and we became good friends. We are together all the time. The girls here are different than back home in Holland and that was really difficult for me to get used to. In Holland how you look is important of course, but here the girls go too far sometimes. They are so concerned with how they look and they spend more time thinking about boys than about school. And the girls say they are equal to boys and they say they want respect but they certainly don't act that way ... I don't know it's weird. I don't want to be like that you know? [whispering] Kissing every guy, I am not like that at all and a lot of the girls are ... So I stay with the exchange student from Germany because she is more like me. (Feena, 31 March 2009)

That these stories were told by girls is not coincidental. The girls who participated in the Fredericton case study have found it far more challenging to meet people and make friends than the boys. With the exception of two male participants – one who had just arrived in Fredericton two weeks before I interviewed him, and the other, who while incredibly astute and articulate, is also shy and withdrawn – the boys have gradually managed to develop relatively strong friendship networks in their schools and in the wider community. Pablo describes meeting his best friend John in grade 6 as his "proudest moment," and Musi and Kito seem to have had a seamless entry into a friendship network at École Sainte Anne that includes both New Brunswick-born adolescents and other immigrants from the Congo. In the university, Fajar enjoys the social benefits of resident life at UNB and "going out and doing fun things" with members of the marketing club.

The immigrant adult participants, all but one of whom are men, also spoke enthusiastically about their networks of friends in Fredericton. For Leeder making friends was easy. "I didn't have to put any special effort into making friends, but this is something that comes naturally to me. I am very social and as such there were many people here who appreciated that and I got to know many people very quickly as I settled in" (Leeder, 10 November 2008). And, according to Paul: "Having a lot of friends is a big accomplishment. I am an only child so having good, lifelong friends is really important to me. For me it was easy to make friends even though I spoke very accented English when I arrived from Poland, but again I was very lucky because of my involvement in Characters Incorporated and other theatre related activities in Fredericton" (Paul, 5 December 2008).

The idea that immigrant girls often experience a more difficult adjustment to the receiving community is discussed in literature on immigrant acculturation and adolescent development. Girls tend to have more household responsibilities and experience more parental control than boys, and they are more likely to take on the role of cultural broker (i.e., parenting the parents) than their brothers are.[36] My own findings do not reveal a big difference between girls and boys in this regard. The boys who participated in the case study of Fredericton talked about their parents as much as did the girls, and none of the adolescents described cultural or generational conflicts with their parents. The girls take their education more seriously and make higher grades in school than the boys, but it is not clear to me how much control parents have over their study habits. Most of the immigrant adolescents who participated in my study come from urbanized families, where traditional norms dictating the differential treatment of boys and girls are not practiced as much as they once were. My findings generally correspond with studies showing that immigrant girls have a pattern of greater susceptibility to life events and their negative impact, and demonstrate lower self-esteem and higher self-awareness.[37] They contradict a recent study conducted in Calgary by Yvonne Hébert, which revealed that immigrant girls have a higher number of friends outside their own ethnic groups than immigrant boys. According to Hébert, "girls are more flexible to changing circumstances, more open to new things, more willing to accept the new ideas; thus, they find it easier to make friends and make bridging transitions."[38] This is not the case in Fredericton. Adjusting to life in Fredericton and making friends may merely be a matter of time for the girls, but it is clear that formal program providers need to make a greater effort to include girls in a wider range of extracurricular activities in the city.

My findings suggest that sports, and especially soccer, play an important role in the creation of bridging social capital for immigrant boys in Fredericton. Team sports such as soccer offer a meeting place where social interactions with local peers are stimulated, and where an immigrant adolescent can be noticed, respected, and appreciated by peers despite his or her perhaps low level of fluency in English or French. While all but one of the boys who participated in the case study play soccer, none of the girls are involved in team sports. Two of the girls dance and one has recently discovered a passion for running, but neither of these activities are done in groups. This situation is best illustrated by the photographs of soccer fields taken by the boys versus the photographs of libraries taken by the girls depicted in chapter 2. It is also a topic touched on by some of the community organization participants. Philip Sexsmith, for example, has found that immigrant boys make connections in the school faster than the girls do and they are more likely to break out of their little ethnic groups and make friends with the local students (Philip Sexsmith, 8 January 2009). According to Kimberley Graham, "I can think straight away of soccer. Soccer is the one international game that everybody is very keen to play, and you don't need to speak English to play it ... The girls seem to struggle a bit more. They don't integrate themselves as easily and they tend to form cliques according to their ethnic group." And Dexter Noel, former president of the MCAF board of directors notes that, "being a good soccer player will at least postpone the surprise and the feelings of unease that people may have when newcomers arrive in the community" (Dexter Noel, 21 January 2009).

FLORENCEVILLE-BRISTOL

In Florenceville-Bristol immigrant adolescents appear to have greater access to bridging social capital than do their counterparts in Fredericton because local residents are easier to meet and there is a more obvious effort all around to form a diverse set of relationships. Bonding social capital is further fostered in Florenceville-Bristol by the existence of a critical mass of people from the same country (and city) of origin.

Family Ties and Ethnic Networks

Like their economic and refugee counterparts in Fredericton, the thirteen immigrant adolescent participants in Florenceville-Bristol did not choose to relocate to rural New Brunswick; that choice was made for them by their parents. Yet, the adolescents say they are grateful for their new lives, and look forward to the educational and career opportunities that lay ahead. Dianne Lord describes what she views as their situation at home:

> I suspect when they are at home their life is very different than the children here. Our children take an awful lot for granted. They just assume you are going to put a roof over their head, food on their plate, and clothes on their back, and the best clothes not just any clothes. I think a lot of the children I have met who have come from other countries; they feel it is their responsibility to work in the home, to help at home. There seems to be a real partnership in these families, that everybody does their part for the family to be successful. So as a result of that I don't think that they go home, drop their book bag on the floor and flop on the couch. Just the way they even speak of their parents, or God forbid I ever threaten to call home to report them. I can just see the look on their faces. They don't want to disappoint their parents. They want their parents to be proud of them. (Dianne Lord, 10 April 2009)

The Colombian participants, in particular, expressed appreciation that their families now live in spacious houses rather than tiny apartments; they own cars and luxury items, and they have more time to spend together as families. The importance of spending time together as a family was a recurrent idea throughout the interviews, as demonstrated, for example, by Monica's comments in chapter 2. It is important to note, however, that not all of the families arrived in Florenceville-Bristol intact. Of the nine Latin American participants, three live with both parents and siblings; one lives with both parents, but left her older sibling at university in Colombia; and one lives with both parents, but lost his sibling to violence in Colombia. This latter boy shares his home with his cousin, who also participated in the case study. The remaining Latin American participants are from single parent and blended families. One lives with his mother and visits his father in Colombia on holidays; another was given the choice to remain in Colombia with her father or immigrate with her mother and stepfather; and one arrived with both parents and a younger sibling, but the parents split up soon after arrival and now reside in separate houses. The adolescents from India and Moldova live in two-parent homes, and the two Korean participants live with guardians. Overall, the family situations of the immigrant adolescents in both Fredericton and Florenceville-Bristol paint an interesting picture of the motivations for immigrating, the impact of violence on people's lives, and the toll that migration can take on marriage.

All of the immigrant adolescents who participated in the case study spoke with conviction about the importance of family and about their parents' role in shaping their values and identities. Discussions about family revolved around making parents proud by mastering English and excelling in school. But, perhaps even more striking were the discussions about safety and security that were alluded to earlier in this book. With the exception of Stefan who says his native Moldova is similar to Canada in many ways, every adolescent expressed tremendous relief that their parents no longer have to worry about their safety in Florenceville-Bristol. "My mom really likes it here because it is so peaceful and safe and everyone kind of watches out for us," says Stefanie (Stefanie, 1 April 2009). And as Cristina points out: "It is safe and peaceful here. We can go wherever we want and our parents don't have to worry about us like they did in Colombia. Back in Medellín kidnappings happened all the time and our parents worried about us and kept us inside. Now I am free" (Cristina, 1 April 2009).

The issue of parenting parents by translating or language brokering did not come up during the interviews in Florenceville-Bristol, most likely because at least one parent spoke English upon arrival. Worrying about parents did come up, however. While the adolescents enjoy their new-found freedom and personal security in this small rural setting, their parents do not necessarily hold their own new lives in such high regard. Three of the adolescent participants conveyed concern and sadness about their mothers experiencing culture shock, social isolation, loneliness, anxiety, and depression. While five mothers work outside of the home (two at McCain Foods, Ltd), the rest stay at home alone while their husbands work and their children attend school. Unable to learn English at the same pace as the rest of the family, and in some cases unable to afford or even drive a car, these women live a lonely existence with MACC acting as the only link to their new community. Claudia describes the situation as follows:

> My mom doesn't feel comfortable here. She has been thinking about moving back to Mexico. But I keep telling her that now is not a good time to go back to Mexico because it is getting really dangerous there. The violence is everywhere in Mexico now, even in the peaceful provinces ... It is really scary ... Mom is really depressed lately because she feels alone. She has friends here but it is not the same as in Mexico. She is also thinking about moving to a bigger city in Canada where there are more people from Mexico. (Claudia, 1 April 2009)

Monica tells a similar story and also refers to her mother's unease that her daughter's integration is moving at such a fast pace. She is becoming too much like the local girls: "My mom has a hard time here. She has not learned very much English and can't communicate well with the people here ... She worries about me becoming too much like the Canadian girls ... My mom thinks my friends here are reckless and she doesn't trust them" (Monica, 1 April 2009).

When these women do leave the homes their limited proficiency in English limits them to only interacting with their own small ethnic groups. The immigrant women maintain an orientation to their home countries and have little contact with the larger community. Many of them live for the moment of return migration, or migration to a bigger urban centre in Canada. The stories told by the immigrant adolescents correspond with literature on immigrant mothers. One Canadian study by Sandra Kouritzin (2000) found that the immigrant mother has two distinct, often contradictory roles: the expectation that she carry the main responsibility for the cultural socialization of children and the expectation that she attend to children's academic development. To accomplish one she feels she must be seen to reject the English language and cultural mores of the receiving society in favour of those of her culture of origin; to accomplish the other she feels she must integrate as quickly as possible into the new life, acquiring the English language and customs so as to benefit her children and maximize the social resources available to the family.[39]

Since both McCain Foods, Ltd and the long-haul trucking companies, the largest of which is itself a division of McCain Foods, Ltd, target certain regions of the world as an employment strategy, there are now enough people from the same source countries to establish small ethnic communities in Florenceville-Bristol. The most obvious of these is the Colombian community. I refer to the "Colombian" community and not the Spanish-speaking or Latin American community, because the Cuban and Mexican families in Florenceville-Bristol are not necessarily part of this growing enclave. Two of the immigrant adolescents and the community organization participants referred to a dispute between a Colombian family and a Mexican family that has resulted in an ethnic community united by nationality rather than a common language. The other tiny ethnic communities consist of the handful of Indian families, and the Eastern European families from Moldova, Romania, and the Ukraine who arrived over the past three years.

As previously mentioned, the immigrant adolescents associate with their ethnic communities, but have nevertheless shifted their orientation from their place of origin to their new community. Andrés, Stefanie, and Vanessa described their families as spending almost every weekend together and as hosting Colombian celebrations at their homes; Heena mentioned an adult role model at the Global Technology Centre who is also from New Delhi; Stefan described getting to know and speaking Russian with families from the Ukraine; and though dating a local boy, Ale says her family tends to stay only with the foreigners at McCain Foods, Ltd "We have more things in common with the foreigners. It doesn't matter which country they come from, we just relate to them more than the local people" (Ale, 1 April 2009).

Transnational ties with the countries of origin are also more obvious and easier to trace in Florenceville-Bristol. Transnational theory locates migration flows within a complex system of linkages between people across borders of nation-states.[40] Once an employee is recruited to the Florenceville-Bristol area from Medellín, Mexico City, or New Delhi, that employee will assist the international recruiter to hire a former colleague, friend, or relative from the same cities, resulting in the phenomena of chain migration. Upon hearing of her impending move to New Brunswick, for example, Ale encountered Julia (the fourteenth immigrant adolescent who was not present during the interviews) on the internet. The two girls stayed in touch with each other while still in Medellín and finally met in person when they arrived in Florenceville-Bristol. The presence of two South Korean adolescents in the community is also an interesting exercise in transnationalism. Upon graduating from university, a local man moved to South Korea to teach English at a Seoul preparatory school. While there he convinced his student Eric to travel to Florenceville-Bristol, reside with his parents, and attend Carleton North High School. Eric subsequently called for his friend Alex to join him on his adventure. Both boys plan to attend medical school, apply for permanent residency, and practice medicine in Canada.

Neighbours

In the rural setting of Florenceville-Bristol most of the houses are situated too far apart to be considered "next door" or adjacent to one another. While the empty spaces can be disconcerting for the immigrant adolescents, the following quotation by Ale demonstrates an understanding that neighbourliness and sense of community can exist without close physical proximity:

> Here the houses are so far apart that you can't get to know your neighbours, because you don't actually have neighbours. Sometimes I think that if I die in my house no one will ever know. My house is surrounded by so many trees. But I guess all the people here are united enough to be considered neighbours, or at least they treat each other like neighbours. Community is not about the place it is about the people. It can be small and rural and the worst place to live, but the people make the place special. (Ale, 1 April 2009)

So in this respect the citizens of Florenceville-Bristol are neighbours and where there are neighbours there are cakes, pies, cookies, and even entire roast turkeys. Food dominated the responses of the immigrant adolescents and adults when asked about their welcome and inclusion in the community. "When we moved into our house, people brought food over to us to introduce themselves and make us feel welcome," says Andrés (Andrés, 1 April 2009). Adwoa notes that "whenever there was a loss or need in the community, the way neighbours came together to help each other made me feel good about living there. For example, there was a time when my mother was quite ill; people came by continually with home cooked meals, offers to help out around the house and kind words throughout her lengthy recovery" (Adwoa, 18 May 2009). And, according to Stefan:

> A welcoming community? Well I can say that when we arrived at our house, the first day at our house, all the neighbours came with cookies, and pies, and gifts for us. It was very welcoming. I liked it so much. And now with a couple of neighbours we are almost best friends. One of the neighbours has a girl a year or two older than my sister. They are best friends. They go over to each other's houses and everything is very good and I have friends in the neighbourhood and they are very welcoming. They brought us a turkey at Christmas and well; they are very good to us. (Stefan, 1 April 2009)

In describing what a welcoming community means to them, the community organization participants made an interesting observation about the balance between living on newcomers' doorsteps and not leaving them alone to live their lives, and being so polite that they ignore them altogether. "I guess you have to be careful that you don't overdo it and not give the people any privacy, but the other extreme is that in trying not to impose you don't do anything," says Calvin Brymer. "I think that the residents of Florenceville-Bristol have somehow managed to strike that balance; perhaps without even thinking about it" (Calvin Brymer, 14 April 2009). And for local resident Troy Evans, "neighbours take you in as one of their own in this community and make you feel like you are part of a big family. You are not judged or ridiculed in any way for looking different or speaking with an accent. You are treated with the same respect as a family member, and that includes respect for privacy" (Troy Morgan, 9 May 2009).

Friends

The difficulties associated with making friends in Fredericton were not central to my discussions with the immigrant adolescents in

Florenceville-Bristol. Friendliness and curiosity on the part of the local adolescents in the latter case community appear to have eased the development of close friendships with the immigrant adolescents. The lack of separate EAL classrooms in the Florenceville-Bristol schools has further facilitated contact across the two groups and provided the immigrant adolescents with a sense of inclusion or membership in the school community. The immigrant adolescents in Florenceville-Bristol have therefore been afforded a network of knowledgeable local peers who support them in their adjustment to school and the wider community – it is precisely this network, and the bridging social capital embedded in it that many of their Fredericton counterparts are missing.

School was central to my discussions with the immigrant adolescents in this case study. They describe New Brunswick-born friends at school as providing an emotional sense of belonging and acceptance, as well as tangible help with homework assignments, language translations, orientation to school, and advice about university and potential careers. Stefan, for example, found comfort and common interests amid the confusion of arriving at a new school in a new country:

When I first got here I was pretty confused because everything is different, and though I spoke English I wasn't used to having it around me all the time. Some kids in the school helped me out and made me feel comfortable. They showed me where the classes are and what to do when each bell rings. It is not difficult to make friends here. I guess teenagers everywhere are the same. We can come from different cultures and speak different languages but we can still have the same interests. So yes I made friends here with teenagers who I have things in common with. (Stefan, 1 April 2009)

Ale says she goes to friends for advice, "especially friends who are from here because they know more than me about how things are done around here" (Ale, 1 April 2009). When Jorge needs advice about school or what to do when he finishes school he goes to his local female friends in particular because "my female friends are more serious about school than the boys. They always seem to know what they are doing. Sometimes we [the boys] all joke around and say we are going to end up working at McDonalds [laughing]"

(Jorge, 1 April 2009). And for Heena, having a close friend in Florenceville-Bristol simply makes her life easier:

> My best friend means everything to me. We tell each other everything. She gives me some tough advice and I appreciate that even when I don't want to take it. I am pretty confident in myself now, but it was a lot more difficult when I was fourteen or fifteen and I had just arrived here from India. I wanted to fit in and do what the local kids were doing. But in the end my best friend helped me to make the right decisions and I didn't go in those directions. I dealt with all of those issues and got through them. It makes my life easier to have her. We will soon be going to different universities in different provinces and that will be hard on us. (Heena, 1 April 2009)

This is not to say that making friends in Florenceville-Bristol is instantaneous; it is still a process that develops gradually as the immigrant adolescents become more fluent in English and communication becomes more effortless. While Stefan and Heena spoke English when they arrived in the community and the Spanish-speaking teens could turn to each other initially to enhance their sense of identity and security; Eric and Alex (who arrived a year apart) were left to their own devices and found it much more difficult to form relationships: "It is easy to make friends but hard to really get to know them and become real friends, because I have little English and I can't communicate well with them," says Alex (Alex, 14 April 2009). And for Eric "it was really hard. I was the first Korean to come to this school and I couldn't speak English at all. It was the language barrier that made things difficult. If I would have spoke English I am sure I would have made friends right away; eventually I did make close friends" (Eric, 1 April 2009).

The immigrant girls in Florenceville-Bristol, contrary to those in Fredericton, spoke with just as much enthusiasm about their friends as the boys. The girls said nothing to indicate that the process of forming relationships with their New Brunswick-born peers was more difficult for them. As demonstrated by the photograph taken by the teens, there are no obvious differences between the integration of the girls and boys into the community. There appear to be two reasons why immigrant girls have an easier time fitting into Florenceville-Bristol than Fredericton. First of all there are more of them. Of the fourteen immigrant adolescents in the community, nine of them are girls. The middle school has had so many immigrant girls arrive in grade 6 over the years that the staff has had little experience dealing with immigrant boys. Secondly, the girls are more involved in their schools, and the sports teams may be less competitive and more welcoming to the girls. The two schools also emphasize music, dance, and drama, and the cheerleading team is popular amongst the girls at the middle school. It is not that the Florenceville-Bristol schools offer more activities for girls than the larger schools in Fredericton; the teachers and administrators are merely better at recognizing interests and talents and encouraging the girls to participate in the activities that are offered.

The one challenge facing the immigrant girls in Florenceville-Bristol that is consistent with Fredericton is finding common ground with respect to beliefs and values. This clash of values was evident in the interview transcripts from five of the girls, though the issue appears to have as much to do with small town versus big city as with cultural differences. Claudia, for example, notes that "the girls here like to party a lot and they drink and smoke at a very young age. In Mexico City they don't do that as much. I am not really different from the other girls here. I have noticed that the differences have more to do with me being from a much bigger city" (Claudia, 1 April 2009). Heena also picks up on this concern:

> I had to try so hard to fit in. And also coming from a big city to a tiny little village is a huge transition. Finding things to do has always been difficult. I come from a very different culture with different traditions and values. Some of the things the kids my age do, I have to really think twice about. I have been brought up with specific rules, for example I would never drink. Not drinking alone leaves me out of a big group of people. My classmates go out drinking every weekend because they are bored, and I have to really think about that. Little things like that make a big difference. (Heena, 1 April 2009)

And as previously mentioned Monica has found common ground with her local peers much to the dismay of her mother who does not approve of her daughter's choice of friends. Ale and Ana Lucia, on the contrary, have found that their modern, urban upbringings are an uncomfortable fit in a community where the behaviour of many girls is influenced by the teachings of the Pentecostal church: "The girls don't want a career when they finish school and I don't think the women in Florenceville work anywhere. I thought in Canada all the women are professionals," says Ale (1 April 2009). And Ana Lucia notes that "in Colombia my mom works in business and she wears a suit and my dad is a teacher. Sometimes, in a small place like this I think the women are more traditional. They stay at home and maybe teach their daughters to stay home too" (Ana Lucia, 1 April 2009).

Despite cultural or urban-rural differences, friendships between the immigrant and local adolescents have been made in Florenceville-Bristol. Perhaps someday the teens will go off to university and look back on their time in the community as Shreyans does:

> I still consider Florenceville my home. I had good friends there. We played lots of sports in the community, everything from badminton to cricket. Summers were a good time in Florenceville ... When the Tim Hortons was built me and my friends pretty much moved in there [laughing], like any other Canadian I enjoyed Tim Hortons. When I go home for summer vacation and my friends are home as well we still gather at Tim Hortons or play sports together. (Shreyans, 6 May 2009)

Or perhaps the local residents will look out the window and continue to observe scenes like this one: "I was out at the local hardware store [on Saturday]. I looked outside and noticed two girls from our school walking together. One was a local girl and the other I think was Cristina. They were walking down the street arm in arm laughing and drinking their cans of 7-Up. They are obviously friends" (Meg Pryde, 14 April 2009).

CONCLUSION

This chapter demonstrated how the immigrant adolescents are taking advantage or attempting to take advantage of available resources in order to facilitate integration into the community. When immigrant adolescents accumulate social capital through social networks in schools and neighbourhoods, integration and self-identification with the receiving community are more likely to occur. Citizen engagement, the topic of the next chapter, is a pivotal component of social capital at the community level.

Feeling Like We Are Part of Something
Citizen Engagement

In small towns across America, Alexis de Tocqueville (1835, republished 1994) found that the foundation of civil society rested on a constellation of small shop owners, public forums, and citizens' propensity to interact. Almost two hundred years later, findings from the General Social Survey on Social Engagement in Canada (Statistics Canada 2003) demonstrate a strong association between residence in smaller communities, volunteering, and greater attendance at public meetings. Political scientists – most notably Robert Putnam (1993; 1995; 2000) – equate social capital with levels of "civicness" in communities. In practice this community-level social capital is associated with levels of associational involvement and participatory behaviour in a community, and is measured by such indicators as newspaper reading, membership in voluntary organizations, and expression of trust in political authorities.[1] Putnam maintains that communities with high levels of social capital are marked by extensive civic engagement and patterns of mutual support. He uses the analogy of bowling together to argue that social interaction increases our willingness to rely on others and to participate in collective endeavours. Connections among individuals function as "social glue" and play a critical role in people's ability to cooperate with one another for the benefit of all. Putnam believes that suburbanization, long commute times, television, and an array of other factors have caused these connections to break down in North America essentially leaving people "bowling alone."[2]

Putnam's argument has been criticized for its logical circularity. As a property of communities rather than individuals, social capital is simultaneously a cause and an effect. Yet the idea that civic engagement is a precursor to social capital remains credible. "We can think of it [civic engagement] as analogous to static electricity – inert energy that has not yet been directed into current. Social capital, on the other hand, is created when this civic engagement is 'excited' by some catalytic issue or event and directed toward a particular end or purpose," writes James Hyman.[3] A community's ability to adapt to change and take advantage of opportunities depends not just on its stock of cultural, economic, political, and social assets, but also on whether or not it can activate these assets to solve a problem or achieve desired outcomes."[4]

FREDERICTON

In Fredericton, non-European immigrant adolescents and adults were the only participants in my case study who suggested that citizens stay in their houses and keep to themselves. The data collected from community organization members, local residents, and the four European immigrant participants in no way indicate that the citizens of their city are bowling alone.[5] These participants overwhelmingly portray the citizens of Fredericton as deeply engaged in their community and with each other. Generally speaking, they know what is going on around them; they are aware of events at the local, provincial, and national levels, though to a lesser extent at the international level. They read newspapers, watch the news, and are one of the most engaged constituencies in Canada with respect to voting in elections. Citizens of Fredericton are described by many of the participants as good, friendly, and tolerant people who have shown themselves on numerous occasions to be very capable of uniting together to achieve a common goal or to focus on a common cause. Participants referred to emergency situations such as the flood of 2008 and the Christmas holiday season as times when citizens demonstrated commitment to act responsibly as members of the community.

The difference in responses between the non-European and European participants may reflect their differing views on what constitutes citizen engagement. People in Northern Europe, for example, do not participate in collective activity to the same degree as those in Southern Europe and Latin America. So those participants from Northern Europe will tend not to see as much of a difference between their societies and New Brunswick society, as might the Latin Americans. Yet, even if the citizens of Fredericton are as engaged as the European participants claim them to be, that engagement does not appear to extend to the integration of immigrants.

Outside of the schools and MCAF, few relationships are being cultivated with immigrant adolescents. The apparent shortage of engaged citizens puts a great deal of pressure on teachers and guidance counsellors in the schools, and on the small number of staff and volunteers at MCAF, to take an active role in the lives of immigrant adolescents. It also frees citizens in the wider community of any responsibility toward them. The topic of adult role models, for example, came up only a few times during interviews with immigrant adolescent participants, and, as the Fredericton High School guidance counsellor pointed out in chapter 2, those individuals who are involved with immigrant adolescents form a small cohort of socially conscious people who have either travelled extensively, or are immigrants or second-generation immigrants themselves. A lot of this gap in citizen engagement probably comes down to an underdeveloped public awareness about immigration and cultural diversity in Fredericton.

Making an Effort

A 2006 survey of public attitudes toward immigration and diversity in Atlantic Canada undertaken by the Bristol Group indicates that 79 per cent of respondents in New Brunswick "agree or strongly agree that immigrants would have a positive influence on their local economies," and 71 per cent say "Canada should encourage qualified immigrants to move here." Yet, a majority of people also want immigrants to "fit in." Sixty-three per cent of respondents in New Brunswick say that "immigrants should completely accept the customs and traditions of Canadians; 45 per cent, meanwhile, agree that "Canadians should completely accept the customs and traditions of immigrants."[6] According to Bristol Group's analyses, "this shows us two things about attitudes to welcoming newcomers to our communities. When it comes to immigration, many people clearly feel that cultural adaptation should be a two-way street. The second is that our tolerance often has limits – or is at least conditional."[7]

John W. Berry defines acculturation as the "process of cultural and psychological change following contact between cultural groups and their individual members."[8] Cultural changes include alterations in an individual's customs, and in their economic and political life. Psychological changes include alterations in individuals' attitudes toward the acculturation process, their cultural identities, and their social behaviours in relation to the groups that individual is in contact with.[9] Both newcomers and established residents in a society undergo the acculturation process, though one group is usually dominant over the others. Members of the receiving society have more control over, and influence, on the definition of the inter-group relationship. Their attitudes toward immigrants play a key role not only in the outcomes of their own acculturation processes, but also in those of the immigrants.[10] The reality is that the acculturation process is often unidirectional, with changes and accommodations occurring almost entirely on the part of immigrants. Immigrants are expected to acquire the cultural attributes of the receiving society, which are assumed to be different from that of their own culture.[11] As such, studies of immigrant adjustment suggest that the forces of assimilation are strong in Canadian society and that over time immigrants do become similar to native-born Canadians in many aspects of life.[12] "In the long run," writes Peter S. Li, "immigrants in Canada and their identifiable social features are as much a product of what they were when they first settled in Canada as what Canada made them to be."[13]

On the topic of active engagement with immigrant adolescents, all categories of participants in Fredericton debated the question "who should reach out to whom?" or "where should that effort come from?" All participants acknowledged that the effort is "lopsided" with immigrants expected to adjust, change, and integrate into Fredericton, while local residents go on with their lives in their normal fashion. The immigrant adolescents, in particular, feel like the effort to fit in with their New Brunswick-born peers rests solely with them. They have to learn enough English to understand and be understood then work extremely hard at fitting in and making friends. Yet, a small number of them are not socially savvy enough to connect with others and even after three years in the city they do not have friends. In an ideal situation immigrant adolescents' attempts at learning about their new society and its institutions would be matched by attempts by their New Brunswick-born peers to learn more about them.

The absence of such attempts suggests more than a lack of public awareness and an ambivalent attitude toward immigrants; it suggests a specific lack of desire and commitment on the part of established residents to reach out to immigrants to the same degree as they expect immigrants to adapt to the mainstream. Heo contends that among peers at school the interest to meet newcomers simply is not there: "There are many students there and when new students come to the school from different countries the other students don't take interest in them; they aren't interested in new stuff or new people" (Heo, 31 January 2009). Other immigrant adolescent participants argue that connections with local peers can be made, but it takes time and a great deal of effort on their part. Mai, for example, describes the process of making connections as time and energy consuming, but rewarding in the end:

> Over time I learned more English. I talked to them and we slowly became friends. It just takes time that's all. You have to make a big effort and talk to them. Even if my English isn't good, if I make the effort and I show my kindness to people, then they will know me, and they will realize I am making that effort and they will be my friends. So when I began talking to people, and when I started being friendly they were friendly back. They accepted me. (Mai, 10 December 2008)

And less effort appears to be necessary for those participants who arrive at a younger age, and who already speak the language, as noted by Kito:

> When I came to Fredericton I was very worried because I had to start all over again. But I arrived in grade 6 and I made friends almost right away. It wasn't that bad. Maybe it is easier to make friends at École Sainte Anne and also I spoke French already because we speak French in the Congo. Everyone came to me and asked me to join them. I joked around with them. I can stick a pencil in my hair and it will stay. My friends tried that and they couldn't. They thought I was funny [laughing]. I felt very happy. I also taught my friends how to say words in Swahili. Now they will say hello and stuff in Swahili and that makes me so proud. It's me, I'm the one that taught them to speak in Swahili! [laughing]. (Kito, 14 February 2009)

Referring to a general lack of motivation on the part of adults in the schools and wider community to engage with immigrant adolescents, Janis Boston, a volunteer with MCAF, argues that "people think that reaching out and getting to know this diverse bunch of newcomers is such hard work, but it really is not" (Janis Boston, 4 November 2008). And the international student advisor at UNB maintains that making an effort requires nothing more than some facilitation:

> There are all kinds of simple things that can be done to connect immigrant adolescents with the broader community: arrange a meal every month with a local family in the community, invite an international student for Christmas dinner at your home; volunteer to help immigrant adolescents with their homework at the multicultural association; drop off some chocolate chip cookies and introduce themselves to the new family from China, Liberia, or Iran who moved in down the street; break away from your small group at church and sit beside someone new; and when they see an immigrant in the aisle of the supermarket look him or her in the eye and say "hello." (International Student Advisor, unb, 7 November 2008)

On a similar note "the social structures and tight-knit relationships that already exist in the community could make immigrant adolescents feel even more lonely and isolated," says George Feenstra. "But if the citizens of Fredericton were intentional and skilful at making newcomers feel like they belong, it would be much easier to build and maintain face to face relationships in such a small city" (George Feenstra, 29 August 2008). Finally, former president of the Fredericton Islamic Association, Naveed Majid, points out that most Muslim people in Fredericton, adolescents included, have generally accepted that no one is going to make the effort to reach out to them:

> But sometimes we receive a pleasant surprise. The fact that you [the researcher] are here at this Mosque with your head covered asking these types of questions is a big effort in our eyes. There are a few people in this community, just a handful, for example like yourself, who are out there seeking knowledge about us. That is a very Islamic trait to seek knowledge and to seek change. And that gesture is so appreciated that it makes up for all the rest of the challenges we face. (Naveed Majid, 7 January 2009)

Adult Role Models

When we look back on the experiences that shaped us as young people, we frequently report our relationship with a positive adult role model – whether a teacher, older neighbour, community member, or another caring adult – as being important in shaping our positive values. Adult role models appear frequently in literature on social infrastructure and developmental assets for adolescents. "How young people understand what it means, and what it takes to be productive and civically engaged citizens, as well as their belief in themselves as people who can achieve those goals, depends to a large extent on the cumulative influence of all the adult role models and connections they have."[14] As discussed in the previous chapter, James Coleman wrote that one of the major mechanisms of developmental influence is adult-youth interactions, through which skills, culture, values, standards, ideas and information are transmitted.[15] While Coleman was referring mainly to parents and other adult relatives, the literature suggests that, across many contexts, caring non-parental adults can be important developmental resources in the lives of adolescents.[16] Therefore, in this context strengthening social infrastructure requires considerable civic engagement by adults in the lives of children and adolescents, which in turn requires social norms favouring civic engagement, and the desire by most community residents to connect and engage.[17] As a result, "adult role models" was one of only a few codes that I took with me when collecting data in the field – that is, it was an *a priori* code taken from the literature rather than an *inductive* code that emerges from the data.

To my surprise adult role models rarely came up in interviews with immigrant adolescent participants in Fredericton. When they were mentioned, they were for the most part limited to school and MCAF. The immigrant adolescents who attend Fredericton High School spoke highly of their EAL teacher and guidance counsellor, who act as their entry points into the school and community. Teachers in general are important to these teens. Caroline, from Belgium, Callie from Liberia, and Mai from Taiwan describe female teachers who were nice to them and looked after them when they arrived, and Feena emphasizes that "here the teachers care about their students. They care if we are making high grades or if something is bothering us; it is easier to like school here and to feel like you are an important part of that school" (Feena, 31 March 2009).

The immigrant adolescent participants also describe relationships with the staff and volunteers coordinating youth activities at MCAF. Several of the teens are involved in Cesar Morales' music classes where they have learned to play various instruments and genres of music, and have recently begun to perform for large audiences. Others have joined Andrew's "Youth Splash" group where they have developed leadership skills, built confidence, and "found their own voices" (Andrew, 12 July 2009). And, some of the boys are coached in soccer by Otto Morales who says that "there are lots of opportunities in this community to use your skills to do what you are good at. You can offer those skills to immigrant youth and it is really appreciated. It makes me and the young newcomers feel like we are a valuable part of the community" (Otto Morales, 4 September 2008). It is important to acknowledge that all of these exceptional adult role models are themselves immigrants who arrived in Fredericton as adolescents and young adults, and all are men. The only two immigrant adolescent participants who mentioned adult role models outside of school and MCAF were Lucus, who spoke of elderly neighbours who look out for him, and Abo who has formed an interesting relationship with members of the Fredericton police force: "The funny thing is while the police officers were arresting me they befriended me and now they kinda look out for me. I talk to them and they let me handle the police dogs sometimes. One of the officers said I should join the police force or the RCMP when I am done school because I would be good at it" (Abo, 28 February 2009).

Yet, overall, it is peers and not adults who matter most to the young newcomers. Those community organization participants who have the most contact with immigrant adolescents argue that it is natural for adolescents to turn to their peers for advice and support instead of adults, and immigrant adolescents are no exception. Immigrant adolescents who arrived as refugees, moreover, are even less likely to turn to adults for support. "Young people who come from countries with a lot of political strife, often have a lot of suspicion of authority and power, so that would make it very difficult for them to go to an adult in a position of responsibility and power due to trust issues" (George Feenstra, 29 August 2008). In this situation, my concern as a researcher was what happens to the immigrant adolescents who do not have peers or adults to turn to? I later realized that immigrants take care of other immigrants, that is, they have each other. The warmth and comradeship demonstrated by the teens participating in the focus groups did not go unnoticed, nor did this comment made by the international student advisor at UNB:

The immigrant and international students had to struggle much more than they should have in Fredericton and in that struggle the relationships they developed with each other were very deep and they were able to overcome so many obstacles together. I know of international students who became permanent residents, and are working here or in other parts of Canada who are now financing the studies of other international students who they befriended. (International Student Advisor, UNB, 7 November 2008)

Success in Spite of Us

Citizens of Fredericton may not be doing enough to purposefully create opportunities for positive interaction with immigrant adolescents. The words "success in spite of us" were mentioned by the International Student Advisor at UNB, the Fredericton High School guidance counsellor, Jeremías Tecu, and Philip Sexsmith, and they stayed with me as I continued to collect data. Some of the immigrant adolescents who participated in the case study have to deal with more adversity than others, including poverty, racism, poor housing, post-traumatic stress disorder, and family strife, yet by and large they say that they are doing *okay*. The teens are gradually becoming more involved in their schools and in the wider community, and all could name at least one extracurricular activity they are involved in. In some cases, I was able to observe the immigrant adolescents as they participated in extracurricular activities at MCAF. Research on the effects of youth community involvement on later development and social outcomes has found that high school students who are involved in community service are less likely to exhibit deviant behaviour compared with other students;[18] and that involvement with church and volunteer activities in the community is associated with positive educational trajectories and low rates of risk-taking.[19]

Van Anh and Mai are active in Christian community outreach activities through the Meeting Place and Baptist Church, and Lucus, Musi, and Jaime have expanded their initial involvement in MCAF youth activities to take part in other youth leadership programs as well. They also mentor children in the Children's International Village summer camps, which take place in Fredericton. Heo volunteers at the Public Library, and Mateo and Fajar are both proctors in the UNB residences and active in student marketing clubs. Feena, Caroline, and Auma practice music and dance, Abo is an aspiring actor, Luis has started a Spanish club at Fredericton high school, and Musi, Kito, Pablo, and Mark are becoming well known in the city for their soccer skills. Perhaps the effort made by that small cohort of engaged citizens has been enough to pull the immigrant adolescents along in the right direction, or perhaps the immigrant adolescents are pulling each other along. Many of these teens also possess the kind of individual-level characteristics that will make them resilient and resourceful despite their circumstances. In other words, they may be successful in spite of us and not because of us.

FLORENCEVILLE-BRISTOL

The portrayal of rural and small towns as fertile grounds for community involvement is largely consistent with data collected in Florenceville-Bristol. The interview transcripts retrieved from the participants collectively portray a community spirit of pride, kindness, and voluntarism. Community organization members described fund-raising for the Northern Carleton County Civic Centre and membership in the Carleton Victoria Arts Council. Local residents spoke of bringing food and clothing to families in need, the involvement of parents in the schools, and the involvement of the schools in the wider community. Local adolescents described getting together on Halloween to transform the Bristol Shogomoc railway site into a haunted train for the local children; and the immigrant adolescents told stories of people watching out for them, taking an interest in them, and generally recognizing their talents and abilities. Participants also mentioned the presence of the McCain family in the community and they contend that, because the owners and managers of McCain Foods, Ltd are also citizens of Florenceville-Bristol, they serve to strengthen ties between the workplace and the community.

The local residents and community organization members say they believe in strength in numbers, and so every effort is made to include immigrant families in activities and decision-making processes in Florenceville-Bristol. "We are a small number of people and we realize if we don't accept newcomers we become a smaller number of people. So out of necessity we end up being inter-dependent and getting to know one another, and ultimately work-ing together to achieve common goals for the community," says Dianne Lord (Dianne Lord, 14 April 2009). And with respect to immigrant adolescents, Meg Pryde maintains that "in a small com-munity like Florenceville-Bristol there is more chance for them to become involved. They are almost forced out of their own little worlds because there are not enough people from their own culture for them to be with. They have to become part of the community. I think a small community pushes them to integrate" (Meg Pryde, 14 April 2009). Citizen engagement in the Florenceville-Bristol case study is therefore associated with three sub-themes: (1) "Making an Effort"; (2) "Adult Role Models"; and (3) "Finding their Way."

Making an Effort

The effort being made by the two schools in Florenceville-Bristol to welcome and include immigrant adolescents has been noted in chap-ter 2 and does not warrant reiteration here. The big question is why that effort is made? What is it about Carleton North High School and Florenceville Middle School that makes them so welcoming? A number of factors may be interrogated, including the small size of the schools and their deep connection with the local community, but it is the students who populate the schools who really stand out in the data:

> Well of all of the age groups to have to pack up and move here, adolescence is the worst. It doesn't matter what your back-ground, it is very difficult to handle the change. But, saying that, I still think we are really good at embracing new people and making sure they are okay. We have really great kids in this school and they are very good at reaching out to newcomers and helping them to settle in. Before you know it they are a group of friends and away they go. (Dianne Lord, 14 April 2009)

It is not clear why the local adolescents are so friendly and accom-modating toward their immigrant peers. Many of their parents likely work with the immigrant parents at the McCain Foods, Ltd Global Technology Centre; perhaps the schools have also created safe, healthy, and inclusive learning environments that teach the teens to respect one another. Whatever the reason, the local adolescents truly shine in this case study. Stefanie describes their efforts as follows:

> I think this school can be called a welcoming community because it is full of people who help you and people who don't judge you because you come from a different country and speak a different language. The teachers here and some of the kids try and communicate with you no matter what and don't give up. They have their doors open for you all the time even after you have been here for a while ... I think people were patient with us as we learned the language and culture. (Stefanie, April 1, 2009)

Another prominent feature of these schools appears to be their informal nature. While informal learning environments usually refer to activities outside of formal schooling, such as after-school clubs whose mission includes learning and development, the schools in Florenceville-Bristol seem to bring those informal elements into the school setting. This informality is most evident in their inspired efforts to communicate with and teach the immigrant adolescents, as well as their efforts to include them in a wide array of extracurricular activities. In his study of the integration of immigrant youth in Israel, Reuvin Kahane (1986) found that the greater the presence of informal elements in a particular social structure, the greater the probability of fair encounters between local residents and immigrant youth. Kahane noticed that immigrant students integrated better into schools with less formal curricula and teaching methods because they provided a context in which young immigrants could meet local youth and adults on their own terms and on a relatively equal footing. The immigrant adolescents in Florenceville-Bristol may actually be benefiting from the deficiency of formal programs for their integration into the schools. In particular, further study is needed on the benefits and drawbacks of separate EAL classes for small numbers of immigrant students in middle and high schools because in this case the adolescents seem to be doing just fine without them.

Adult Role Models

Unlike their counterparts in Fredericton, the immigrant adolescents in the Florenceville-Bristol case study put equal weight on the role of peers and adults in their lives. Almost all of them spoke of the support and guidance they receive from teachers and administrators. "The teachers understand the students better and have more respect for them," says Andrés. "When we get into trouble the teachers make it easier on us. Discipline here is not harsh like it is in Colombia." (Andrés, 1 April 2009). For Alex the teachers make school far more tolerable since Korean schools emphasize academic achievement to the point of causing distress for students: "In Korea I studied all the time. I studied from early morning to midnight every day. Friends didn't matter. The teachers taught me that other kids my age were competition not friends. Here the teachers care about me. They want me to work with the other kids in class and be friends with them. They make us feel like we are a team" (Alex, 14 April 2009).

Adult role models outside of the school include the parents of New Brunswick-born friends (for three of the immigrant adolescents) and adult friends in the same ethnic community (for two of the immigrant adolescents). Additionally, Eric mentioned the role of his family doctor in helping him to choose a medical school: "I did research on the internet and learned that Dalhousie University has a well-known medical school ... I talked to my family doctor. He went to Dalhousie and also recommended that I go there. My family doctor is nice to me and he has even let me observe him at his practice" (Eric, 1 April 2009). And according to Adwoa, "the Baptist Church community was very important to me as an adolescent in Florenceville. Adults in my church community served as positive role models who encouraged and supported me" (Adwoa, 18 May 2009).

Finding Their Way

The thirteen immigrant adolescents interviewed for this research are not only adapting and integrating into Florenceville-Bristol, they are flourishing. Every one of them is involved in activities in school and in the wider community. At the schools, I was able to observe the teens participating in extracurricular activities in the gym (at Florenceville Middle School), and in classrooms and the cafeteria (at Carleton North High School). Eric plays badminton, basketball, rugby, and soccer at school; Andrés and Alex play soccer and Claudia is honing her soccer skills so that she can try out for the Carleton North High School team next year; Jorge plays basketball at the Florenceville Ark and practices mixed martial arts in Woodstock; Vanessa and Stefanie were on the cheerleading team at Florenceville

Middle school and also play recreational soccer and basketball; Ale plays in the school band and volunteers at the local nursing home; Stefan also plays in the school band and he and his father recently joined a community curling team. Heena is a dancer. When she is not dancing, she is on the student council and in the organization Students Taking Action; she also participated in the school pageant and volunteers at MACC and the Little Spuds Daycare. The three girls at Florenceville Middle School: Monica, Ana Lucia, and Cristina are on their school's cheerleading team. Shreyans, an adult, maintains that he was more involved in Florenceville-Bristol as an adolescent due to the small size of the community: "It is so much easier to know everyone, to make friends and to become involved in the community. I actually don't go out in Ottawa as much as I did in Florenceville because I can't be bothered taking the bus and spending all that time driving places" (Shreyans, 6 May 2009).

While each immigrant adolescent was at a different stage of adaptation depending on the amount of time he or she had been in the community at the time of interview, it was evident during the interviews that they all have personality and family traits that would probably bring them success regardless of the community they reside in. With only one parent working in most cases, these teens are by no means wealthy, but they are more self-selected than many of their immigrant peers in Fredericton. As the dependents of economic immigrants, they were favourably selected for labour market success by Canadian immigration officials and judged to be middle class by their parents' level of education, the physical conditions in which they work, and by their consumption habits. The parents (and the adolescents themselves) are believed to be more able, ambitious, aggressive, entrepreneurial, or otherwise more favourably selected than similar individuals who choose to remain in their place of origin.[20] Highly educated parents, moreover, have the financial or nonmonetary cultural capital to invest in their children's abilities early on, and such investments place the children on track for the pursuit of higher education.[21] Studies in the United States show that young immigrants with the lowest levels of academic achievement are the ones with low-skilled parents at the time of arrival.[22]

The immigrant adolescent participants in Florenceville-Bristol are high academic achievers, sociable, and talkative, and despite often feeling lonely and somewhat out of place in such a tiny community, they all have a tremendously positive attitude and sense of adventure. Social networking is valued and taught in educated middle class families. These adolescents learn from their parents how to talk with adults as equals and negotiate to get favourable outcomes in any situation. Even the youngest of the immigrant adolescent participants appear to be knowledgeable about maneuvering through the academic landscape of university applications and financial aid. While the data clearly demonstrate the important role played by engaged citizens in their lives, it is equally clear that the teens are skilled at taking advantage of the social capital available in social networks discussed in the previous chapter.

CONCLUSION

Although both Fredericton and Florenceville-Bristol are home to engaged citizens, the citizens of Florenceville-Bristol, especially its adolescent citizens, are more proactive in engaging in actions that facilitate immigrant adolescents' involvement in the community. The community appears to have the kind of social organization that provides the context for both the sources and effects of social capital to materialize, including an acceptance of diversity, a sense of inclusiveness, and quality social networks.

6

Are We Home Yet?

Sense of Belonging and Summary

Finding a sense of belonging to a community involves building confidence in one's own identity and connecting oneself to the surrounding environment, people, and social institutions. Young people from other cultural backgrounds face the additional challenge of deciding about their ethnic identity. This can lead to an identity crisis as they attempt to work out their affiliation to their culture of origin and their place within the dominant culture.[1] Positive ethnic identity is an important first step in immigrant adolescents' quest for belonging. Jean Phinney refers to *ethnic identity* as the degree to which individuals have explored their ethnicity, are clear about what their ethnic group membership means to them, and can identify with their ethnic group.[2] She conceptualizes ethnic identity in terms of a progression, with an individual moving from the unexamined attitudes of childhood, through a moratorium or period of exploration, to an achieved, secure ethnic identity at the end of adolescence. The final stage of identity achievement is a peaceful one in which youth stop comparing themselves to the dominant cultural group and begin to perceive themselves as unique individuals who are part of a multicultural community.[3]

The expectation is that positive psycho-social outcomes for immigrant adolescents will be related to strong identifications with both their ethnic group and the larger receiving society.[4] Consequently, the implications for the settlement and adaptation of immigrant adolescents are clear: they should be encouraged to retain both a sense of their own heritage cultural identity, while establishing close ties with the larger receiving society.[5] A bicultural orientation has been shown to be conducive to better school performance,[6] and fluent bilingualism is associated with higher educational achievement and more ambitious plans for the future.[7] The view of immigrants as bringing their culture and a fixed, stable identity with them, moreover, has been replaced by the postmodern conception of a continuous process of identity formation and the weaving together of elements of the old and new culture. Thus, over time these young immigrants learn to become part of a new society, peer group, and school, while continuing to develop identities related to their home country, culture, language, and religion. They are not isolated in a narrow regional universe, and they see this hybridization as a source of enrichment and greater skill, which is helping them to develop an open-minded, outward-looking attitude – valuable qualities in a globalizing world.[8]

Finding a sense of belonging to Fredericton and Florenceville-Bristol is a lengthy process for the immigrant adolescents who participated in this research, and as in Alejandro Portes and Min Zhou's (1993) theory of segmented assimilation, the process of achieving this sense of belonging follows a bumpy path rather than a straight line. But, in the end all thirty-three immigrant adolescents were able to make, or are in the process of making, connections with a variety of people in the two communities. The data suggest that for the thirty-three immigrant adolescents I interviewed, there are at least four states of belonging.

(1) Bicultural and Well-Adjusted

Eight immigrant adolescent participants who have been in the receiving community for more than three years appear in the data to be happy, well-adjusted teens. Having arrived when they were entering adolescence, at around grade 6 or 7, they have adopted a bicultural identity and appear to be confident, comfortable, and fulfilled by their new lives. The teachers who participated in the case studies of Fredericton and Florenceville-Bristol have commented that they can see these students growing, finding their place in the school, and beginning to have a bicultural attitude whereby they celebrate their own selves, appreciate their roots, but learn to love this culture as well. These adolescents speak with poise; they appear to possess a deep self-understanding, and are astute and observant of their surroundings. Although they admit to being bored at times, they regard themselves as active and valued members of their communities. Heena, for example, arrived in Florenceville in grade 6 and at the time of our interview was preparing to graduate from Carleton North High School and leave the town for university in Ontario: "I have strong family values. I know who I am and what is expected of me. I want to become something important and be successful in life ... Yes I come from an entirely different culture, but this town feels like home now. I can't go anywhere without wanting to go back home to Florenceville" (Heena, 1 April 2009).

Two other participants, who appear to fit this state of belonging, arrived in the receiving community more recently as older adolescents. Ale immigrated to Florenceville-Bristol less than a year before our interview, in grade 11. She is still developing fluency in English and can find plenty of things wrong with the small rural town, yet she simultaneously demonstrates that same confidence, comfort, and contentment with her new life:

> It has been difficult, very difficult. I needed to learn the language, break that wall of culture, and try and figure out the rules of what to say and when to say it; those unwritten rules that every culture has. You have to think and analyze the culture first and then try and find your place in it. I don't think though that being from a different country makes me a different person. I am still the same person no matter where I live. I think what is important is how you were raised and the values you have. Those values will always stay the same. My parents taught me how to see the world. I am a very proud Colombian and I will go back to Colombia someday, but for now I want to stay in Canada and study and work. Canada has given to me and now I want to give back to Canada. I think it is important to give back to the country that takes you in as an immigrant. (Ale, 1 April 2009)

The last example of a bicultural, well-adjusted immigrant adolescent is Stefan, despite the fact that he had only been in Florenceville-Bristol for a matter of weeks when I interviewed him. Stefan's enthusiastic responses to the interview questions, moreover, may reflect the early phase of what Adrian Furnam and Stephen Boschner (1992) describe in the literature as a U-shaped curve of adjustment in which immigrants initially feel optimism and joy, followed by confusion and frustration, which eventually becomes satisfaction and confidence.

The stories told by immigrant adults coincide with the length of time they had spent in their community. All of the immigrant adults interviewed reported having a strong sense of belonging to Fredericton and Florenceville-Bristol. Three of these adults migrated from the communities in pursuit of opportunities in Montreal and Ottawa, and they claim that their sense of belonging was left behind in New Brunswick. While active in their new communities and comfortable as Canadians, the immigrant adults express pride in having retained their ethnic identities. Leeder, for example, cites the retention of his Persian Baha'i beliefs and values as his biggest accomplishment:

I am still the same person. I really believe that. I have set the goals on how I am supposed to behave and it is easy to get caught up in life and ambitions and get distracted from those goals. But I am happy that my core values and beliefs are intact and I can raise my children in the appropriate manner. Canadian-born people may take things for granted and I try not to do that. (Leeder, 10 November 2008)

(2) Torn Between Two Cultures

These immigrant adolescent participants had been in the community for less than three years when I interviewed them. They too are in the process of constructing a bicultural identity for themselves, but they do not understand exactly what that identity is and what they should do with it. The teens are beginning to meet people and feel comfortable in Fredericton and Florenceville-Bristol, but also miss "home" so they feel torn between two cultures and unsure if they belong to either. They feel compelled to choose between embracing Canadian mainstream culture and the values and traditions of their home countries. Seven of the immigrant adolescents describe being in this cultural dilemma. Van Anh actually has an acronym for it: "I feel like a 'TCK' kid, a 'third culture kid' because when I go home to Vietnam I'm too Western and I don't fit with Vietnamese people, but I don't fit here either because I have had an entirely different life experience" (Van Anh, 5 November 2008). The participants admit to feeling unsure if a bicultural identity is "acceptable." By way of illustration, Jorge had been in Florenceville-Bristol for two years at the time of our interview. While he blends in with his local peers with

respect to dress, accent, and shared interests, he still claims to live
between two cultures:

> Well I have travelled and I have seen different cultures and that
> makes me a really different person than the kids my age who were
> born here. I tell them about other cultures and they are interested
> in learning about them. They ask me to tell stories about my life
> in Colombia, about my family and I teach them words in Spanish.
> My friends love to learn words in Spanish, especially bad words
> [laughing]. So that makes me different. But different in a good
> way I think. So sometimes I do belong here sometimes I don't. I
> think I belong to two different places. Is that okay? It feels weird
> sometimes like I am living in half a culture. Maybe someday I will
> feel more comfortable living in two cultures, but as a teenager it
> just feels complicated. (Jorge, 1 April 2009)

(3) Struggling but Optimistic

Fourteen (almost half) of the participants who had been in the community for less than three years and still identify primarily with
their home culture do not feel like they belong to Fredericton or
Florenceville-Bristol and do not feel at home in the communities.
However, they express optimism about their future in New Brunswick and are confident that a sense of belonging will come with
time. The teens are aware that being in the province will offer them
excellent opportunities and they are ready to "fulfill their dreams."
Most of the immigrant adolescents who fit into this category are
refugees in Fredericton. They have made few friends outside of their
ethnic groups and are not necessarily happy in their school or neighbourhood, but they feel safe and know that if they persevere there
is light at the end of the tunnel. Abo, for example, has had a tough
three years in Fredericton. Having "gotten in with a bad group of
kids," and having found himself in more than one sticky situation
with law enforcement, Abo has learned the hard way that not all
social networks are beneficial to him. He now spends more time
alone exercising, writing, and he hopes to take acting classes. He
seems to be more aware of who he is and where he needs to go:

> I want to be an actor. I want to be famous. But when I am
> famous I will still be the same person. I will appreciate what I

have here, but I won't forget where I come from. I won't forget
my family back home. I will visit them and give them money.
I want to take advantage of all the opportunities here so I can
make lots of money and send it to Sierra Leone where they can
use it to buy artificial limbs for people. Because you know in
Sierra Leone during the war they cut people's hands and arms
off, and also they can use it to start a national soccer team. (Abo,
28 February 2009)

The immigrant adolescents who, at the time of our interview, had
recently arrived as the dependents of provincial nominees also fit in
this category in Fredericton, but less so in Florenceville-Bristol where
they appear to be more content and at ease. Their parents made the
decision to immigrate to Canada to take advantage of educational
opportunities for their children and give them better lives. The adolescent children did not ask to come here and, while their parents
have their best interests at heart, the adolescents have not necessarily
"bought into their program yet." Heo, for example, knows why she
is here and she plans to make the most of the experience:

No, I don't think I belong here, but maybe someday I will
belong. My parents came here so that me and my brother can
have better opportunities. It hasn't been easy though and now
my parents and my brother are not sure if they want to stay
here, but I think despite everything and despite the fact that I am
lonely here, I will stay because there will be more opportunities
here for me. In my country it is very hard to get into university
and to get a good job when we graduate. (Heo, 31 January
2009)

In all of these states of belonging, but especially this one, a positive,
optimistic attitude can make a big difference. The guidance counsellor at Fredericton High School touched on this optimism in his interview, and looking back on my own exchange year in Mexico, I am
inclined to agree:

I remember when I was abroad I was so excited. Every time I
opened the door I would think "what is going to happen today?"
I was open to all of those new and wonderful experiences. But it
was my decision to go to South Korea. I think for many of these

teens the decisions have been made for them and they don't enter these new circumstances with the same enthusiasm. Exchange students are in an entirely different group. They are pumped. Young immigrants on the other hand open the door and think "God, what is going to happen to me today?" (Guidance Counsellor, 26 November 2008)

(4) Lost in Translation

Length of time in the communities does not seem to make a difference to the two immigrant adolescent participants who do not feel like they belong, and are pessimistic about ever finding that sense of belonging. The teens have struggled to learn English, overcome culture shock, and make friends in their new community. Mateo, for example, had been in Fredericton for three years at the time of our interview. He arrived in the community from Colombia via Florenceville-Bristol where his family now resides. High grades in university and flawless English aside, I detected sadness between the lines of his interview transcript:

> No, I don't belong here. Not at all … [pause] … I don't have any friends here really. I haven't made friends with any of the local students and I haven't met any of the Latin Americans. I guess I haven't been committed to finding friends. I don't make friends easily … [pause] … I don't know. I understand why my family can't go back to Colombia. I understand why New Brunswick is a better place to raise a family, and to have better opportunities, and I accept that but that doesn't mean I have to be happy about it. After I get my Canadian citizenship I'll probably stay in Canada but I would like to be in a big city like Toronto. (Mateo, 28 October 2008)

Mark had only recently arrived from English-speaking Liberia at the time of our interview. When asked to describe what a welcoming community meant to him he replied with a cracking voice "it means home." Claiming to have no friends and no prospect of meeting peers either in his largely white middle school or in the low-income apartment complex where he resides, Mark wants only to return to Africa.

FACTORS PREDICTING SENSE OF BELONGING

As evident in these categories and in the words spoken throughout this book, social capital, social networks, and the engaged citizens who mobilize them all play into the immigrant adolescents' sense of belonging or lack of belonging to the receiving communities. Individual and group-level factors have also been discussed in the previous chapters. In Fredericton these factors appear to include, in no given order: age at arrival; length of residence in the community; whether the participant is a boy or a girl; personality type; individual resilience and resourcefulness; country of origin; family dynamics; immigrant classification; socio-economic status; race; whether the participant spoke English (or French) upon arrival; and the roles played by neighbourhoods, schools, churches and other social institutions. The most significant contextual factor in Florenceville-Bristol is the role engaged citizens play in the lives of the immigrant adolescents. This is especially true of the New Brunswick-born adolescents and staff in the schools. The individual and group-level factors include fluency in English and, to a lesser extent, length of residence in the community, as well as an apparent institutional culture that accepts immigration and cultural diversity. Class, gender, and race do not appear to play into the argument in Florenceville-Bristol to the extent that they do in Fredericton, but ethnic networks do play a more important role. With respect to immigrant classification and socioeconomic status, the immigrant adolescents in Florenceville-Bristol are a much more homogeneous group than their counterparts in Fredericton. Their middle class, professional backgrounds allow the teens to make contact with local residents on a more equal footing. It is also evident that all of the immigrant families in Florenceville-Bristol place great importance on education and know how to navigate the school system.

Qualitative research cannot tease out each variable to determine which one holds the most weight in relation to the others. Nor can it determine without a doubt that the sense of belonging the immigrant adolescents acquire predicts adaptation and integration, or vice-versa. Qualitative research *can* collect people's feelings and perceptions about some of those variables. In describing their experiences integrating into the two communities, the immigrant adolescents gave me the privilege of listening to their beliefs, dreams, and

motivations. From their words, and the words of the other participants, I came to have a better understanding of what matters to them.
There is no doubt that forming relationships with active, engaged
citizens in school and the wider community *matters* to them.

SUMMARY OF THE FINDINGS

Using the voices of participants as much as possible, the preceding
chapters presented the findings of case studies of Fredericton and
Florenceville-Bristol, New Brunswick. Interviews with participants
were guided by the question: How do the actions of engaged citizens
of a community factor into immigrant adolescents' sense of belonging? Based on a small body of literature on adolescent development
and community development focusing on informal social infrastructure, I entered data collection with the premise that contact with
immigrant adolescents, and increased awareness about their circumstances, would cause citizens – adolescent citizens, but especially
adult citizens – to make an effort to become engaged in their lives.
This active engagement on the part of citizens would expand social
networks for the immigrant adolescents, which in turn would create or trigger social capital and ultimately facilitate their sense of
belonging to the community.

The data collected in Fredericton suggest that there is little purposeful contact between the established citizens and the immigrant
adolescents. There is also an underdeveloped public awareness
about immigration and cultural diversity, which is either the result
of this lack of contact, or the cause of it. Citizens of Fredericton are
engaged in the community and with each other, but that engagement
for the most part does not appear to reach the immigrant adolescents. The data further suggest that the immigrant adolescents are
dependent upon Fredericton's formal social infrastructure to support them in the integration process. This finding contradicts Grace
Pretty and colleagues' (1996) argument regarding sense of belonging
to a community: "if adolescents feel accepted as members of a community, they will be more likely to access the resources and opportunities afforded by that community." The reality is they may seek
out the resources even more if they are not as integrated into the
community; those immigrant adolescents without informal supports
in Fredericton turn to the formal ones – through which they access a
variety of resources and opportunities.

Given that the twenty immigrant adolescents who participated in the Fredericton case study are gradually becoming involved in the community and are, for the most part, finding their way, this situation may be entirely acceptable. The formal programs in place for the settlement and integration of immigrants in Fredericton are evolving over time and are functioning as they should, although they are also overburdened (in the case of MCAF) and were initially unprepared (in the case of the schools). Outside of the formal infrastructure, friends and friendship networks mean the world to these immigrant adolescents, and are pivotal to their welcome and inclusion in Fredericton. But the teens have found meeting local peers and making friends to be difficult. Ultimately, most of them did make friends with local peers and with other immigrant adolescents. However, making friends should be a natural act that does not consume so much time and energy. The majority of the immigrant adolescent participants in Fredericton (both refugees and provincial nominees) have yet to find a sense of belonging to the receiving community, but are optimistic that the sense of belonging will come with time. As noted in this chapter, this lack of belonging depends on a variety of factors besides connections with engaged citizens.

The Fredericton data have therefore answered the second set of questions guiding the research: What is the relative weight of formal services and programs for immigrant adolescents compared with the more intangible and informal actions of engaged citizens in a community? And, do young immigrants have to be included in formal activities and community structures or is it more important to make them *feel* like they belong in some larger sense? The answer, however, is not straightforward. Undoubtedly formal programs and services for immigrant adolescents in Fredericton carry more weight than the more intangible and informal actions of engaged citizens. Most of the immigrant adolescent participants spoke of the need to be included in formal groups and activities in school and the wider community, but some did also pick up on the feeling of belonging or being excluded. The older adolescents, in particular, were able to capture that more abstract feeling in their stories.

Throughout the chapters, I have highlighted the effects of sociodemographic characteristics such as class, gender, and race on social infrastructure for immigrant adolescents in Fredericton. Low socioeconomic status appears to be associated with less access to recreational activities in the city, since families who cannot afford a

vehicle of their own must make do with poor public transportation. Friendly, helpful neighbours, moreover, do not appear to be
prevalent in the city's low-income apartment complexes. Given that
most of the refugees in Fredericton are members of visible minority
groups of low socioeconomic status, class and race may be associated with their difficulties making friends and accessing social capital and social networks. A gender difference was noted between the
immigrant girls and immigrant boys, with girls being less involved
in extracurricular and recreational activities in the city and finding
it more difficult to meet local peers and make friends. The data further indicate that cultural stereotyping and racial name-calling are
unfortunate features of Fredericton's middle and high schools.

Attentive to the fact that a town the size of Florenceville-Bristol
would have limited experience with a relatively big cohort of immigrant adolescents, and few or no programs targeted at that age-
group, I doubted my original premise and felt that perhaps there
would actually be a rural disadvantage with respect to young immigrants. The literature, after all, led me to believe that small town
Atlantic Canada lacks the capacity to attract and integrate immigrants,[9] as well as the ability to retain its young adult population.[10]
Yet the Florenceville-Bristol data are astoundingly consistent with
my original premise.

As it turns out, the recent increase of immigrant adolescents settling in Florenceville-Bristol and attending school there seems to
act as the catalyst that motivates citizens of the community – the
school community especially – to become engaged with the teens.
This engagement facilitates the development of social capital and
social networks for the immigrant adolescents, and these assets in
turn assist them in finding acceptance and membership in the community. The lack of programs targeted at immigrant adolescents in
fact appears to heighten the feeling of responsibility the local residents have toward the young newcomers. This is not to argue, of
course, that cutting back programs for the integration of immigrants
would have the unintended reverse effect of actually improving their
integration outcomes. MACC's programs are critical to the integration of immigrants, especially the mothers of the immigrant adolescents. It is also apparent that the residents of Florenceville-Bristol
go out of their way to get to know and assist everyone, not only
immigrants. I initially assumed, moreover, that if community members were at all engaged, then those members would be adults. The

effort being made by the New Brunswick-born adolescents to reach out and include their immigrant peers came as a pleasant surprise.

There is definitely something more intangible at work in Florence-ville-Bristol. As mentioned in chapter 1, even the formal social institutions of MACC and the schools have an air of informality about them. All of the discussions with participants touched on the idea of recognizing the strengths and abilities of the immigrant adolescents (and immigrants in general) and including them in activities and structures where they would have the best fit. Like the Fredericton case study, the more analytical adolescents were better able to articulate a larger and more abstract feeling of belonging to the community, but for the most part belonging was associated with inclusion in community activities and institutions.

As previously noted, class, gender, and race do not appear to affect social infrastructure for the immigrant adolescents in Florenceville-Bristol to the same extent as they do in Fredericton. All thirteen immigrant adolescents are relatively homogeneous with respect to their urban, professional, middle class family backgrounds. Gender difference was insignificant for the teens with respect to their involvement in extracurricular and recreational activities, or their ability to make friends with local peers, but it was perceived in stories of their mothers' adjustment to the community. While racism is undoubtedly present in rural Carleton County, few of the immigrant participants actually regard themselves as members of a visible minority group. Class and race do, however, play into how local residents of Florenceville-Bristol perceive the immigrant adolescents. In chapter 3, I suggested that individuals from working class backgrounds may be more likely to accuse immigrants of taking their jobs and decreasing their wages, and some individuals see the immigrants as members of visible minority groups despite their fair complexions.

As noted in chapter 2, face-to-face contact in Florenceville-Bristol anchors the other themes and sub-themes, including the sense of belonging, but it may also romanticize participants' perceptions of life in small town New Brunswick. Many of the quotations from community organizers and local residents, although lovely and hospitable, denote power relationships between the "helpers and the helped." Both Florenceville-Bristol and Fredericton appear to encourage the adaption and integration of immigrants using what is becoming known in the literature as an *immigrant deficit model*. This model of working with immigrants tends to regard them as a series of needs to be met by the local communities or serviced by government-funded agencies.[11] With any luck this needs-based perspective will evolve into a more progressive community model, which recognizes the newcomers as full citizens, accords them respect, and welcomes them as valued and equal partners in the progressive development of the communities.[12]

7

There's No Place Like Home
Discussion and Implications of the Research

At a time when the federal and provincial governments are looking at ways of balancing the distribution of immigrants across Canada and outside of the largest metropolitan centres, *Getting Used to the Quiet* focuses on the integration experiences of an understudied age group of immigrants in a small city and rural town in New Brunswick. The research was undertaken to enhance the understanding of how citizens mobilize to facilitate the adaptation and integration of immigrant adolescents into their communities. Semi-structured interviews and focus groups were conducted with six categories of volunteer participants over an eleven-month period in 2008–09. The study borrowed the concept of social infrastructure from the literature on adolescent development and community development to describe the relationship being built between immigrant adolescents and the receiving community. It distinguished between "formal social infrastructure" – community resources such as immigrant settlement and integration programs – and "informal social infrastructure" – engaged citizens, social capital, and social networks – and it paid particular attention to informal social infrastructure. Five core themes emerged from the analysis of the interview transcripts. These themes branched into a hierarchy of sub-themes and codes.

This concluding chapter will examine the findings of the Fredericton and Florenceville-Bristol case studies, and in doing so will: (1) Respond to the final question that guided the research "Is the social infrastructure for the adaptation and integration of immigrant adolescents the same in an urban and rural setting?"; (2) Move beyond the data to link the individual experiences presented in the previous chapters to broader societal themes; (3) Demonstrate how this research contributes to our understanding of the adaptation and integration of immigrant youth in small communities, particularly those in Atlantic Canada; and (4) Outline the limitations of the research and explain how further academic study could advance knowledge of immigration in Canada and beyond.

My study of social infrastructure for the integration of young immigrants in a city with a population of 50,535 and in a rural town of 1,500 has brought to light parallels and contrasts. I anticipated that the data would demonstrate the existence of an urban-rural divide in New Brunswick on the policy and programming related to immigration. This was not the case. Although Florenceville-Bristol does not have the formal programs for immigrant adolescents that a city the size of Fredericton is able to deliver, the citizens of Florenceville-Bristol compensate for this absence by generally being more involved in the settlement and integration of these immigrant adolescents than the citizens of Fredericton. The resources and mechanisms appear to be in place in Florenceville-Bristol to encourage collective action by its citizens. Their purposeful and continuous engagement with immigrant adolescents facilitates the inclusion of the adolescents in social networks and the development of social capital. The social capital and social networks, in turn, assist the adolescents in finding a sense of belonging to the community. This collective action is especially apparent in the schools where staff and students have made a major effort to reach out to, include, and communicate with the immigrant adolescents. The resources and mechanisms for collective action are in place in Fredericton as well, but there appears to be a disconnection between citizen engagement and the integration of immigrants into the community. A lack of personal interaction and public awareness in Fredericton fosters a greater sense of indifference and ambivalence, which hinders the mobilization of citizens to act collectively toward the goal of integrating immigrants. The larger size of the city and the fact that immigrants are not central to the city's major industries – government and education – reduces the pressure to engage newcomers.

The data suggest that social infrastructure for the inclusion of immigrant adolescents in a small urban community is quite different from that of a rural community, with the former depending upon formal programs and organized youth activities, and the latter turning to the more informal and spontaneous efforts of friendly, engaged citizens. Despite this difference, the immigrant adolescents in both communities appear to undergo similar journeys to belonging which result, for the most part, in relatively positive outcomes. It would be incorrect to state at this juncture that all of the immigrant adolescents who participated in the research are part of peer networks and are happy with their new lives. However, almost all of them are involved in activities in their schools and wider community. They are generally doing well in school, and every one of the adolescents say that they would like to have the opportunity to pursue post-secondary education.

Immigrant adolescents in Fredericton comprise a more diverse group than their counterparts in Florenceville-Bristol due to the addition of refugees to the population. Nevertheless, if I remove the ten refugees from the Fredericton sample, and compare only the ten economic immigrants (including the international students) with the thirteen economic immigrants in Florenceville-Bristol, my findings would remain the same. The five provincial nominees in Fredericton do not experience the same discrimination and economic hardship as the ten refugees, but they are equally lonely, friendless, and unsure of their sense of belonging. The citizens of Fredericton are not only ambivalent toward refugees, they are ambivalent toward the economic immigrants as well – and especially those from non-European source countries. Yet, ambivalence aside, Fredericton still has an advantage over small rural communities like Florenceville-Bristol. The city is more likely to retain its immigrant adolescents for a longer period of time by encouraging them to attend university or community college there or by presenting them with the opportunity to return after they migrate to other cities to pursue studies and careers. Once immigrant adolescents leave Florenceville-Bristol, they are not likely to return; and more often than not, immigrant parents follow their grown children to other parts of Canada. Parallels and contrasts are also evident in each of the five core themes of the research as noted here and in Table 13 shown in the Appendix.

MAKING CONTACT

Although not a sizeable urban centre by any means, established residents and recent immigrants in Fredericton do not usually come into daily contact with one another. Work appears to influence people's associations within and beyond the workplace. Established residents are also committed to their families, devoting much of their nonworking hours to family time. Combined with few common spaces and organized events where the various cultures can interact, as well as a shortage of affordable housing and public transportation for some immigrants, this local focus on the private domestic sphere reduces the opportunities available for wider social activities and the personalization of relationships. Immigrant adolescents spoke of not being seen or heard by local residents, particularly their local peers, and of not being included in groups and activities. The small size of Florenceville-Bristol, in contrast, is more conducive to daily contact between cultures along with the fact that a single large corporation employs the adolescents' parents and a large number of the town's residents. A healthy sense of curiosity in the schools encourages staff and students to accept the immigrant adolescents, and to recognize and draw on their strengths and abilities to achieve common goals.

PUBLIC AWARENESS

Citizens of Fredericton are knowledgeable regarding the province's immigration goals and the economic reasons why immigrants are needed, but they are not necessarily aware of who is in their community now and where they are from. The local adolescents in the schools appear to be insular, with apparently little interest in learning about the world. Immigrant adolescents described cultural stereotypes, misunderstandings, and racist name-calling in the schools. Local residents maintained that they lack experience welcoming immigrants, but would like to improve the circumstances of immigrant adolescents if given the chance to do so. They believe that the inclusion of immigrants in the life of the city will come with increasing immigration levels and with the passage of time. Florenceville-Bristol, on the contrary, is small enough to make word of newcomers travel fast. Most citizens are aware of their presence and, despite some concerns that immigrants are coming to compete for their jobs, are nonetheless accepting of them. Learning about the source countries and cultures of the immigrant adolescents is now part of the school curriculum, and residents of all ages voluntarily partake in Spanish classes and multicultural celebrations in the community.

SOCIAL CAPITAL AND SOCIAL NETWORKS

In both communities the immigrant adolescents care deeply for their parents, and some worry that their parents are not adjusting to their

new lives as well as they should. Ethnic networks appear to play a
larger role in the adolescents' lives in Florenceville-Bristol because
there is now a critical mass of people in the town from the same
country. Social support provided by neighbours was mentioned by
the dependents of economic immigrants who live in those Fredericton
neighbourhoods with relatively high household socioeconomic levels, but not by the dependents of refugees who reside in low-income
neighbourhoods. In Florenceville-Bristol, all citizens are regarded as
"neighbours." Friends and their social networks mean a great deal
to the immigrant adolescents, though making friends across groups
in Fredericton has been, according to the youth, an exceedingly difficult task. A gender difference was also noted in Fredericton, with
the boys having an easier time socializing and making friends than
the girls. In Florenceville-Bristol making friends has been less prob-
lematic and there were no obvious gender differences.

CITIZEN ENGAGEMENT

Outside of the formal social infrastructure of school and the multicultural association, few relationships are being built with immigrant
adolescents in Fredericton. The Multicultural Association of Fredericton is an important source of adult role models for the adolescents. These role models are also immigrants who settled in the city
as adolescents and young adults. Immigrant adolescents claim that
the effort to fit into their schools and wider community rests solely
with them, but having made that effort, most of them have slowly
acquired friends and have become involved in a variety of activities.
In Florenceville-Bristol, adults tend to look out for the immigrant
adolescents (as they would any adolescent) and act as the primary
agents of social control in the community. The most engaged citizens
are local adolescents in the schools who have reached out to their
immigrant peers in an effort to include them in their social networks.

SENSE OF BELONGING

The final theme represents more of a parallel than a contrast. Over
half of the immigrant adolescents in the two case communities have
achieved the bicultural identity and integration profile which the literature describes as ideal. Some still struggle with that identity, while
others are at peace with it. The two additional states of belonging
consisted of "not belonging with optimism that it will come with

time" and "not belonging with the expression of doubt that it will come with time." Immigrant adolescents experiencing these additional states of belonging are largely refugees and provincial nominees in Fredericton who are really struggling to make friends and fit into the community.

BROADER SOCIETAL THEMES

Broader societal themes also influence how members of the two case communities behave toward the immigrant adolescents. These themes make a subtle appearance in or go beyond the verbal data of the interview transcripts. C. Wright Mills identifies three separate, but interconnected levels of analysis: (1) The biography, or the inner lives of individuals; (2) The small-scale milieux, or everyday worlds of individuals; and (3) The broad structural forces most evident in patterns of historical change.[1] The everyday experiences of the immigrant adolescents and the other participants displayed throughout this book are shaped by the community in which they live, work, and go to school. The community and its social institutions, in turn, are shaped by forces operating in the larger society within a given historical period.[2] These forces include the local economy and labour market in the community, the larger role of class and race in society, and the position of migrants and the receiving society within the increasing connectivity and interdependence of the world's markets, cultures, values, and ideas, better known as globalization.

LOCAL ECONOMY AND LABOUR MARKET

Florenceville-Bristol is a one-industry town. Its citizens are dependent on the farming, manufacturing, and professional support divisions of a single employer – McCain Foods, Ltd. Not only does McCain Foods, Ltd determine, to a great extent, the economic and social well-being of the citizens of Florenceville-Bristol, by employing the majority of these citizens either directly or indirectly, it also shapes their view of the world. In chapter 1, I noted that the organizational culture of McCain Foods, Ltd spreads to the community, resulting in a general acceptance and promotion of cultural diversity by authorities, institutions and the social and cultural norms that guide them. Put another way, the citizens of Florenceville-Bristol were likely not given the choice to welcome or not welcome immigrant families.

If the managers of McCain Foods, Ltd decide to recruit employees and their families from around the world, then it is best to treat
them with fairness and respect because if the Colombians cannot be
brought to Florenceville-Bristol, in the era of globalization, the company's entire information technology division can always be outsourced to Colombia.

My findings have been incontestably affected by Florenceville-
Bristol's single industry status. The community is so heavily dominated by the corporation that hired most of the immigrant adolescents' parents that it increases the likelihood that their families
will interact with each other and be more easily integrated into the
community. This situation is not unique to Florenceville-Bristol, but
likely exaggerated due to the sheer size of McCain Foods, Ltd, and
the fact that it is privately owned by a family that maintains deep
connections to the community. Unless immigrants are farmers – and
few of them are – they would not settle in a rural area but for the
presence of jobs. Several rural towns and small cities across Canada
and the United States are home to a single industry that employs
large numbers of people. Manitoba's success at dispersing immigrants to small towns outside of Winnipeg through its provincial
nominee program has been described and celebrated in numerous
reports and presentations. Winkler, Portage la Prairie, and Steinbach,
for example, offer newcomers jobs at Triple E Recreational Vehicles
(500 employees), the McCain Foods, Ltd potato processing centre
(500 employees), and Loewen Windows (1,500 employees).

The idea that immigrants bring the strength of numbers to collective community efforts in Florenceville-Bristol is also characteristic
of a one-industry town.[3] The high population turnover in the small
town creates a great expense for McCain Foods, Ltd with respect to
the hiring and training of human resources; it also inhibits community development and makes long-range community planning difficult.[4] Citizens are aware they have to capitalize on the experience,
skills, investment, and creativity that is available through immigrants moving to the community. It is in their best interest to be
involved in the integration of immigrant adolescents, so that they
can keep the young immigrants and their families in the community
for as long as possible.

In Fredericton, it is difficult to discern exactly why citizens are so
uninterested and ambivalent toward immigrant adolescents, beyond
the larger size of the community. The argument seems to centre on

why the contact hypothesis – discussed in chapters 2 and 3 – appears to work in Florenceville-Bristol, but not in Fredericton. In the latter community at least two, if not all, of Gordon Allport's (1954) "four necessary conditions for contact to result in the reduction of prejudice" are not as developed as they are in the former. The first, "making contact as relative equals," is discussed in the next section on social class and race; the second, that "contact between the groups be supported by authority figures, institutions, and social and cultural norms," is elaborated on here.

As mentioned in chapters 4 and 5, Fredericton has relatively active and engaged citizens, social networks, and other social resources, yet somehow fails to connect immigrant adolescents with them. Citizens of Fredericton are friendly, but relationships between them are fundamentally shaped by professional affiliations in a largely white-collar, service-based economy. Whether they are university professors, civil servants, or healthcare professionals, their social networks tend to be small, interconnected, and difficult for newcomers to penetrate. Most of the parents of the immigrant adolescent participants in Fredericton do not work in institutions where they could interact with local residents with similar professional backgrounds. Instead they are self-employed, unemployed, or still learning English at the Multicultural Association. Authority figures (namely the various levels of government) and social and cultural norms dictate that immigrants of all ages be accepted in Fredericton, but few people have given much thought to providing opportunities for them to become more involved in the community's institutions and, subsequently, to become embedded in diverse social networks. Schools, churches, and voluntary associations are not as proactive as they could be when including immigrants. As noted by Andy Scott, "we certainly don't have a policy that if you are East Indian you can't be part of our club, but I don't think anyone is sitting around at a Rotary Club meeting on a Thursday afternoon saying 'there are no East Indians here we need to go out and find some.' We need to do exactly that" (Andy Scott, 18 December 2008).

SOCIAL CLASS AND RACE

Social class is another structural force that permeates the data in subtle ways. The occupational position of the immigrant adolescents' parents determines the social position of their families in both

Florenceville-Bristol and Fredericton. In Florenceville-Bristol, class divisions are largely determined by McCain Foods, Ltd, with the sharpest distinction being between management and the processing-plant workers. The less technically skilled temporary migrants driving trucks for McCain Foods, Ltd also fall at the lower end of the salary structure. Local residents participating in my research rightly or wrongly made reference to the "good office jobs" in the professional support divisions of the company being filled primarily by the provincially nominated immigrants at the expense of the local labour force. Yet despite perceived competition for some jobs, contact between newcomers and established residents has largely been made on an equal footing because all of the immigrant adolescent participants come from middle class professional families. Provincially nominated immigrant parents working as systems engineers and computer programmers at the McCain Foods, Ltd Global Technology Centre, moreover, would ultimately develop close ties with other middle class educated professionals allowing the parents to gain access to a broad range of social resources and information channels, which may prove useful to their adolescent children as they integrate into the community.

In Fredericton, the economic and provincially nominated immigrants have gradually joined or will gradually join the ranks of Fredericton's university-educated, middle class professionals, along with the international students who choose to remain in the city after they complete their degrees. The addition of refugees to the population of immigrant adolescents in Fredericton, however, makes social stratification more probable. The dire economic situation of many refugee families, combined with their struggle to start from scratch and get ahead – or at the very least to survive – place them at the bottom of the community's social hierarchy. In accordance with Fernando Nunes' (2003) study of academically underachieving Portuguese youth in Canada, some refugee parents are unable to provide their sons and daughters with the experience, knowledge, contacts, habits, and resources, or "cultural capital" which middle class families take for granted. Those refugee families who come from urban, professional, middle class backgrounds in their country of origin will already possess much of the cultural capital to be able to integrate more readily into middle class Canadian society. What they lack are the social and economic contacts. Once they make those contacts they are more able to navigate middle class society, get good jobs, and participate culturally and politically in their communities. Refugee families from predominantly working class and rural refugee populations, however, tend to have a much harder time achieving this life, even if their children become university educated. Their children will not have developed this cultural capital.[5]

Race also defines the self-worth and aspirations of many of the refugee adolescents who participated in my research in Fredericton, making community resources and a network of social support that much more critical for them to achieve their full potential in life. Black parents may face additional child rearing challenges compared to parents from other racial cultural groups because of the disadvantaged position they often occupy within their communities.[6] Studies show that visible minorities (especially black men, both foreign and native-born) encounter a significant disadvantage in the labour market;[7] others conclude that Canada's labour market is usually characterized by the overrepresentation of racialized women in low paid, low end occupations.[8] Extensive research also documents the barriers faced by racialized groups within the school system, including the absence of visible minority teachers, lower expectations by teachers and counsellors, "colour coded" streaming, and Eurocentric curricula.[9]

In short, non-white refugee adolescents of low socioeconomic status in Fredericton are not making contact with their white, middle class peers as relative equals. Furthermore, most research evidence surrounding contact hypothesis tends to ignore the issue of race, and the effect of institutionalized racist practices and policies on the relationships between people. For example, if it were really true that existing stereotypes start to break down with increased contact between people, then in places like the Southern United States, there would be a perfect relationship of trust between the African American and white communities, but this is not the case.[10]

LIVING IN A GLOBALIZED WORLD

Globalization's effect on international migration and the receiving society is the last structural force worth emphasizing here. Over the last three decades the economies of the advanced industrial countries of the North have undergone massive restructuring and transformation. These changes have had an enormous impact on the structure of labour, both on the domestic and on the international level.[11]

Canada and other industrialized countries are benefiting from international migration by receiving highly trained human capital from developing regions of the world. As noted by Peter S. Li, the social worth of immigrants is largely evaluated on their ability to augment the country's productivity so that those already in the country can benefit from immigration. Accordingly, immigrants at the very least cannot be burdens to those already in the country.[12] As discussed in chapter 6, my research in New Brunswick offers insights into what a "welcoming community" might consist of; nonetheless it is not easy to move beyond a needs-based analysis of this concept. In her recent article about the reception of immigrants in New Zealand, Avril Bell suggests that relations of hospitality are in fact power relations: "The act of welcome invokes a spatialized relationship between the established resident who is at home and the newcomer/guest who arrives from elsewhere ... What hospitality does the host offer? What are the limits to that hospitality? And how long are guests welcome to stay?"[13] Even in the friendly, small-town atmosphere of Florenceville-Bristol, the actions of engaged citizens still call attention to the dominant culture – "us" – reaching out to the racially, culturally, and linguistically different immigrants – "them" – to help further their adjustment to *our* way of life. Clearly our communities need to be welcoming, but they must also encourage a sense of agency in immigrants. This would allow immigrants to find their own identity and sense of belonging so that they could reach their full potential and be able to contribute their creativity and enthusiasm to society.

It is also important to note that these immigrants are settling in a province that has not kept pace with the rest of Canada with respect to employment, income, trade, and productivity.[14] Globalization has dealt New Brunswick the complicated task of preparing an under-educated aging labour force for the transition from a natural resource-based economy to a knowledge-based economy that requires more sophisticated literacy and numeracy skills than the workers currently possess. Further still, the demographic reality of slowing population growth, rapid population aging, declining labour force participation, significant out-migration (particularly of young adults), and difficulty in attracting immigrants poses a danger to New Brunswick's economic prosperity and social security system. In a nutshell, at the regional level it is apparent that "Decades of out-migration have not served the region very well as a development strategy";[15] and (2) The region may be a "stop over place for immigrants at best."[16]

Classic social theorist Robert E. Park (1969) viewed migrants as potential wanderers. He delineated the concept of the "sojourner" as a way to understand the personal struggles immigrants engage in as they constantly re-evaluate whether to stay in a new community, return to their community of origin, or migrate to another new community.[17] The immigrant adolescents (mostly the dependents of economic immigrants and the international students, but also some of the refugees) are adventurous, ambitious, confident citizens of the modern, urban world. They can study, work, and make themselves at home in any city, province, or country of their choosing. Some are the children of parents in what Richard Florida (2002, 2005) calls the "creative class": professional, highly skilled, specialized and flexible workers who can find opportunity, build support structures, be themselves, and not get stuck in any one place or identity. For many of these adolescents, Florenceville-Bristol and Fredericton are merely stops on the journey to pursuing their dream wherever it works for them. Their experiences in these two New Brunswick communities are changing them as they transition from childhood to adulthood; and hopefully their presence, if only temporary, is changing the communities as well.

CONTRIBUTION TO EXISTING KNOWLEDGE

Getting Used to the Quiet strengthens and expands our understanding of immigrant youth by placing what is known about their general psycho-social adaptation and integration into the context of two small communities that are relatively unaccustomed to receiving immigrants. By examining the everyday worlds of immigrant adolescents as they adapt to their new lives and build networks of social support around them, my research shows integration as it occurs at both the individual and local community levels; that is, it shows the young immigrants and the local residents interacting with one another and the gradual changes that occur as a result of that interaction.

At the individual level, the four states of belonging outlined in chapter 6 are supported by John W. Berry and colleagues' (2006) findings from an international study of the acculturation of immigrant youth, which concluded beyond a doubt that youth should be encouraged to retain a sense of their own ethnic identity while establishing close ties with the larger national society. Accordingly, immigrant adolescents in Fredericton and Florenceville-Bristol who have adopted a bicultural identity, regardless of whether or not they are secure with that identity, correspond with Berry and colleagues' "integration profile," which indicates high involvement in both national and ethnic cultures. Those adolescents who do not identify with their receiving community, but are optimistic that that sense of belonging will come with time, correspond with an "ethnic profile," which represents young people who are largely embedded within their own culture and show little involvement with the larger receiving society. Those who have marginalized themselves from both the national and ethnic communities (either by choice or by force) fit what Berry and colleagues describe as a "diffuse profile," whereby the youth reported low national identity and few national peer contacts, but they also reported a low ethnic identity and few ethnic peer contacts.

Research across the social sciences has explored the various ways in which immigrants begin to make sense of both their heritage culture and the new society in which they now live, but very few studies have focused on changes occurring at the level of the receiving community.[18] Those studies that do deal with how immigrants might influence the receiving community[19] still emphasize the power and influence of institutionally complete ethnic communities and enclaves, which are far from robust and vigorous in the communities I examined. No study, to my knowledge, focuses specifically on the other side of acculturation: the gradual changes that occur in the dominant culture as it comes into contact with minority cultures. Through rich descriptions, and the incorporation of interview excerpts into the analytical themes derived from the data, my research takes community context out of the background and places it at the forefront of the immigrant adolescents' adaptation and integration experiences.

Because they lack contact with and knowledge about the new community members, citizens of Fredericton have been ambivalent about immigrants. Newcomers and established residents coexist primarily (though perhaps unconsciously) by maintaining distance from each other. The data reveal that few opportunities for inter-group interaction exist so occasions and places for group interaction, such as schools and the Multicultural Association, have had to absorb the strains of cultural and linguistic differences. Sheer numbers of immigrant families settling in the city and the passage of time will likely thrust the citizens of Fredericton out of placidity and into action. Immigrant adolescent participants in Fredericton spoke of friendships made with each other and, ultimately, with New Brunswick-born peers. They described adult role models in the community and worldviews beginning to broaden, especially amongst a small group of civically engaged, socially conscious peers and adults. However, the most fundamental changes in this small city have been more formal in nature. The increasing numbers of immigrants have created a sense of urgency to set up or improve programs and to introduce interventions in the schools, such as providing newcomer students with a full-time settlement worker. Exposure to new cultures in Florenceville-Bristol has also resulted in the implementation of new programs by MACC and various spontaneous school-wide initiatives, but participants in this case study spoke in greater length about the development of diverse social networks in the community, close friendships, and the infiltration of a new language – Spanish – into schools, churches, and other public places.

As noted in chapters 1 and 4, many scholars have documented the importance of communities and neighbourhoods on adolescents' social outcomes, including their mental and physical health, and more specifically their identity and sense of belonging.[20] Studies of community effects on immigrant adolescents' social outcomes usually emphasize the role played by ethnic communities rather than that of local citizens.[21] This book attempts to explain why some smaller receiving communities are more successful than others at advancing the adaptation and integration of immigrant adolescents. Citizens of Florenceville-Bristol and, to a lesser extent, Fredericton are endeavouring to engage the young immigrants, and to recognize their value as members of the communities. As a result, they are beginning to fill the void of bounded social networks and bonding social capital offered by well-established ethnic communities. Parents are still the most influential people in the lives of the immigrant adolescents and within-family social capital or cultural capital likely factors heavily into academic and other social outcomes. Nevertheless, these young people are gradually developing positive relationships with adults and peers in the communities, who in turn connect them with more diverse social networks; opportunities for personal interaction across cultural groups are progressively occurring; schools are now more prepared to handle an influx of non-English and French-speaking students from a variety of cultural and socioeconomic backgrounds; and most churches appear to be welcoming and inclusive. The programmed elements of social infrastructure stand out in Fredericton, while the more informal elements prevail or are more magnified in the smaller community of Florenceville-Bristol.

Jeffrey Reitz (2003) presents four dimensions of the receiving society that facilitate or hinder the integration of immigrants: (1) Differences in labour markets and related institutions, which may lead to different outcomes amongst immigrants; (2) The impact of government policies and programs, including immigration policies and programs for immigrant integration, which in many cases are closely connected to the labour market; (3) The changing nature of international boundaries as part of the process of globalization, which brings opportunities and constraints operating to regulate the flow of persons, goods, and information between countries; and (4) Preexisting ethnic or race relations within the host population, which Reitz argues provide the social framework within which integration occurs.[22] While the broader societal themes discussed earlier in this chapter touch on Reitz's analysis, my research takes this analysis from the macro-level of society to the micro-level of the community.

The case studies of Fredericton and Florenceville-Bristol reveal that the foundations of a welcoming community lie in the willingness of the people who reside there. The adaptation and integration of immigrant adolescents might be best advanced in communities where, among other conditions: (1) Citizens are involved in the life of the community and are committed to act upon a sense of responsibility as members of that community; (2) Citizens recognize immigrant families as active contributors to the community, and they are willing to hire qualified immigrant parents and include parents and children in associations, groups, and activities; (3) Citizens know how to, and do, make an effort to communicate with individuals who speak limited English or French; (4) Schools maintain a positive and informal school climate that emphasizes the personalization of relationships. They are able to make changes to accommodate and utilize the immigrant adolescents' strengths and talents; (5) Schools take advantage of peer interaction by improving the integration of EAL students in mainstream classrooms and by creating a collaborative, inclusive learning environment in which all students participate as equal partners; (6) Schools, churches, voluntary associations and other institutions treat all people fairly regardless of race, ethnicity, language, and social class; (7) Churches and other religious centres provide spaces where immigrant families can meet each other and also locally born residents, and where they can receive formal, and especially informal assistance, in the settlement and adaptation process. (8) Voluntary associations, both ethnic and mainstream, play a constructive role in the lives of immigrant families;[23] (9) Ethnic communities are respected and supported, and encouraged to grow and flourish;[24] and (10) Immigrant youth are, in turn, encouraged to draw resources from both their small ethnic community and mainstream society.

Immigration and the ensuing diversity have provided both case communities with an opportunity for change. The problem they now face is how to anticipate, perceive, and engage in practices to deal with this change. As Atlantic Canada continues its difficult transition to a knowledge-based economy, some cities and towns will absorb large numbers of newcomers and respond to this economic, social, and technological change, while others will stagnate and decline. Resiliency is "the ability to respond or perform positively in the face of adversity, to achieve despite the presence of disadvantages, or to significantly exceed expectations under given negative circumstances."[25] At the community level, resiliency is a "measure of the robustness and buffering capacity of a community in a changing system."[26] Flora and Flora and colleagues (1992, 1993) found that resilient communities with viable local economies maintain high levels of citizen engagement, are accepting of differing citizen perspectives, and have a community-level orientation toward inclusiveness rather than exclusiveness.[27] These scholars claim that the most creative and effective solutions emerge when citizens from diverse perspectives actively engage in initiatives to address local concerns. For communities to maintain a sufficiently high quality of life, people who know one another must work together to achieve common goals and those who do not know one another must have ways to discover their common interests and concerns.[28] These chapters have demonstrated that the same community attributes which Flora and Flora and their colleagues outline make small cities and towns more welcoming to immigrants and more able to foster a sense of belonging amongst immigrant adolescents.

LIMITATIONS AND FURTHER RESEARCH

My case studies were limited by the age-range of the immigrant participants; my sampling technique, including the categories of immigrants I chose to study; the qualitative nature of the data; and the borders of the case communities and province. As such, I discerned four issues that went beyond the scope of this book and subsequently warrant further study:

(1) Focus on Immigrant Adults

My research focused on a specific age group of immigrants – adolescents ages twelve-twenty. The challenges and opportunities immigrant adolescents face are not the same as those which immigrant adults face. Just because the adolescents have achieved, or are in the process of achieving, a sense of belonging to these communities does not mean that their parents are in the same state of mind. Their parents might be miserable. Further study on the economic, social, cultural, and political integration of immigrant adults into small cities and rural towns across Canada is needed.

(2) Sampling Decisions

Purposive sampling is customary practice in qualitative research. It is doubtful that other methods could have produced the diversity and richness of detail I was aiming for. Nevertheless, as mentioned in chapter 1, the type of people who were available and willing to participate in the study may have been different from those in the population who could not be located, and this might have introduced a source of bias. Because I was unable to recruit economic immigrants of African descent who I know resided in Fredericton at the time of data collection, all of the immigrant adolescent participants from Africa were refugees from low socioeconomic households. Therefore it is difficult to distinguish which variable, race or social class, played the more powerful role in my Fredericton data.

The inclusion of refugee adolescents in the study also constitutes a limitation. Many refugee youth have been through extremely traumatic experiences, which may cause them to relate differently to their receiving societies. This consequently may have affected the data. However, I purposefully included ten young refugees in my

Fredericton case study because I think their stories are important to tell; indeed, the data would be incomplete without them. The refugees are different from the economic class immigrants, but in many ways, they are also the same. As noted in chapter 6, many of the economic and provincially nominated adolescents and refugee adolescents in Fredericton did not choose to settle in New Brunswick; that choice was made for them by their parents and, in the case of the refugees, by the Canadian government. Fourteen of these adolescent participants share a state of belonging in which they do not feel like they belong to the community, but are optimistic that sense of belonging will come with time. A study focusing specifically on the integration experiences of refugees of all ages would make a valuable addition to my research and the existing body of literature on immigrants in Canada.

(3) Quantitative Research

The case studies are qualitative, largely based on the analysis of interview transcripts. Adding quantitative methods to a qualitative study, i.e. a mixed method approach, or a purely quantitative approach to studying immigrant adolescents would give the researcher the ability to separate and tease out the variables I encountered in my research. Statistical analysis might allow the researcher to discern which variables hold more weight in relation to the others. A longitudinal study tracking a cohort of immigrant adolescents through the school-to-work transition would also be a valuable addition to the existing knowledge base.

(4) Grow the Research

The experiences of immigrant adolescents in small cities and towns outside of Toronto, Montreal, and Vancouver represent new terrain for researchers. The findings of the few published studies currently available support those discussed in this book. Lloydetta Quaicoe (2008), for example, noted in her study of immigrant adolescents in St John's Newfoundland and Labrador that participants also had a difficult time making connections with local peers in school. Myriam Simard's (2007) article about the lives of immigrant adolescents in areas of Quebec outside of Montreal demonstrates the emergence of a bicultural or transcultural identity driven by daily interactions with the local receiving society. By virtue of their socialization in two or more cultural systems, these young people are undergoing a unique recombining of culture and identity. Yatta Kanu's (2008) investigation of the educational needs and barriers for African refugee students in two inner-city high schools in Winnipeg reveals that academic, economic, and psychosocial challenges facing African refugee students adversely affect their ability to integrate and cope well in school, thereby significantly reducing their socioeconomic opportunities. And Yvonne Hébert's (2005) analysis of immigrant youth in Calgary shows the significance of social capital in shaping the youth's identity and their sense of place in the majority culture. These youth make use of social capital as a resource in order to cope with the difficulties of adjusting to a new setting, and to ease anxiety and isolation. Social networks, in turn, are used as adaptive strategies by the immigrant youth, helping them make friends across groups and improve social status.

Research on immigrant adolescents in small cities and rural towns is more commonplace amongst American researchers. In rural United States, immigration has largely been the result of recruitment efforts by the agri-food industry beginning in the early 1980s. Seeking labour to meet their productivity needs, agricultural operations located in small rural communities have used existing immigrant networks to recruit a steady stream of workers mainly from Mexico and Central America, but also from Somalia and parts of India. Some of the receiving communities very quickly doubled in size and minority representation, which challenged the existing infrastructure and forced local residents to scramble to meet pressing community needs.[29] The so-called "browning of the Midwest" has, according to some reports, led to increasing conflict between immigrants and established residents in many towns, some of which have seen their Hispanic population rise by 200 to 500 per cent since 1990.[30]

It is within this context that James G. Gimpel and J. Celeste Lay (2008) found hostility to immigrants among rural adolescents concentrated among youth from well-rooted and more affluent families, and not adolescents from working class families (as appears to be the case in Florenceville-Bristol). Lower income local adolescents in rural schools share classes and school activities with the immigrant youth, while the children of farmers and those whose families are well-rooted in the community go to different schools and have far fewer of these classroom and neighbourhood interactions. In his study of school attachment among Hispanic youth in rural Minnesota, Joseph D. Diaz (2005) found that students born outside the United States had a greater level of attachment to school than students born in the United States. Since many Hispanic immigrants came to work in meat-processing plants, where the work is difficult and offers little financial security, a commitment to school might be seen by the family as a means of increasing the youth's future chances of securing employment with a higher salary and better working conditions. Linda K. Ko and Krista M. Perreira (2010) looked at the migration and acculturation experiences of Hispanic youth in a newly emerging Hispanic community in North Carolina; this is an area that historically has had low levels of immigration. The authors pick up on many of the themes highlighted in my research including the challenge of going to school and learning English, building a bridge between the cultures and values of their home countries and those of their new communities, making connections with local peers, fitting in, isolation at school, confronting racism, and shaping a positive ethnic identity. Finally, in an effort to explain why Sikh students frequently outperform majority white and other minority students at high school in an agricultural community in central California in the early 1980s, Margaret Gibson (1988) argues that Punjabi Sikh students succeed in school by employing a strategy of accommodation and acculturation without assimilating into the mainstream dominant culture. Sikhs view the acquisition of important cultural tools, such as standard English as additive rather than subtractive from their own identity.

My research was conducted within the municipal limits of Fredericton and Florenceville-Bristol and within the boundaries of the province of New Brunswick. Fredericton's white-collar, service-based economy and status as a provincial capital, the circumstances surrounding Florenceville-Bristol's one-industry local economy, and New Brunswick's demographic and economic challenges mean that lessons learned in this study may not necessarily hold true for immigrant adolescents elsewhere. Expanding a similar study to small cities and towns across Canada, and ultimately also to the United States and other immigrant receiving countries would enhance the knowledge gained from my research and ultimately affect policy and programming targeted at immigrant adolescents.

CONCLUSION

Twenty years after I experienced the process of adjusting to a new language and culture in Mexico, I continue to wonder why the citizens of that dusty town in Zacatecas have had such a big impact on my life. Did they welcome me out of curiosity? Was it a desire to learn about the world outside of their borders? Or was it merely a warm, friendly culture that takes the expression "*mi casa es su casa*" ("my home is your home") very seriously? But today I am not wondering about the characteristics of a welcoming community. As I fix my host-sister Lucy's veil and help her into her ivory satin wedding gown, I am not asking why her family and several others reached out to me when I was an adolescent. No, today I am not analyzing. On this sweltering hot June afternoon I am counting my blessings that every once in a while I am welcome to return to that little Mexican town, which is now my home away from home.

This research has revealed that welcoming immigrant adolescents calls for a strong emphasis on how communities behave toward them. Engaged, attentive citizens build the social infrastructure that makes communities receptive to change and diversity so that they can become "home" to these young people in the same way that the small community in Mexico became home to me. Formal programs play a critical role in the adaptation and integration of immigrant adolescents in the receiving community, but it is informal relations that really count when one is searching for a sense of belonging and that feeling of being at home. What is required are the forms of social organization that make these informal relations flourish.

Appendix: Tables

Table 1
Immigrant Adolescents, Fredericton

Sex	Age	Source Country	Mother Tongue	Official Language	Immigrant Classification
M	14	Congo	French/ Swahili	French English	Refugee
M	12	Congo	French/ Swahili	French English	Refugee
M	12	Liberia	English	English	Refugee
M	13	Colombia	Spanish	English	Refugee
M	17	Sierra Leone	English	English French	Refugee
M	16	Guatemala	Spanish	English	Refugee
F	13	Sierra Leone	English	English French	Refugee
F	13	Liberia	English	English	Refugee
F	14	Liberia	English	English	Refugee
M	17	Colombia	Spanish	English	Refugee
M	19	Colombia	Spanish	English	Provincial Nominee (dependent)
F	15	Netherlands	Dutch	English	Provincial Nominee (dependent)
F	14	Belgium	Dutch	French English	Provincial Nominee (dependent)
F	17	Iran	Farsi	English	Provincial Nominee (dependent)
F	17	South Korea	Korean	English	Provincial Nominee (dependent)
F	15	Venezuela	Spanish	English French	Economic (dependent)
F	17	Taiwan	Mandarin Chinese	English	Economic (dependent)

Table 1   (continued)

Sex	Age	Source Country	Mother Tongue	Official Language	Immigrant Classification
M	15	Iran	Farsi	English	Student (sibling guardian is a permanent resident)
F	20	Vietnam	Vietnamese	English French	Student (applying for permanent residency)
M	18	Indonesia	Indonesian	English	Student (applying for permanent residency)

Total in sample: 20

Table 2
New Brunswick-Born Adolescents, Fredericton

Sex	Age	Source Country	Mother Tongue	Official Language
F	15	Canada	English	English French
F	15	Canada	English	English French
F	14	Canada	English	English
M	14	Canada	English	English
M	14	Canada	English	English
M	15	Canada	English	English French

Total in sample: 6

Table 3
Immigrant Adults, Fredericton (Stayed)

Current Residence	Sex	Age	Source Country	Year of Arrival	Mother Tongue	Immigrant Classification
Fredericton	M	20s	Colombia	2003	Spanish	Economic
Fredericton	M	30s	Peru	1990	Spanish	Economic
Fredericton	M	30s	Poland	1989	Polish	Economic
Fredericton	M	20s	Sierra Leone	2005	English	Refugee
Fredericton	M	30s	Guatemala	1990	Spanish	Refugee
Fredericton	F	30s	El Salvador	1991	Spanish	Refugee

Total in sample: 6

Table 4
Immigrant Adults, Fredericton (Left)

Current Residence	Sex	Age	Source Country	Year of Arrival	Mother Tongue	Immigrant Classification
Ottawa	M	40s	Iran	1989	Persian	Refugee
Montreal	M	30s	Colombia	1990	Spanish	Economic

Total in sample: 2

Table 5
Community Organization Members Fredericton

Sex	Age	Organization	Source Country	Mother Tongue
M	60s	MCAF	Trinidad	English
M	40s	MCAF	Guatemala	Spanish
F	60s	MCAF, Chinese Cultural Association	Singapore	Mandarin Chinese
F	40s	MCAF	Bosnia	Croatian
F	50s	MCAF	Canada	English
M	30s	Fredericton High School	Canada	French English
M	30s	Leo Hayes High School	Canada	English
M	40s	Fredericton Islamic Association	Pakistan	Urdu Arabic
M	50s	United Church of Canada	Netherlands	Dutch
F	50s	School District 18	Canada	English
M	50s	School District 18	Canada	English
M	50s	School District 18	Canada	
F	30s	University of New Brunswick	Canada	English
F	40s	YMCA, Public Library	Canada	English

Total in sample: 14

Table 6
Local Residents Fredericton

Sex	Age	Source Country	Mother Tongue
M	40s	Canada	English
M	30s	Canada	English
M	50s	Canada	English
F	60s	Canada	English
F	40s	Canada	English
F	40s	Canada	English
F	30s	Canada	English, French

Total in sample: 7

Table 7
Immigrant Adolescents Florenceville-Bristol

Sex	Age	Source Country	Mother Tongue	Official Language	Immigrant Classification
M	15	Colombia	Spanish	English	Provincial Nominee (dependent)
M	17	Colombia	Spanish	English	Provincial Nominee (dependent)
M	16	Moldova	Russian	English	Provincial Nominee (dependent)
M	19	South Korea	Korean	English	Student (applying for permanent residency)
M	20	South Korea	Korean	English	Student (applying for permanent residency)
F	14	Colombia	Spanish	English	Provincial Nominee (dependent)
F	14	Colombia	Spanish	English	Provincial Nominee (dependent)
F	14	Colombia	Spanish	English	Provincial Nominee (dependent)
F	13	Colombia	Spanish	English	Provincial Nominee (dependent)
F	13	Colombia	Spanish	English	Provincial Nominee (dependent)
F	17	Colombia	Spanish	English	Provincial Nominee (dependent)
F	15	Mexico	Spanish	English	Provincial Nominee (dependent)
F	18	India	Hindi	English	Provincial Nominee (dependent)

13 interviewed from total of 14

Table 8
New Brunswick-Born Adolescents Florenceville-Bristol

Sex	Age	Source Country	Mother Tongue	Official Language
F	14	Canada	English	English
F	14	Canada	English	English
M	15	Canada	English	English
M	15	Canada	English	English

Total in sample: 4

Table 9
Immigrant Adults Florenceville-Bristol (Stayed)

	Current Residence	Sex	Age	Source Country	Year Arrival	Mother Tongue	Immigrant Classification
Stayed Total 0							

Table 10
Immigrant Adults Florenceville-Bristol (Left)

Current Residence	Sex	Age	Source Country	Year Arrival	Mother Tongue	Immigrant Classification
Ottawa	M	20s	India	2003	Hindi	Provincial Nominee
Saint George's Grenada	F	20s	Ghana	1997	English	Economic

Total in sample: 2

Table 11
Community Organization Members Florenceville-Bristol

Sex	Age	Organization	Source Country	Mother Tongue
F	50s	Multicultural Association Carleton County (macc)	Canada	English
F	20s	MACC	Canada	English
F	40s	MACC	Canada	English
F	50s	Carleton North High School	Canada	English
F	50s	Florenceville Middle School	Canada	English
M	50s	Florenceville Middle School	Canada	English

Total in sample: 6

Table 12
Local Residents Florenceville-Bristol

Sex	Age	Source Country	Mother Tongue
M	20s	Canada	English
M	30s	Canada	English
F	50s	Canada	English
F	30s	Canada	English
F	30s	Canada	English

Total in sample: 5

Table 13
Matrix of Findings

Theme	Fredericton	Florenceville-Bristol
Making Contact	Little contact between immigrant adolescents (and immigrants in general) and local residents. People "keep to themselves." Few public spaces where immigrants and established residents interact or immigrant adolescents cannot access the public space.	Daily contact inevitable in small town. People are "out and about." Immigrant adolescents have support of ethnic community, but also mix with their local peers in variety of extracurricular activities.
	Local adolescents ambivalent to presence of immigrant peers, they do not reach out to them or include them in groups and activities.	Local adolescents curious and excited about immigrant peers. They learn about them, engage with them, and include them in those groups and activities that best match their interests and talents.
	Local residents think it is responsibility of formal programs to include immigrant adolescents; or they are "new at this" and unsure of their responsibility.	Local residents (adults) generally watch out for and engage with all adolescents.
	Polite local residents do not want to intrude.	Local residents polite but also curious and friendly.
	Immigrant adolescents want people to listen to their stories. Language barrier hinders communication and relationship building.	Local adolescents want to learn about their immigrant peers. Adolescents and adults in the school find creative, innovative ways to overcome language barrier.
Public Awareness	Cultural stereotypes and racism prevalent in the schools.	"Immigrants take away our jobs." Sector of population misunderstands why immigrants are recruited.
	Local residents are "new at this," they lack experience dealing with immigrant adolescents. Schools lack experience accommodating immigrant students who speak little English, but are becoming more organized.	Local residents are "getting better at this" and claim to treat immigrants like any other resident. Schools have had to figure out how to accommodate EAL students.
Citizen Engagement	Citizens are engaged, but disconnected with immigrant adolescents.	Citizens engaged with immigrant adolescents, especially adults and adolescents in schools.

Table 13   (continued)

	Immigrant adolescents make effort to befriend local peers.	Local adolescents make effort to engage with immigrant peers, but become frustrated with language barrier. Immigrant adolescents make effort when they are more confident with language.
	Adult role models limited to teachers and mcaf staff (who are also immigrants).	Adult role models mostly limited to teachers, but also parents of local and immigrant adolescents and ethnic network.
	"Success in spite of us": immigrant adolescents finding their way on their own, with formal programs there to support them.	"Success with our help": immigrant adolescents finding their way with the support of engaged citizens.
Social Capital Social Networks	Immigrant adolescents make parents proud, worry about parents, and "parent" parents.	Immigrant adolescents make parents proud, worry about parents, especially mothers' experiencing depression.
	Ethnic networks only mentioned in relation to Korean adolescents. There are however, ethnic communities in the city.	Colombian adolescents rely on each other, but ethnic networks only mentioned with regard to parents.
	"Neighbourly neighbours" depends on which neighbourhood participant resides in. Neighbourhoods are divided by SES, and refugees tend to be of lower SES.	All citizens of community considered "neighbours." Discussion of neighbours revolved around the sharing of food.
	Extremely difficult for immigrant adolescents to make friends. Boys ultimately do befriend local peers, while girls have a more difficult time. Boys are more involved in activities than girls, especially sports.	Easy to make friends once adolescents are able to communicate. Network of local friends help immigrant adolescents at school. No obvious difference between boys and girls. Girls play soccer and basketball as much as boys.
Sense of Belonging	Bicultural or transcultural identity, confident, comfortable, fulfilled.	Bicultural or transcultural identity, confident, comfortable, fulfilled.
	Living in between two cultures and unsure of identity	Living in between two cultures and unsure of identity.
	Do not feel sense of belonging but optimistic that it will come with time.	
	So not feel sense of belonging and doubtful that it will come with time.	

Notes

CHAPTER ONE

1 Susan Smith, "Immigration and Nation-building in Canada and the United Kingdom," in *Construction of Race, Place, and Nation*, eds Peter Jackson and Jan Penrose (Minneapolis: University of Minnesota Press, 1993), 50.

2 Peter S. Li, *Destination Canada: Immigration Debates and Issues* (Oxford: Oxford University Press, 2003), 98.

3 Li, *Destination Canada*, 55.

4 Paul Anisef and Kenise M. Kilbride, *The Needs of Newcomer Youth and Emerging 'Best Practices' to Meet Those Needs* (Toronto: Joint Centre of Excellence for Research on Immigration and Settlement (CERIS), 2000, http://ceris.metropolis.net/frameset_e.html, accessed March 23, 2007); Paul Anisef et al., *Between Two Worlds: The Experiences and Concerns of Immigrant Youth in Ontario* (Toronto: Joint Centre of Excellence for Research on Immigration and Settlement (CERIS), 2001, http://www.ceris. metropolis.net/Virtual%20Library/other/kilbride2.html, accessed October 9, 2007); Paul Anisef et al., *Parenting Issues of Newcomer Families in Ontario* (Kitchener: Centre for Research and Education in Human Services and Centre of Excellence for Research on Immigration and Settlement, 2001); Morton Beiser et al., "Poverty and Mental Health Among Immigrant and Non-immigrant Children," *American Journal of Public Health* 92, no. 2 (2002); Morton Beiser et al., "The New Canadian Children and Youth Study: Research to Fill a Gap in Canada's Children's Agenda," *Canadian Issues/Themes Canadiens, Special Issue on Immigration and Intersections of Diversity* (May 2005); Joanna Ochochka, *Pathways to Success: Immigrant Youth in High School* (Kitchener: Centre for Research and Education in Human Services, 2006, http://www.

communitybasedresearch.ca/resources/Pathways%20to%20Success%20
Immigrant%20Youth%20at%20School%20Final%20Report.pdf ,
accessed November 4, 2010); Vappu Tyyskä, "Parents and Teens in Immigrant Families: Cultural Influences and Material Pressures," *Canadian
Diversité Canadienne* 6, no. 2 (2008).

5 Andrew J. Fuligni, "The Adjustment of Children from Immigrant Families," *Current Directions in Psychological Science* 7 (1998); Leslie Andres
et al., "The Persistence of Social Structure: Cohort, Class, and Gender
Effects on the Occupational Aspirations of Canadian Youth," *Journal
of Youth Studies* 2, no. 3 (1999); Paul Anisef et al., *Negotiating the Life
Course: Structure, Agency and the Class of '73* (Toronto: University of
Toronto Press, 2000); Monica Boyd, "Educational Attainments of Immi-
grant Offspring: Success or Segmented Assimilation?," *International
Migration Review* 36, no. 4 (2002); Ronit Dinovitzer, John Hagan, and
Patricia Parker, "Choice and Circumstance: Social Capital and Planful
Competence in the Attainments of Immigrant Youth," *Canadian Journal of
Sociology* 28 (2003); David E. Hayes-Bautista, *La Nueva California: Lat-
inos in the Golden State* (Berkeley: University of California Press, 2004);
Grace Kao and Marta Tienda, "Optimism and Achievement: The Educa-
tional Performance of Immigrant Youth," in *The New Immigration: An
Interdisciplinary Reader*, eds Marcelo M. Suárez-Orozco, Carola Suárez-
Orozco, and Desiree Qin-Hilliard (New York: Taylor & Francis Group,
2005); Harvey Krahn and Alison Taylor, "Resilient Teenagers: Explaining
the High Educational Aspirations of Visible Minority Immigrant Youth in
Canada," *Journal of International Migration and Integration* 6, nos 3–4
(2005); Cynthia García Coll, "Cuando se Convierte la Cultura en un Factor de Riesgo Contextual?," in *Factores de Riesgo en Psicopatología del
Desarrollo*, ed. E. L. Ezpeleta (Barcelona: Masson, 2005); Huong Nguyen,
"Acculturation in the United States" in *Cambridge Handbook of Accul-
turation Psychology*, eds David L. Sam and John W. Berry (Cambridge:
Cambridge University Press, 2006); John W. Berry et al., *Immigrant Youth
in Cultural Transition: Acculturation, Identity, and Adaptation Across
National Contexts* (Mahwah: Lawrence Erlbaum and Associates, Inc,
2006); Leslie Andres et al., "Educational Expectations, Parental Social
Class, Gender, and Post Secondary Attainment: A Ten Year Perspective,"
Youth and Society 39, no. 2 (2007); Andrew J. Fuligni and Krista Perreira,
"Immigration and Adaptation" in *Handbook of U.S. Latino Psychol-
ogy, Developmental and Community-based Perspectives*, eds Francisco A.
Villaruel et al. (Thousand Oaks: Sage Publications, 2009).

6   Mythili Rajiva, "Brown Girls, White Worlds: Adolescence and the Making of Racialized Selves," *The Canadian Review of Sociology and Anthropology* 43, no. 2 (2006): 166.

7   Mythili Rajiva, "Bridging the Generation Gap: Exploring the Differences Between Immigrant Parents and Their Canadian-born Children," *Canadian Issues* (Spring 2005).

8   Jacquelynne S, Eccles and Bonnie L. Barber, "Student Council, Volunteering, Basketball, or Marching Band: What Kind of Extracurricular Involvement Matters?," *Journal of Adolescent Research* 14 (1999); Peter C. Scales and Nancy Leffert, *Developmental Assets* (Minneapolis, Minnesota: Search Institute, 1999); James Youniss et al., "The Role of Community Service in Identity Development: Normative, Unconventional, and Deviant Orientations.," *Journal of Adolescent Research* 14 (1999); Peter C. Scales et al., "Contribution of Developmental Assets to the Prediction of Thriving Among Adolescents," *Applied Developmental Science* 4, no. 1 (2000); James Youniss, Jeffrey A. McLellan, and Barbara Mazer, "Voluntary Service, Peer Group Orientation, and Civic Engagement," *Journal of Adolescent Research* 16, no. 5 (2001); Michelle Crozier Kegler et al., "Relationships Among Youth Assets and Neighbourhood and Community Resources," *Health Education and Behavior* 32 (2005).

9   M.H. Grace Pretty et al., "Sense of Community and its Relevance to Adolescents of All Ages," *Journal of Community Psychology* 24, no. 4 (1996).

10   See Lloydetta Quaicoe, "Canadian Heritage in the Atlantic Region: Engagement with the Multicultural Community – From Research to Practice: Immigrant and Refugee Children's Need to Belong," *Our Diverse Cities* 5 (2008); Myriam Simard, "Immigrant Integration Outside Montreal," *Our Diverse Cities* 3 (2007); Yvonne Hébert et al., "Relational Citizenship as Social Networks: Immigrant Youth's Maps of Their Friendships," *Encounters on Education* 4 (Fall 2003).

11   Timothy J. Hatton and Andrew Leigh, *Immigrants Assimilate as Communities, Not Just as Individuals.* CEPR Discussion Papers 547 (London: Centre for Economic Policy Research, 2007).

12   Pilar A. Parra and Max J. Pfeffer, " New Immigrants in Rural Communities: The Challenges of Integration," *Social Text* 24, no. 3 88 (2006).

13   Jon H. Rieger and J. Allen Beegle, "The Integration of Rural Migrants in New Settings," *Rural Sociology* 29, no. 1 (1974); Gil-Soo Han and John S. Humphreys, "Overseas-trained Doctors in Australia: Community Integration and Their Intention to Stay in a Rural Community," *Australian Journal of Rural Health* 13, no. 4 (2005).

14 See for example Government of New Brunswick 2008.

15 Additional funding for immigrant settlement and adaptation in New Brunswick comes from a variety of sources, including other federal government departments (Human Resources and Skills Development Canada, Canadian Heritage, and Industry Canada), the provincial government, municipalities, and community charities and foundations.

16 Louis Swanson, "Rural Social Infrastructure," in *Foundations of Rural Development Policy*, eds J. Norman Reid et al. (Boulder: Westview Press, 1992).

17 Peter L. Benson, "Developmental Assets and Asset-building Community: Conceptual and Empirical Foundations," in *Developmental Assets and Asset-building Communities: Implications for Research, Policy, and Practice*, eds Richard M. Lerner and Peter L. Benson (New York: Kluwer Academic/ Plenum Publishers, 2003).

18 Cornelia Butler Flora and Jan L. Flora, "Entrepreneurial Social Infrastructures: A Necessary Ingredient," *The Annals of the American Academy of Political and Social Science* 529 (1993); Cornelia Butler Flora and Jan L. Flora with Susan Fey, *Rural Communities: Legacy and Change*, 2nd ed. (Boulder: Westview Press, 2004).

19 John W. Berry, "Immigration, Acculturation, and Adaptation," *Applied Psychology: An International Review* 46 (1997).

20 Berry et al., *Immigrant Youth in Cultural Transition*.

21 David Walters, Kelli Phythian, and Paul Anisef, "The Acculturation of Canadian Immigrants: Determinants of Ethnic Identification with the Host Society," *Canadian Review of Sociology* 44, no. 1 (2007).

22 John W. Berry et al., "Comparative Studies of Acculturative Stress," *International Migration Review* 21 (1987); Berry, "Immigration, Acculturation, and Adaptation,"; John W. Berry and David L. Sam, "Acculturation and Adaptation," in *Handbook of Cross-Cultural Psychology: Social Behaviour and Applications*, Vol. 3, eds John W. Berry, Marshall H. Segall, and Cigdem Kagitcibasi (Boston: Allyn & Bacon, 1997); Rhoda E. Howard, "Being Canadian: Citizenship in Canada," *Canadian Studies* 2 (1998).

23 See for example Elizabeth Ruddick, "Immigrant Economic Performance," *Canadian Issues* 5 (2003); Harvey Krahn, Tracey Derwing, and Baha Abu-Laban, "The Retention of Newcomers in Second- and Third-tier Cities in Canada," Edmonton: Prairie Centre of Excellence for Research on Immigration and Integration, University of Alberta. Working Paper series no. WP01-03 (2003); Victoria M. Esses et al., "Characteristics of a Welcoming Community," Canada. Citizenship and Immigration Canada (2010).

24   Ruddick, "Immigrant Economic Performance."

25   Margaret Conrad and Heather Steel, "They Come and They Go: Four Centuries of Immigration to New Brunswick," in *Rendez-vous Immigration 2004: Enjeux et Défis de l'Immigration au Nouveau-Brunswick /Immigration in New Brunswick Issues and Challenges*, eds Hélène Destrempes and Joe Ruggeri (Fredericton: Policy Studies Centre, University of New Brunswick, 2005), 48.

26   Ibid, 62.

27   Barry R. Chiswick, ed., *Immigration, Language, and Ethnicity: Canada and the United States*. (Washington: The AEI Press, 1992).

28   Citizenship and Immigration Canada 1956, cited in Heather Steel, "Where's the Policy? Immigration to New Brunswick, 1945–1971," *Acadiensis* 35, no. 2 (2006): 86.

29   Steel, "Where's the Policy?," 105.

30   The New Brunswick Provincial Nominee program includes streams both for individuals with job offers to work in New Brunswick, and for business applicants who wish to invest or manage businesses in the province.

31   Bruce Hutchison, *The Unknown Country: Canada and her People* (New York: Coward-McCann, Inc, 1942), 223.

32   Katherine Ashenburg, "A Loyalist Legacy in Fredericton," *New York Times* (New York), November 30 1997.

33   The IT professionals are initially given a temporary contract by McCain Foods Ltd, after which they are given permanent residency in New Brunswick through the Federal Skilled Worker or Provincial Nominee Program. Many of the temporary long-haul truck drivers also become permanent residents following probationary contracts.

34   Bruce L. Berg, *Qualitative Research Methods for the Social Sciences* (Boston: Allyn and Bacon, 2001).

35   This may have been the case for the adolescent children of two UNB instructors from Ghana and Nigeria who resided in Fredericton, but declined to participate in the study.

36   I also interviewed students from École Sainte Anne, though the interviews did not take place on school premises.

37   Adolescent and some adult participants have been given pseudonyms to protect their identities.

38   Leo R. Chavez, "The Power of the Imagined Community: The Settlement of Undocumented Mexicans and Central Americans in the United States," *American Anthropologist* 96, no. 1 (1994): 53.

39   David W. McMillan and David M. Chavis, "Sense of Community: A Definition and Theory," *Journal of Community Psychology* 14 (1986).

40 Seymour B. Sarason, *Work, Aging, and Social Change: Professionals and the One-Life One Career Imperative* (New York: Free Press, 1977); Susan Farrell, Tim Aubry, and Daniel Coulombe, "Neighborhoods and Neighbors: Do They Contribute to Well-being," *Journal of Community Psychology* 32, no. 1 (2004).

41 David M. Chavis and Abraham Wandersman, "Sense of Community in the Urban Environment: A Catalyst for Participation and Community Development," *American Journal of Community Psychology* 18 (1990); William B. Davidson, Patrick Cotter, and James Stovall, "Social Predispositions for the Development of Sense of Community," *Psychological Reports* 68 (1991); Miretta P. Prezza et al., "Sense of Community Referred to the Whole Town: Its Relations with Loneliness, Life Satisfaction and Area of Residence," *Journal of Community Psychology* 29, no.1 (2001); M. Loreto Martínez, Maureen Black, and Raymond H. Starr, "Factorial Structure of the Perceived Neighbourhood Scale (OPNS): A Test of Longitudinal Variance," *Journal of Community Psychology* 30, no. 1 (2002); Christopher C. Sonn, "Immigrant Adaptation. Understanding the Process Through Sense of Community," in *Psychological Sense of Community: Research, Applications and Implications*, eds Adrian T. Fisher, Christopher C. Sonn, and Brian J. Bishop (New York: Plenum Publishers, 2002).

42 Grace M. H. Pretty, Lisa Andrewes, and Chris Collett, "Exploring Adolescents' Sense of Community and its Relationship to Loneliness," *Journal of Community Psychology* 22 (1994).

43 Pretty, Andrewes, and Collett, "Exploring Adolescents'"; Ricardo Stanton-Salazar and Sanford M. Dornbusch, "Social Capital and the Reproduction of Inequality: Information networks among Mexican-origin High school Students," *Sociology of Education* 68 (1995); Pretty et al., "Sense of Community"; Ricardo Stanton-Salazar, "A Social Capital Framework for Understanding the Socialisation of Racial Minority Children and Youths," *Harvard Educational Review* 67 (1997); Daniel Solomon et al., "A Six-district Study of Educational Change: Direct and Mediated Effects on Child Development," *Social Psychology of Education* 4 (2000); Heather M. Chipuer, "Dyadic Attachments and Community Connectedness: Links with Youth's Loneliness Experiences," *Journal of Community Psychology* 29, no. 4 (2001); James W. Ainsworth, "Why Does it Take a Village? The Mediation of Neighbourhood Effects on Educational Achievement," *Social Forces* 81, no. 1 (2002); Lee Tennent et al., "Social Capital and Sense of Community: What Do They Mean for Young Children's Success at School?," in *Proceedings Australian Association for Research in Education*

(AARE) International Education Research Conference, (Sydney Australia, 2005, www.aare.edu.au/05pap/ten05115.pdf, accessed July 18, 2009).

44 Carol Goodenow and Kathleen E. Grady, "The Relationship of School Belonging and Friends' Values to Academic Motivation Among Urban Adolescent Students," *The Journal of Experimental Education* 62 (1993); Karen F. Osterman, "Students' Need for Belonging in the School Community," *Review of Educational Research* 70, no. 3 (2000); Xin Ma, "Sense of Belonging to School: Can Schools Make a Difference?," *The Journal of Educational Research* 96, no. 6 (2003); Jon Douglas Willms, *Monitoring School Performance: A Guide for Educators* (London: Falmer Press, 1992); David Kember, Kenneth Lee, and Natalia Li, "Cultivating a Sense of Belonging in Part-time Students. International Journal of Lifelong Education" 20, no. 4 (2006).

45 Osterman, "Students' Need for Belonging"; Willms *Monitoring School Performance*.

46 Urie Bronfenbrenner, *The Ecology of Human Development: Experiments by Nature and Design* (Cambridge: Harvard University Press, 1979); Christopher Jencks and Susan E. Mayer, "The Social Consequences of Growing Up in a Poor Neighbourhood," in *Inner-City Poverty in the United States*, eds Laurence E. Lynn and Michael G. H. McGeary (Washington: National Academy Press, 1990); Catherine L. Garner and Stephen W. Raudenbush, "Neighbourhood Effects on Educational Attainment: A Multilevel Analysis," *Sociology of Education* 64, no. 4 (1991); James Gabarino, *Children and Families in the Social Environment*, 2nd ed. (New York: Walter de Gruyter., Inc, 1992); Jeanne Brooks-Gunn et al., "Do Neighborhoods Influence Child and Adolescent Development?," *American Journal of Sociology* 99, no. 2 (1993); Dale A. Blyth and Nancy Leffert, "Communities as Contexts for Adolescent Development," *Journal of Adolescent Research* 10 (1995); Carol S. Aneshensel and Clea Sucoff, "The Neighborhood Context of Adolescent Mental Health," *Journal of Health and Social Behavior* 37, no. 4 (1996); Karen Bogenschneider, "An Ecological Risk/Protective Theory for Building Prevention Programs, Policies, and Community Capacity to Support Youth," *Family Relations* 45, no. 2 (1996); J. Lawrence Aber et al., "Development in Context: Implications for Studying Neighborhood Effects," in *Neighborhood Poverty: Context and Consequences for Children*, eds Jeanne Brooks-Gunn, Greg J. Duncan, and J. Lawrence Aber, (New York: Russell Sage Foundation, 1997); Peter L. Benson, *All Kids Are Our Kids: What Communities Must Do To Raise Caring and Responsible Children and Adolescents* (San Francisco: Jossey

Bass, 1997); Tama Leventhal and Jeanne Brooks-Gunn, "The Neighbor-hoods They Live: The Effects of Neighbourhood Residence on Child and Adolescent Outcomes," *Psychological Bulletin* 126, no. 2 (2000); Eric P. Baumer and Scott J. South, "Community Effects on Youth Sexual Activ-ity," *Journal of Marriage and Family* 63 (2001); Robert J. Sampson, "How Do Communities Undergird or Undermine Human Development? Rel-evant Contexts and Social Mechanisms," in *Does It Take a Village? Com-munity Effects on Children, Adolescents, and Families*, eds Alan Booth and Nan Crouter (Mahwah: Lawrence Erlbaum Associates, Publishers, 2001); Susan Averett, Daniel I. Rees, and Laura M. Argys, "The Impact of Government Policies and Neighbourhood Characteristics on Teen-age Sexual Activity and Contraceptive Use," *American Journal of Public Health* 92, no. 11 (2002); Bruce H. Rankin and James M. Quane, "Social Contexts and Urban Adolescent Outcomes: The Interrelated Effects of Neighborhoods, Families, and Peers on African-American Youth," *Social Problems* 49, no. 1 (2002); Robert J. Sampson, Jeffrey D. Morenoff, and Thomas Gannon-Rowley, "Assessing Neighborhood Effects: Social Pro-cesses and New Directions in Research," *Annual Review of Sociology* 28 (2002); Peter C. Scales, Nancy Lefert, and Renee Vraa, "The Relation of Community Developmental Attentiveness to Adolescent Health," *Amer-ican Journal of Health Behavior* 27, Suppl. 1 (2003); Robert J. Chaskin, "Building Community Capacity for Children, Youth, and Families," *Chil-dren Australia* 34, no. 1 (2009): 4

47 John P. Kretzmann and John L. McKnight, *Building Communities from the Inside Out* (Evanston: Center for Urban Affairs and Policy Research, Northwestern University, 1993); Ross J.Gittel and Avis Vidal *Commun-ity Organizing: Building Social Capital as a Development Strategy* (Thou-sand Oaks: Sage, 1998); Robert J. Chaskin et al., *Building Community Capacity* (Hathorne, NY: Aldine de Gruyter); Mark E. Warren, *Democracy and Association* (Princeton: Princeton University Press, 2001); Michelle Crozier Kegler et al., "Relationships Among Youth Assets," *Health Educa-tion and Behavior* 32 (2005), as cited in Chaskin, 2009.

48 Greg J. Duncan and Stephen W. Raudenbush, "Neighborhoods and Ado-lescent Development: How Can We Determine the Links?," in *Does it Take a Village? Community Effects on Children, Adolescents, and Fam-ilies*, eds Alan Booth and Nan Crouter (State College: Pennsylvania State University Press, 2001).

49 Bronfenbrenner, *The Ecology of Human Development*, 3.

50 Seyda Aksel et al., "Migration and Psychological Status of Adolescents in Turkey," *Adolescence* 42, no. 167 (2007): 589.

51 Jodie L.Roth and Jeanne Brooks-Gunn, "Youth Development Programs: Risk, Prevention and Policy. *Journal of Adolescent Health* 32 (2003): 172.

52 Jane Kroger, *Identity Development: Adolescence Through Adulthood*, 2nd edition (Newbury Park: Sage Publications, 2007).

53 Alejandro Portes, "An Enduring Vision: The Melting Pot That Did Happen," *International Migration Review* 34 (2000).

54 Jodie L. Roth and Jeanne Brooks-Gunn, "Youth Development Programs and Healthy Development: A Review and Next Steps," in *Reducing Adolescent Risk: Toward an Integrated Approach*, ed. Daniel Romer, Thousand Oaks: Sage Publications (2003).

55 Kathryn Harker, "Immigrant Generation, Assimilation, and Adolescent Psychological Well-being: The Importance of Mediating Factors," *Social Forces* 79, no. 3 (2001); Nora E. Thompson, and Andrea G. Gurney, "'He is Everything': Religion's Role in the Lives of Immigrant Youth," *New Directions for Youth Development* 100 (2003).

56 Department of Canadian Heritage; Status of Women Canada; Services Canada; Canadian Women's Foundation; Post Secondary Education and Training, and Labour New Brunswick; New Brunswick Population Growth Secretariat; New Brunswick Multicultural Council; Fredericton Community Foundation; Muriel McQueen Fergusson Foundation; City of Fredericton; UPS.

57 Some of the temporary migrants working as truck drivers in the Florenceville-Bristol area did bring their families with them. The ages of their children, however, do not fit the range of 12–20 years old so they were not included in the case study.

58 MACC is funded by Citizenship and Immigration Canada and the New Brunswick Population Growth Secretariat.

59 Roth and Brooks-Gunn, "Youth Development Programs: Risk," 171.

60 Richard M. Lerner and Peter L. Benson.. *Developmental Assets and Asset-Building Communities* (New York: Kluwer Academic/Plenum Publishers, 2003), 37.

61 Lyn Richards, *Handling Qualitative Data: a Practical Guide* (London: Sage, 2005).

62 Patricia Ann Bazeley, *Qualitative Data Analysis with NVivo* (Thousand Oaks: Sage, 2007), 70.

CHAPTER TWO

1 Li, *Destination Canada*; Peter S. Li, Deconstructing *Canada's Discourse of Immigrant Integration.* (Metropolis Prairie Centre of Excellence Working

Paper No. WP04-03, 2003) http://pcerii.metropolis.net/WorkingPapers/
WP04-03.pdf (accessed November 5, 2010); Jeffrey G. Reitz, *Warmth of
the Welcome: The Social Causes of Economic Success in Different Nations*
(Boulder: Westview Press, 1998); Jeffrey G. Reitz, ed., *Host Societies and
the Reception of Immigrants* (San Diego: Center for Comparative Immigration Research, 2003); Jeffrey G. Reitz, "Tapping Immigrants' Skills:
New Directions for Canadian Immigration Policy in the Knowledge Economy," *IRPP Choices* 11, no. 1 (2005).

2   Wsevolod Isajiw, *Understanding Diversity: Ethnicity and Race in the Canadian Context* (Toronto: Thompson Educational Publishing, 1999), 25.

3   Donn Byrne, *The Attraction Paradigm* (New York: Academic Press, 1971);
James S. Coleman, "Social Capital in the Creation of Human Capital,"
American Journal of Sociology 94, Supplement: S95-S-120 (1988); Amitai
Etzioni, "The Responsive Community: A Communitarian Perspective,"
American, Sociological Review 61(1996); Eric M. Uslaner, *The Moral
Foundations of Trust* (Cambridge: Cambridge University Press, 2002).

4   Jeffrey G. Reitz and Rupa Banerjee, "Racial Inequality, Social Cohesion,
and Policy Issues in Canada," in *Belonging? Diversity, Recognition and
Shared Citizenship in Canada*, eds Keith Banting, Thomas J. Courchene,
and F. Leslie (Montreal: Institute for Research on Public Policy, 2007);
Robert D. Putnam, "E Pluribus Unum: Diversity and Community in the
Twenty-first Century the 2006 Johan Skytte Prize Lecture," *Scandinavian
Political Studies* 30, no. 2 (2007).

5   Alberto Alesina and Eliana La Ferrara, "Who Trusts Others?," *Journal of
Public Economics* 85 (2002); Putnam, "E Pluribus Unum."

6   Serge Guimond, Douglas L. Palmer, and Guy Bégin, "Education, Academic
Program and Intergroup Attitudes," *Review of Sociology and Anthropology* 26, no. 2 (1989); Douglas L. Palmer, "Prejudice and Intolerance in
Canada," in *New Faces in the Crowd: Economic and Social Impacts of
Immigration*, ed. Economic Council of Canada (Ottawa: Economic Council of Canada, 1991); Augie Fleras and Jean Leonard Elliot, *The Challenge of Diversity, Multiculturalism in Canada* (Toronto: Nelson Canada,
1992); Rudy Kalin and John W. Berry, "Ethnic and Multicultural Attitudes," in *Ethnicity and Culture in Canada: The Research Landscape*, eds
John W. Berry and Jean Laponce (Toronto: University of Toronto Press,
1994); Geoffrey Eley and Ronald Grigor-Suny, eds, *Becoming National*
(New York: Oxford University Press, 1996); Thomas F. Pettigrew, "Generalized Inter-group Contact Effects on Prejudice," *Personality and Social
Psychology Bulletin* 23, no. 2 (1997); Isajiw, *Understanding Diversity*;
Will Kymlicka, *Finding our Way: Rethinking Ethnocultural Relations in*

Canada (Don Mills: Oxford University Press, 1998); Will Kymlicka, "Well Done, Canada: Multiculturalism is Working," *Globe and Mail* (2007, December 1); Abdolmohammad Kazemipur, "A Canadian Exceptionalism? Trust and Diversity in Canadian Cities," *Journal of International Migration and Integration* 7, no. 2 (2006).

7   Gordon W. Allport, *The Nature of Prejudice* (Reading, MA: Addison-Wesley Publishing Company, 1954, 1979); Stuart W. Cook, "Experimenting on Social Issues: The Case of School Desegregation," *American Psychologist* 40 (1985); Thomas F. Pettigrew, "The Inter-group Contact Hypothesis Revisited," in *Contact and Conflict in Inter-Group Encounters*, eds Miles Hewstone, and Rupert J. Brown (Oxford: Blackwell, 1986); Walter G. Stephan and John C. Brigham, "Intergroup Contact: Introduction," *Journal of Social Issues* 41, no. 3 (1985).

8   Michele Andrisin Witting and Sheila Grant-Thompson, "The Utility of Allport's Conditions of Inter-group Contact for Predicting Perceptions of Improved Racial Attitudes and Beliefs – Contact Hypothesis," *Journal of Social Issues*, Winter (1998) http://findarticles.com/p/articles/mi_m0341/is_4_54/ai_54422539/pg_14/ (accessed February 8, 2011).

9   Godfrey Baldacchino, *Coming to, and Settling on, Prince Edward Island: Stories and Voices: A Report on Recent Immigrants to PEI, Canada* (Charlottetown: University of Prince Edward Island with the support of the Prince Edward Island Population Secretariat, 2006).

10 Carey M. Noland, "Auto-photography as Research Practice: Identity and Self-esteem Research," *Journal of Research Practice* 2, no. 1 (2006).

11 Researchers use socioeconomic status (SES) to refer to the relative position of a family or individual on a hierarchical social structure, based on their access to or control over, wealth, prestige, and power. Operationally the SES of pupils is ascribed to a wide range of background measures describing the occupational prestige, educational levels, and economic positions of pupils' parents (Willms 1992, 50).

12 See Kalman J. Kaplan, "On the Ambivalence-indifference Problem in Attitude Theory and Measurement: A Suggested Modification of the Semantic Differential Technique," *Psychological Bulletin* 77, no. 5 (1972); Irwin Katz and R. Glen Hass, "Racial Ambivalence and American Value Conflict: Correlational and Priming Studies of Dual Cognitive Structures," *Journal of Personality and Social Psychology* 55 (1988); Alice H. Eagly and Shelly Chaiken, *The Psychology of Attitudes* (Fort Worth: Harcourt Brace Jovanovich College Publishers, 1993); James M. Olson and Mark P. Zanna, "Attitudes and Attitude Change," *Annual Review of Psychology* 44 (1993); Megan M. Thompson, Mark P. Zanna, and Dale W. Griffin,

"The Conflicted Individual – Personality-based and Domain-specific Antecedents of Ambivalent Social Attitudes," *Journal of Personality* 63 (1995).

13 Laurie Olsen, "Learning English and Learning America: Immigrants in
the Center of a Storm," *Theory into Practice* 39, no. 4 (2000); Mustafa
Koc and Fernando Nunes, *Newcomer Youth at Risk in the School System*
(Toronto: Joint Centre for Excellence for Research on Immigration and
Settlement (CERIS) and Citizenship and Immigration Canada, 2001); Jenny
Hsin-Chun Tsai, "Xenophobia, Ethnic Community and Immigrant Youths'
Friendship Network Formation," *Adolescence* 4, no. 162 (2006); Quaicoe,
"Canadian Heritage."

14 Jim Cummins, "Cognitive/Academic Language Proficiency, Linguistic
Interdependence, the Optimum Age Question and Some Other Matters,"
Working Papers on Bilingualism No. 19 (1979); Jim Cummins, "Age on
Arrival and Immigrant Second Language Learning in Canada. A Reassess-
ment," *Applied Linguistics* 2 (1981); Jim Cummins, "Language and Lit-
eracy Acquisition in Bilingual Contexts," *Journal of Multilingual and
Multicultural Education* 10 (1989); Wayne P. Thomas and Virginia P.
Collier, *School Effectiveness for Language Minority Students* (National
Clearinghouse for English Language Acquisition (NCELA) Resource Col-
lection Series, No. 9, December 1997); Kenji Hakuta, Yuko Goto Butler,
and Daria Witt, *How Long Does It Take English Learners to Attain Proficiency?* (University of California Linguistic Minority Research Institute
Policy Report 2000–1, 2000).

15 Min Zhou, "Growing Up American: The Challenge Confronting Immigrant Children and Children of Immigrants," *Annual Review of Sociology*
23 (1997); Marcelo M. Suárez-Orozco, Carola Suárez-Orozco, and Irina
Todorova, "Moving Stories: Immigrant Youth Adapt to Change," *Du Bois
Review* 4 (2007), 256.

16 Ana F. Muñoz-Sandoval et al., *Bilingual Verbal Ability Tests* (Itasca, IL:
Riverside Publishing, 1998); Carola Suárez-Orozco et al., "Academic Trajectories of Newcomer Immigrant Youth," *Developmental Psychology* 46,
no. 3 (2010).

17 Helen M. Marks, "Student Engagement in Instructional Activity: Patterns in the Elementary, Middle, and High School Years," *American Educational Research Journal* 37, no. 1 (2000); Jennifer A. Fredericks, Phyllis
C. Blumenfeld, and Alison H. Paris, "School Engagement: Potential of
the Concept, State of the Evidence," *Review of Educational Research* 74
(2004); National Research Council, *Engaging Schools: Fostering High
School Students' Motivation to Learn* (Washington: National Academies

Press, 2004), as cited in Carola Suárez-Orozco et al., "Academic Trajectories."

18 Arlene G. Muchnick and David E. Wolfe, "Attitudes and Motivations of American Students of Spanish," *The Canadian Modern Language Review* 88 (1982); Elaine K. Horwitz, Michael B. Horwitz, and Joann A. Cope, "Foreign Language Classroom Anxiety," *Modern Language Journal* 70 (1986); Peter D. MacIntyre and Robert C. Gardner, "Methods and Results in the Study of Anxiety and Language Learning: A Review of the Literature," *Language Learning* 41, no. 1 (1991).

19 Richard Clément and Robert C. Gardner, "Second Language Mastery," in *The New Handbook of Language and Social Psychology*, eds W. Peter Robinson and Howard Giles (London: Wiley, 2001), 504.

20 Laura Weiss Roberts, John Battaglia, and Richard S. Epstein, "Frontier Ethics: Mental Healthcare Needs and Ethical Dilemmas in Rural Communities," *Psychiatric Services* 50 (1999).

21 William Nelson, "Addressing Rural Ethics Issues," *Healthcare Exec*: 1936–1937 (2004).

22 Robert J. Sampson, Jeffrey D. Morenoff, and Felton Earls, "Beyond Social Capital: Spatial Dynamics of Collective Efficiency for Children," *American Sociological Review* 64, no. 5 (1999): 635.

23 James S. Coleman, "Some Points on Choice in Education," *Sociology of Education* 65, no. 4 (1992).

24 Mateo bridges the two case studies since his family also emigrated to Florenceville-Bristol from Medellín Colombia. He left for UNB shortly after arriving in Florenceville-Bristol.

CHAPTER THREE

1 Baukje Miedema and Nancy Nason-Clark, "Second-class Status: An Analysis of the Lived Experiences of Immigrant Women in Fredericton," *Canadian Ethnic Studies* 21, no. 2 (1989); Julia Noel, "Voices in Health-care: Afro-Caribbean Women's Experiences" (Master's Thesis, Dalhousie University, 1996); Elaine C. Kenyon, "Immigrant Women: Journeying Towards Harmony" (Master's Thesis, University of New Brunswick, 2000); Rosemary Clews. "Diversity, Immigration and Rural Communities: New Brunswick – A Case Study" (Paper Presented at the Fifth International Metropolis Conference November 13–17, 2000, Vancouver. 2000); Rosemary Clews, "Changing the Same Old Story: Mounting a Challenge to Metanarratives About Racism by Exploring Stories in Rural

Communities" (Paper Presented at the International Rural Human Services Conference, Halifax, 2003); Cynthia Baker, Manju Varma-Joshi, and Connie Tanaka, "Sticks and Stones. Racism as Experienced by Adolescents in New Brunswick," *Canadian Journal of Nursing Research* 33, no. 3 (2001, republished 2009); Neyda H. Long and Andrew Hughes, "The Political Integration of Newcomers of Latin American Origin to Canada: An Examination of the Role and Relevance of Prior Knowledge," *Encounters on Education* 4 (2003); Hélène Destrempes and Joe Ruggeri, eds, *Rendez-vous immigration 2004: Enjeux et défis de l'immigration au Nouveau-Brunswick /Immigration in New Brunswick Issues and Challenges* (Fredericton: Policy Studies Centre, University of New Brunswick, 2005); Neyda H. Long, "Conceptions of Political Participation Among Recent Latin-American Newcomers to Canada," in *Ruptures, Continuities, and Re-Learning: The Political Participation of Latin Americans in Canada*, eds Jorge Ginieniewicz and Daniel Schugurensky (Toronto: Transformative Learning Centre, OISE, 2006); Deborah Murray, "Spinning Their Own Webs: An Exploration of English Second Language Learning for Newcomers in New Brunswick" (Master's Thesis, University of New Brunswick, 2006); Neyda H. Long and Benjamin Amaya, "'We' and 'the Others:' Cultural Identity Among Latin Americans in Rural New Brunswick," *Our Diverse Cities* 3 (2007).

2   Jan Pieter van Oudenhoven, Colleen Ward, and Anne-Marie Masgoret, "Patterns of Relations Between Immigrants and Host Societies," *International Journal of Intercultural Relations* 30, no. 6 (2006).

3   Henri Tajfel, ed., *Differentiation Between Social Groups: Studies in the Social Psychology of Intergroup Relations* (London: Academic Press, 1978); Henri Tajfel and John C. Turner, "An Integrative Theory of Intergroup Conflict," in *Psychology of Intergroup Relations*, eds Stephan Worchel and W.G. Austin (Chicago: Nelson-Hall, 1986).

4   Walter G. Stephan and Cookie White Stephan, "An Integrated Threat Theory of Prejudice," in *Claremont Symposium on Applied Social Psychology*, ed. Stuart Oskamp (Hillsdale: Erlbaum, 2000).

5   Walter G. Stephan et al., "Prejudice Toward Immigrants: An Integrated Threat Theory," *Journal of Applied Social Psychology* 29 (1998).

6   Marlene Mulder and Harvey Krahn, "Individual and Community-level Determinants of Support for Immigration and Cultural Diversity in Canada," *The Canadian Review of Sociology and Anthropology* 42, no. 4 (2005): 3.

7   van Oudenhoven, Ward, and Masgoret, "Patterns of Relations"; Gregory R. Maio, David W. Bell, and Victoria M. Esses, "Ambivalence and

Persuasion: The Processing of Messages About Immigrant Groups," *Journal of Experimental Social Psychology* 32 (1996).

8   Kymlicka, *Finding Our Way.*

9   Saskia Sassen, "America's Immigration Problem," *World Policy*, 6 (Fall 1989): 811.

10 Brian K. Obach, "Demonstrating the Social Construction of Race." *Teaching Sociology* 27, no. 3 (1999).

11 Paul Gilroy, *There Ain't no Black in the Union Jack* (London: Routledge, 1987); Martin Barker, *The New Racism* (London: Junction Books, 1981).

12 Eva Mackey, *The House of Difference: Cultural Politics and National Identity in Canada* (Toronto: University of Toronto Press, 2002), 8.

13 Li, *Destination Canada*, 44–5.

14 Margaret Conrad, "They Come and They Go: New Brunswick's Immigration Policy," *Telegraph Journal*, 21 March 2006; see also Barrington Walker, *The History of Immigration and Racism to Canada: Essential Readings* (Toronto: Canadian Scholars' Press, Inc, 2008); Howard Palmer, "Reluctant Hosts: Anglo-Canadian Views of Multiculturalism in the Twentieth Century," in *Immigration in Canada: Historical Perspectives*, ed. Gerald Tulchinsky (Toronto: Copp Clark Longran, Ltd, 1994); Subhas Ramcharan, *Racism: Non-Whites in Canada* (Toronto: Butterworths, 1982).

15 Siobhan Moran et al., "Ethnic Differences in Experiences of Bullying: Asian and White Children," *British Journal of Educational Psychology* 63 (1993); Courtland C. Lee, "Culturally Responsive School Counselors and Programs: Addressing the Needs of All Students," *Professional School Counseling* 4 (2001); Maykel Verkuyten and Jochem Thijs, "Multiculturalism Among Minority and Majority Adolescents in the Netherlands," *International Journal of Intercultural Relations* 26 (2002); Tan Phan, "Life in School: Narratives of Resiliency Among Vietnamese-Canadian Youths," *Adolescence* 38 (2003); Debra J. Pepler, Wendy Craig, and Jennifer A. Connolly, *School Experiences of Immigrant and Ethnic Minority Youth: Risk and Protective Factors in Coping with Bullying and Harassment* (CERIS Research Report. Toronto: Joint Centre for Excellence for Research on Immigration and Settlement (CERIS), 1999); Frances E. Aboud, and Anna Joong, "Intergroup Name-calling and Conditions for Creating Assertive Bystanders," in *Intergroup Attitudes and Relations in Childhood through Adulthood*, eds Sheri R. Levy and Melanie Killen (Oxford: Oxford University Press, 2007).

16 Frank J. Lechner, "Fundamentalism and Sociocultural Revitalization," *Sociological Analysis* 46 (1985).

17 See for example Jake Harwood, "Alienation: American Attitudes Towards Immigrants," *Public Opinion* 6 (1983); Rita J. Simon and Susan H. Alexander, *The Ambivalent Welcome: Print Media, Public Opinion, and Immigration* (Westport: Praeger, 1993); John S. Lapinski et al., "The Polls Trends: Immigrants and Immigration," *Public Opinion Quarterly* 61 (1997); James C. Gimpel and James R. Edwards, Jr., *The Congressional Politics of Immigration Reform* (Boston: Allyn & Bacon, 1999).

18 Peter Burns and James G. Gimpel, "Economic Insecurity, Prejudicial Stereotypes, and Public Opinion on Immigration Policy," *Political Science Quarterly* 115 (Summer, 2000).

19 Guimond, Palmer, and Bégin, "Education."

20 Burns and Gimpel, "Economic Insecurity."

21 Alex Himelfarb, "The Social Characteristics of One-industry Towns in Canada," in *Little Communities and Big Industries*, ed. Roy T. Bowles (Toronto: Butterworth, 1982), 33.

CHAPTER FOUR

1 Jeremy Boissevain, *Friends of Friends: Networks, Manipulators and Coalitions* (Oxford: Basil Blackwell, 1974), 31–33.

2 James Farr, "Social Capital a Conceptual History," *Political Theory* 32, no. 1 (2004): 9.

3 Alejandro Portes, "Social Capital: Its Origins and Applications in Modern Sociology," *Annual Review of Sociology* 24 (1998): 3.

4 See Stephan Baron, John Field, and Tom Schuller, eds, *Social Capital: Critical Perspectives* (Oxford: Oxford University Press, 2000); Nan Lin, *Social Capital, a Theory of Social Structure and Action* (New York: Cambridge University Press, 2001); Ricardo Stanton-Salazar, "Social Capital Among Working-class Minority Students," in *School Connections: U.S. Mexican Youth, Peers, and School Achievement*, eds Margaret A. Gibson, Patricia Gándara, and Jill Peterson Koyama (New York: Teachers College Press, Columbia University, 2004); Robert K. Ream and Gregory Palardy, "Re-examining Social Class Differences in the Availability and the Educational Utility of Parental Social Capital," *American Educational Research Journal* 45, no. 2 (2008).

5 Pierre Bourdieu, *The Forms of Capital*, in *Handbook of Theory and Research for Sociology of Education*, ed. John Richardson (New York: Greenwood Press, 1986), 248.

6 Coleman, "Social Capital," s98.

7 Portes, "Social Capital," 7.

8 Frank F. Furstenberg and Mary Elizabeth Hughes, "Social Capital and Successful Development Among At-risk Youth," *Journal of Marriage and the Family* 57 (1995): 581.

9 Coleman, "Social Capital," s101, as cited in Furstenberg and Hughes, "Social Capital," 581.

10 Robert D. Putnam, *Bowling Alone the Collapse and Revival of American Community* (New York: Simon & Schuster, 2000); Robert G. Croniger and Valirie E. Lee, "Social Capital and Dropping Out of High School: Benefits to At-risk Students of Teachers: Support and Guidance," *Teachers College Record* 103, no. 4 (2001); Anthony S. Bryk and Barbara L. Schneider, *Trust in Schools: A Core Resource for Improvement* (New York: Russell Sage Foundation, 2002); Lucia Tramonte and Jon Douglas Willms. "Cultural Capital and its Effects on Education Outcomes." *Economics of Education Review* 29, no. 2 (2010).

11 Hébert et al., "Relational Citizenship."

12 Carl L. Bankston III and Min Zhou, "Social Capital and Immigrant Children's Achievement," in *Schooling and Social Capital in Diverse Cultures Volume 13*, eds Bruce Fuller and Emily Hannum, (Amsterdam: JAI, 2002).

13 Grace Kao, "Social Capital and its Relevance to Minority and Immigrant Populations," *Sociology of Education* 77 (2004): 174.

14 Nathan Caplan, Marcella H. Choy, and John K. Whitmore, *Children of the Boat People: A Study of Educational Success* (Ann Arbor: University of Michigan Press, 1991); Min Zhou and Carl L. Bankston III, *Growing up American: How Vietnamese Children Adapt to Life in the United States* (New York: Russell Sage Foundation, 1998), as cited in Kao, "Social Capital," 174; see also Ronit Dinovitzer, John Hagan, and Patricia Parker, "Choice and Circumstance: Social Capital and Planful Competence in the Attainments of Immigrant Youth," *Canadian Journal of Sociology* 28 (2003); Carl L. III. Bankston, "Social Capital, Cultural Values, Immigration, and Academic Achievement: The Host Country Context and Contradictory Consequences," *Sociology of Education* 77, no. 2 (2004); H.P.H. Chow, "The Effects of Ethnic Capital and Family Background on School Performance: A Case Study of Chinese-Canadian Adolescents in Calgary," *The Alberta Journal of Education* 50, no. 3 (2004).

15 Igor Ryabov, "The Role of Peer Social Capital in Educational Assimilation of Immigrant Youths," *Sociological Inquiry* 79, no. 4 (2009): 454–5.

16 Grace Kao, "Social Capital," 173.

17 Margaret Gibson, *Accommodation Without Assimilation: Punjabi Sikh Immigrants in an American High School* (Ithaca: Cornell University Press, 1988); Portes, "Social Capital"; Angela Valenzuela and Sanford

M. Dornbush. "Familism and Social Capital in the Academic Achievement of Mexican Origin and Anglo Adolescents," *Social Science Quarterly* 75 (1994); Stanton-Salazar and Dornbusch, "Social Capital"; Steven J. Gold, *From the Worker's State to the Golden State: Jews from the Former Soviet Union in California* (Boston: Allyn & Bacon, 1995); John Hagan, Ross MacMillan, and Blair Wheaton, "The Life Course Effects of Family Migration on Children," *American Sociological Review* 61, no. 3 (1996).

18   Nazli Kibria, "Household Structure and Family Ideology: The Dynamics of Immigrant Economic Adaptation Among Vietnamese Refugees," *Social Problems* 41, no. 1 (1994).

19   Morton Beiser, Angela Shik, and Monica Curyk, *New Canadian Children and Youth Study: Literature Review* (Toronto: Joint Centre of Excellence for Research on Immigration and Settlement (CERIS), 1999).

20   Abdolmohammad Kazemipur and Shiva S. Halli, "Immigrants and New Poverty: The Case of Canada," *International Migration Review* 35, no. 4 (2001); Abdolmohammad Kazemipur and Shiva S. Halli, "The Changing Colour of Poverty in Canada," *Canadian Review of Sociology and Anthropology* 38, no. 2 (2001).

21   Alejandro Portes, "Immigration Theory for a New Century: Some Problems and Opportunities," *International Migration Review* 31, no. 4, Special Issue: Immigrant Adaptation and Native-Born Responses in the Making of Americans (1997): 814.

22   Fernando Nunes, *Problems and Adjustments of the Portuguese Immigrant Family in Canada* (Porto, Portugal: Secretaria de Estado das Comunidades Portuguesas, 1986); Jeffrey McQuillan and Lucy Tse, "Child Language Brokering in Linguistic Minority Communities: Effects on Cultural Interaction, Cognition, and Literacy," *Language and Education* 9 (1995); Jorge Partida, "The Effects of Immigration on Children in the Mexican-American Community," *Child and Adolescent Social Work Journal* 13, no. 3 (1996); Lucy Tse, "Language Brokering in Linguistic Minority Communities: The Case of Chinese- and Vietnamese-American Students," *The Bilingual Research Journal* 20 (1996); Raymond Buriel et al., "The Relationship of Language Brokering to Academic Performance, Biculturalism, and Self-efficacy Among Latino Adolescents," *Hispanic Journal of Behavioral Sciences* 20 (1998); Maria Elena Puig, "The Adultification of Refugee Children: Implications for Cross-cultural Social Work Practice," *Journal of Human Behavior in the Social Environment* 5 (2002); Robert S. Weisskirch and Sylvia Alatorre Alva, "Language Brokering and the Acculturation of Latino Children," *Hispanic Journal of Behavioral Sciences* 24 (2002); Curtis J. Jones and Edison J. Trickett, "Immigrant Adolescents

Behaving as Cultural Brokers: A Study of Families from the Former Soviet Union," *The Journal of Social Psychology* 145, no. 4 (2005).

23 James S. Coleman, *Foundations of Social Theory* (Cambridge: Harvard University Press, 1990, 1994), 318.

24 Bankston III, "Social Capital," 177.

25 Min Zhou and Carl L. Bankston III, "Social Capital and the Adaptation of the Second Generation: The Case of Vietnamese Youth in New Orleans," *International Migration Review* 28 (1994);

26 Dafna Kohen, Clyde Hertzman, and Jeanne Brooks-Gunn, *Neighbourhood Influences on Children's School Readiness* (Ottawa: Strategic Policy. Applied Research Branch. Human Resources Development Canada. Working Paper. 1998).

27 See also Michael H. Boyle and Ellen Lipman, *Do Places Matter? A Multilevel Analysis of Geographic Variations in Child Behaviour in Canada* (W-98-16E. Applied Research Branch, Strategic Policy, Human Resources Development Canada, 1998); Kohen, Hertzman, and Brooks-Gunn, *Neighbourhood Influences*; Thomas P. Vartanian and Philip M.Gleason. "Do Neighborhood Conditions Affect High School Dropout and College Graduation Rates?" *Journal of Socio-Economics* 28, no. 1 (1999); Franklin T. Thompson, "Student Achievement, Selected Environmental Characteristics, and Neighborhood Type," *Urban Review*, 34, no. 3 (2002); Ruth N. López Turley, "When Do Neighbourhoods Matter? The Role of Race and Neighbourhood Peers," *Social Science Research* 32 (2003).

28 Jonathan Crane, "The Epidemic Theory of Ghettos and Neighborhood Effects on Dropping Out and Teenage Childbearing," *American Journal of Sociology* 96 (1991); Brooks-Gunn et al., "Do Neighborhoods Influence"; Abdolmohammad Kazemipur and Shiva S. Halli, "The Colour of Poverty: A Study of the Poverty of Ethnic and Immigrant Groups in Canada," *International Migration* 38, no. 1 (2000).

29 Ricardo Stanton-Salazar and Stephanie Urso Spina, "Adolescent Peer Networks as a Context for Social and Emotional Support," *Youth and Society* 36 (2005): 410.

30 Margaret A. Gibson, Patricia C. Gándara, and Jill Peterson Koyama, "The Role of Peers in the Schooling of U.S. Mexican Youth," in *School Connections: U.S. Mexican Youth, Peers, and School Achievement*, eds Margaret A. Gibson, Patricia C. Gándara, and Jill Peterson Koyama (New York: Teachers College Press, 2004), 5–6.

31 James E. Marcia, "Identity in Adolescence," in *Handbook of Adolescent Psychology*, ed. Joseph J. Adelson (New York: Wiley, 1980); Lyda

Lannegrand-Willems and Harke A. Bosma, "Identity Development-in-context. The School as an Important Context for Identity Development," *Identity: An International Journal of Theory and Research* 6, no. 1 (2006).

32 Carlo Raffo and Michelle Reeves, "Youth Transitions and Social Exclusion: Developments in Social Capital Theory," *Journal of Youth Studies* 3, no. 2 (2000).

33 Carrie Furrer and Ellen Skinner, "Sense of Relatedness as a Factor in Children's Academic Engagement and Performance," *Journal of Educational Psychology* 95 (2003): Fredericks, Blumenfeld, and Paris, "School Engagement"; Suárez-Orozco, Suárez-Orozco, and Todorova, "Moving Stories."

34 Canadian Council on Social Development, *Immigrant Youth in Canada* (Ottawa: author, 2000), 10.

35 Canadian Council, *Immigrant Youth*, 14.

36 Floya Anthias and Nira Yuval-Davis, eds, *Woman-Nation-State* (New York: St Martin's Press, 1989); Mythili Rajiva, "Bridging the Generation Gap: Exploring the Differences Between Immigrant Parents and Their Canadian-born Children," *Canadian Issues* (Spring 2005); Hieu Van Ngo and Barbara Schleifer, "Immigrant Children and Youth in Focus." *Canadian Issues*, (Spring 2005).

37 For example Cristoph Steinhausen, Cinzia Bearth-Carrari, and Christa Winkler Metzke, "Psychosocial Adaptation of Adolescent Migrants in a Swiss Community Survey," *Social Psychiatry and Psychiatric Epidemiology* 44, no. 4 (2008).

38 Yvonne Hébert, "Transculturalism Among Canadian Youth: Focus on Strategic Competence and Social Capital," in *Belongings and Social Capital Among Youth in Comparative Perspective*, eds Dirk Hoerder, Yvonne Hébert, and Irina Schmitt (Toronto: University of Toronto Press, 2005), 123.

39 Sandra Kouritzin, "Immigrant Women Redefine Access to ESL Classes: Contradiction and Ambivalence." *Journal of Multilingual and Multicultural Development* 21, no. 1 (2000): 15.

40 Thomas Faist, *The Volume and Dynamics of International Migration* (New York: Oxford University Press, 2000); Peggy Levitt, "Transnational Migration: Taking Stock and Future Directions," *Global Networks* 1, no. 3 (2001); Nina Glick Schiller, Linda Basch, and Cristina Blanc Szanton, "From Immigrant to Transmigrant: Theorizing Transnational Migration," *Anthropological Quarterly* 68, no. 1, (1995); Luin Goldring, "The Power of Status in Transnational Social Fields," in *Transnationalism From Below*, eds Michael Peter Smith and Luis Eduardo Guarnizo

(London: Transactions Publishers, 1998); Portes "Immigrant Theory"; Sarah Mahler, "Constructing International Relations: The Role of Transnational Migrants and Other Non-state Actors," *Identities: Global Studies in Culture and Power* 7, no. 2 (2000); Steven Vertovec, "Conceiving and Researching Transnationalism," *Ethnic and Racial Studies* 22, no. 2 (1999).

CHAPTER FIVE

1   Portes, "Social Capital," 18.

2   Robert D. Putnam, "Bowling Alone: America's Declining Social Capital," *The Journal of Democracy* 6, no. 1 (1995); Robert D. Putnam, *Bowling Alone*.

3   James Hyman, "Exploring Social Capital and Civic Engagement to Create a Framework for Community Building," *Applied Developmental Science* 6, no. 4 (2002): 197.

4   Ellen M. Donoghue and Victoria Sturtevant, "Social Science Constructs in Ecosystem Assessments: Revisiting Community Capacity and Community Resiliency," *Society and Natural Resources* 20 (2007): 908.

5   Along with the two girls from Belgium and the Netherlands, two of the adult immigrant participants are European. One is from Poland; the other has a Swedish background.

6   Omnifacts Bristol Research, *Bring 'em on Carefully: Excerpt from the Inside Out Report* 3 (2006). The Bristol Group survey included a total of 1,800 respondents in Atlantic Canada, consisting of 800 respondents in each of the following provinces: New Brunswick, Nova Scotia, and Newfoundland and Labrador, and a smaller number in Prince Edward Island. Data was weighted to proportionately represent the populations being surveyed.

7   Omnifacts Bristol Research, *Bring 'em on Carefully*.

8   John W. Berry, "Acculturation: Living Successfully in Two Cultures," *International Journal of Intercultural Relations* 29 (2005): 698.

9   Berry et al., *Immigrant Youth in Cultural Transition*, 305.

10 Silvia Domínguez and Isidro Maya-Jariego "Acculturation of Host Individuals: Immigrants and Personal Networks," *American Journal of Community Psychology* 42, no. 3–4 (2008): 325.

11 Morton Weinfeld and Lori Wilkinson. "Immigration, Diversity and Minority Communities," in *Race and Ethnicity in Canada*, ed. Peter S. Li (Toronto: Oxford University Press, 1999), 66.

12 Li, *Destination Canada*, 52.

13　Ibid, 53.

14　Peter L. Benson et al., "Beyond the 'Village' Rhetoric: Creating Healthy Communities for Children and Adolescents," *Applied Developmental Science* 2, no. 3 (1998): 139.

15　James S. Coleman, *Report of the Panel on Youth of the President's Science Advisory Committee* (Chicago: University of Chicago Press, 1974), 132.

16　Jean Rhodes, Jean B. Grossman, and Jennifer Roffman, "The Rhetoric and Reality of Youth Mentoring." *New Directions for Youth Development* 93 (Spring 2002).

17　Benson et al., "Beyond the 'Village' Rhetoric," 140.

18　James Youniss et al., "The Role of Community Service in Identity Development"; Youniss, Jeffrey A. McLellan, and Mazer, "Voluntary Service."

19　Eccles and Barber, "Student Council."

20　Barry R. Chiswick, "Are Immigrants Favorably Self-selected: An Economic Analysis," in *Migration Theory: Talking Across Disciplines*, eds Caroline D. Brettell and James F. Hollifield (New York: Routledge, 2000); George Borjas, "Immigrants, Minorities, and Labor Market Competition," *Industrial and Labor Relations Review* 40 (1987); Amelie Constant and Douglas S. Massey, "Self-selection, Earnings, and Out-migration: A Longitudinal Study of Migrants to Germany," *Journal of Population Economics* 16, no. 4 (2003).

21　Miles Corak, "Are the Kids All Right: Intergenerational Mobility and Child Well-being in Canada," in *Review of Economic Performance and Social Progress*, eds Keith Banting, Andrew Sharpe, and France St-Hilaire (Montreal and Ottawa: Institute for Research on Public Policy and Centre for the Study of Living Standards, 2001); Teresa Abada and Eric Y. Tenkorang, "Pursuit of University Education Among the Children of Immigrants in Canada: The Roles of Parental Human Capital and Social Capital," *Journal of Youth Studies* 12 no. 2 (2009),

22　Grace Kao and Jennifer Thompson, "Racial and Ethnic Stratification in Educational Achievement and Attainment," *Annual Review of Sociology* 29 (2003).

CHAPTER SIX

1　Karen Bevan, "Young People, Culture, Migration and Mental Health: A Review of the Literature," in *Deeper Dimensions – Culture, Youth and Mental Health*, eds Marie Bashir and David L. Bennett (Sydney: Transcultural Mental Health Centre, 2000).

2 Jean S. Phinney, "Understanding Ethnic Diversity: The Role of Ethnic Identity," *American Behavioral Scientist* 40, no. 2 (1996): 145.

3 Phinney, "Understanding Ethnic Diversity."

4 Teresa LaFromboise, Hardin L. K. Coleman, and Jennifer Gerton, "Psychological Impact of Biculturalism: Evidence and Theory," *Psychological Bulletin* 114, no. 33 (1993); Jean S. Phinney et al., "Ethnic Identity, Immigration, and Well-being: An Interactional Perspective," *Journal of Social Issues* 57, no. 3 (2001).

5 Berry et al., *Immigrant Youth in Cultural Transition*; Andrew J. Fuligni, "Family Obligation and the Academic Motivation of Adolescents from Asian and Latin American, and European Backgrounds," in *Family Obligation and Assistance During Adolescence: Contextual Variations and Developmental Implications*, ed. Andrew J. Fuligni (San Francisco: Jossey-Bass, 2001); Paul A. Singh Ghuman, *Double Loyalties: South Asian Adolescents in the West* (Cardiff: University of Wales Press, 2003); Ruben G. Rumbaut and Alejandro Portes, *Ethnicities: Children of Immigrants in America* (Berkeley: University of California Press and Russell Sage, 2001).

6 Alejandro Portes and Rubén G. Rumbaut, *Immigrant America: A Portrait* (Berkeley: University of California Press, 1990).

7 Alejandro Portes and Richard Schauffler, "Language and the Second Generation: Bilingualism Yesterday and Today," *The International Migration Review* 28 (1994).

8 Myriam Simard, "Immigrant Integration Outside Montreal," *Our Diverse Cities* 3 (2007).

9 John Samuel, "Barriers to Attracting and Retaining Immigrants in Atlantic Canada," in *Rendez-vous immigration 2004: Enjeux et défis de l'immigration au Nouveau-Brunswick / Immigration in New Brunswick Issues and Challenges*, eds Hélène Destrempes and Joe Ruggeri (Fredericton: Policy Studies Centre, University of New Brunswick, 2005); Greg R. Halseth and Laura Ryser, *Service Provision in Rural and Small Town Places: A Report for Mackenzie, British Columbia* (Montreal: Initiative on the New Economy, Project of the Canadian Rural Revitalization Foundation, Concordia University, 2006); Rene Houle, "Secondary Migration of New Immigrants to Canada," *Our Diverse Cities* 3 (2007); Bill Reimer, "Immigration in the New Rural Economy," *Our Diverse Cities* 3 (2007); David Bruce, "The Challenges of Immigration as a Rural Repopulation Strategy in Maritime Canada," *Our Diverse Cities* 3 (2007).

10 Patricia Thornton, "The Problem of Out-migration from Atlantic Canada, 1871–1921: A New Look," *Acadiensis* 15, no. 1 (1985); Margaret Conrad, "The 1950s: The Decade of Development," in *The Atlantic Provinces*

in Confederation, eds E.R. Forbes and Delphin A. Muise (Toronto: University of Toronto Press, 1993, reprinted in 1997); Conrad, "They Come and They Go"; D.J. Savoie, *Visiting Grandchildren: Economic Development in the Maritimes* (Toronto: University of Toronto Press, 2006); Michael Corbett, *Learning to Leave: The Irony of Schooling in a Coastal Community* (Blackpoint: Fernwood Publishing, 2007).

11 Margaret Walton-Roberts, "Regional Immigration and Dispersal: Lessons from Small- and Medium-sized Urban Centres in British Columbia," *Our Diverse Cities* 2 (2006).

12 Kamilla Bahbahani, *The Changing Face of Kelowna: Best Practices for Creating a Welcoming Community* (Kelowna: The Intercultural Society of the Central Okanagan, 2008).

CHAPTER SEVEN

1 C. Wright Mills, *The Sociological Imagination* (New York: Oxford University Press, 1970), 6–7.

2 Roy T. Bowles, ed. *Little Communities and Big Industries* (Toronto: Butterworth, 1982).

3 See Bowles, *Little Communities*, for a discussion of one-industry towns across Canada.

4 Himelfarb, "The Social Characteristics."

5 Fernando Nunes, Personal Communication with the Author, 16 April 2010.

6 Richard N. Lalonde, Janelle M. Jones, and Mirella L. Stroink, "Racial Identity, Racial Attitudes, and Race Socialization Among Black Canadian Parents," *Canadian Journal of Behavioural Science* 40, no. 3 (2008).

7 Krishna Pendakur and Ravi Pendakur, "The Colour of Money: Earnings Differentials Among Ethnic Groups in Canada," *Canadian Journal of Economics* 31, no. 3 (1998); Derek Hum and Wayne Simpson. "Closing the Wage Gap: Economic Assimilation of Canadian Immigrants Reconsidered," *Journal of International Migration and Integration* 1, no. 4 (2000); Jean Lock Kunz, Anne Milan, and Sylvain Schetagne, *Unequal Access: A Canadian Profile of Racial Differences in Education, Employment and Income* (Toronto: Canadian Race Relation Foundation, 2000); Jean Lock Kunz, *Being Young and Visible: Labour Market Access Among Immigrant and Visible Minority Youth* (Ottawa: Human Resources and Skills Development Canada, SP-581-08-03E, 2003); Abada and Tenkorang, "Pursuit of University Education."

8 Grace-Edward Galabuzi, *Canada's Economic Apartheid: The Social Exclusion of Racialized Groups in the New Century* (Toronto: Canadian Scholars' Press, 2006).

9 Edgar G. Epps, "Race, Class, and Educational Opportunity: Trends in the Sociology of Education," *Sociological Forum* 10, no. 4 (1995); George J. Sefa Dei et al., *Reconstructing "Drop-out": A Critical Ethnography of the Dynamics of Black Students' Disengagement from School* (Toronto: University of Toronto Press, 1997); Kenise M. Kilbride, *A Review of the Literature on the Human, Social and Cultural Capital of Immigrant Children and their Families with Implications for Teacher Education*, 2000; David Watt and Hetty Roessingh, "The Dynamics of ESL Drop-out: Plus Ça Change ... " *Canadian Modern Language Review* 58, no. 2 (2001); Anisef and Kilbride, *The Needs of Newcomer Youth*.

10 Fernando Nunes, Personal Communication with the Author, 16 April 2010.

11 Rose Baaba Folson and Hijin Park, Introduction to *Calculated Kindness: Global Restructuring, Immigration and Settlement in Canada*, ed. Rose Baaba Folson (Halifax: Fernwood Publishing, 2004), 12.

12 Li, *Destination Canada*, 11.

13 Avril Bell, "Being 'At Home' in the Nation: Hospitality and Sovereignty in Talk About Immigration," *Ethnicities* 10 (2010): 240.

14 Savoie, *Visiting Grandchildren*.

15 Conrad, "The 1950s," 410.

16 Godfrey Baldacchino et al., *The Host Program and Immigrant Retention on Prince Edward Island* (Charlottetown: University of Prince Edward Island and the Prince Edward Island Association for Newcomers to Canada, 2009), 30.

17 Robert E. Park, *Old World Traits Transplanted* (New York: Arno Press, 1969), as cited in Chavez, "The Power of the Imagined Community," 54.

18 Derek McGhee, "Getting 'Host' Communities on Board: Finding the Balance Between 'Managed Migration' and 'Managed Settlement' in Community Cohesion Strategies," *Journal of Ethnic and Migration Studies* 32, no. 1 (2006); Khanh T. Dinh and Meg A. Bond, "Introduction to Special Section the Other Side of Acculturation: Changes Among Host Individuals and Communities in their Adaption to Immigrant Populations," *American Journal of Community Psychology* 42, no. 3–4 (2008); Silvia Domínguez and Isidro Maya-Jariego, "Acculturation of Host Individuals:Immigrants and Personal Networks," *American Journal of Community Psychology* 42, no. 3–4 (2008).

19 For example, Anthony M. Orum, "Circles of Influence and Chains of Command: The Social Processes Whereby Ethnic Communities Influence Host Societies," *Social Forces* 84, no. 2 (2005); Richard Bourhis et al., "Acculturation Orientations and Social Relations Between Immigrant and Host Community Members in California," *Journal of Cross-Cultural Psychology* 40, no. 3 (2009).

20 For example, Bronfenbrenner, *The Ecology of Human Development*; Urie Bronfenbrenner, *Making Human Beings Human: Bioecological Perspectives on Human Development* (Thousand Oaks: Sage, 2005); Jencks and Mayer, "The Social Consequences"; Gabarino, *Children and Families*; Pretty, Andrewes, and Collett, "Exploring Adolescents' Sense of Community"; Blyth and Leffert, "Communities as Contexts"; Pretty et al., "Sense of Community"; Aber et al., "Development in Context"; Kohen, Hertzman, and Brooks-Gunn, *Neighbourhood Influences*; Duncan and Raudenbush, "Neighborhoods and Adolescent Development"; Sampson, Morenoff, and Gannon-Rowley, "Assessing Neighborhood Effects"; Chaskin, "Building Community Capacity."

21 Zhou and Bankston III, "Social Capital and the Adaptation of the Second Generation"; Zhou and Bankston III, *Growing up American*; Dinovitzer, Hagan, and Parker, "Choice and Circumstance"; Bankston III, "Social Capital, Cultural Values"; Kao, "Social Capital."

22 Reitz, ed., *Host Societies*, 8–13.

23 See Caroline B. Brettell, "Voluntary Organizations, Social Capital, and the Social Incorporation of Asian Indian Immigrants in the Dallas-Fortworth Metroplex," *Anthropological Quarterly* 78, no. 4 (2005).

24 See Irene Bloemraad, "The Limits of de Tocqueville: How Government Facilitates Organizational Capacity in Newcomer Communities," *Journal of Ethnic and Migration Studies* 31, no. 5 (2005).

25 Mark A. Brennan, "Conceptualizing Resiliency: An Interactional Perspective for Community and Youth Development," Special issue of *Child Care in Practice Building – Resilience in Children, Families, and Communities* 14, no. 1 (2008): 56.

26 Fikret Berkes and Carl Folke, *Linking Social and Ecological Systems* (Cambridge: Cambridge University Press, 1998), 12.

27 Flora and Flora, "Entrepreneurial Social Infrastructures," 54.

28 Gittel and Vidal, *Community Organizing*.

29 Robert L. Bach, *Changing Relations: Newcomers and Established Residents in US Communities. National Board of the Changing Relations Project* (New York: Ford. Foundation, 1993); Elzbieta N. Gozdziak and Micah Bump, "Poultry, Apples, and New Immigrants in the Rural Com-

munities of the Shenandoah Valley: An Ethnographic Case Study," *International Migration* 42, no. 1 (2004); Pilar A. Parra and Max J. Pfeffer, "New Immigrants in Rural Communities: The Challenges of Integration," *Social Text* 24 (3 88, 2006).

30 J. Edward Taylor, Philip L. Martin, and Michael Fix, *Poverty Amid Prosperity: Immigration and the Changing Face of Rural California* (Washington: The Urban Institute Press, 1996).

Bibliography

Abada, Teresa, and Eric Y. Tenkorang. "Pursuit of University Education Among the Children of Immigrants in Canada: The Roles of Parental Human Capital and Social Capital." *Journal of Youth Studies* 12 no. 2 (2009): 185–207.

Aber, J. Lawrence, Martha A. Gephart, Jeanne Brooks-Gunn, and James P. Connell. "Development in Context: Implications for Studying Neighborhood Effects." In *Neighborhood Poverty: Context and Consequences for Children.* Jeanne Brooks-Gunn, Greg J. Duncan, and J. Lawrence Aber, chapter 2. New York: Russell Sage Foundation, 1997.

Aboud, Frances E., and Anna Joong. "Intergroup Name-calling and Conditions for Creating Assertive Bystanders." In *Intergroup Attitudes and Relations in Childhood through Adulthood.* Edited by Sheri R. Levy and Melanie Killen, 249–60. Oxford: Oxford University Press, 2007.

Ainsworth, James W. "Why Does it Take a Village? The Mediation of Neighbourhood Effects on Educational Achievement." *Social Forces* 81, no. 1 (2002): 117–52.

Aksel, Seyda, Zubeyit Gun, Turkan Yilmaz Irmak, and Cengelci Banu. "Migration and Psychological Status of Adolescents in Turkey." *Adolescence* 42, no. 167 (2007): 589–602.

Alesina, Alberto, and Eliana La Ferrara. "Who Trusts Others?" *Journal of Public Economics* 85 (2002): 207–34.

Allport, Gordon W. *The Nature of Prejudice.* Reading: Addison-Wesley Publishing Company, 1954, 1979.

Andres, Leslie, Paul Anisef, Harvey Krahn, Dianne Looker, and Victor Thiessen. "The Persistence of Social Structure: Cohort, Class, and Gender Effects on the Occupational Aspirations of Canadian Youth." *Journal of Youth Studies* 2, no. 3 (1999): 261–82.

Andres, Leslie, Maria Adamuti-Trache, Ee-Seul Yoon, Michelle Pidgeon, and Jens Peter Thomsen. "Educational Expectations, Parental Social

Class, Gender, and Post Secondary Attainment: A Ten Year Perspective."
   Youth and Society 39, no. 2 (2007): 135–63.
Andrisin Witting, Michele, and Sheila Grant-Thompson. "The Utility of
   Allport's Conditions of Inter-group Contact for Predicting Perceptions
   of Improved Racial Attitudes and Beliefs – Contact Hypothesis." *Jour-
   nal of Social Issues*, winter (1998). http://findarticles.com/p/articles/mi_
   m0341/is_4_54/ai_54422539/pg_14/ (accessed February 8, 2011).
Aneshensel, Carol S., and Clea Sucoff. "The Neighborhood Context of
   Adolescent Mental Health." *Journal of Health and Social Behavior* 37,
   no. 4 (1996): 293–310.
Anisef, Paul. *Issues Confronting Newcomer Youth in Canada: Alternative
   Models for a National Youth Host Program*, CERIS Working Paper No.
   39. Toronto: Joint Centre for Excellence for Research on Immigration
   and Settlement (CERIS), 2005. http://ceris.metropolis.net/frameset_e.
   html (accessed March 23, 2007).
Anisef, Paul, Paul Axelrod, Etta Baichman-Anisef, Carl James, and Anton
   Turrittin. *Negotiating the Life Course: Structure, Agency and the Class
   of '73*. Toronto: University of Toronto Press, 2000.
Anisef, Paul, and Kenise M. Kilbride. *The Needs of Newcomer Youth and
   Emerging "Best Practices" to Meet those Needs*. Toronto: Joint Cen-
   tre of Excellence for Research on Immigration and Settlement (CERIS),
   2000. http://ceris.metropolis.net/frameset_e.html (accessed March 23,
   2007).
Anisef, Paul, Kenise M. Kilbride, Etta Baichman-Anisef, and Randa Khattar.
   *Between Two Worlds: The Experiences and Concerns of Immigrant
   Youth in Ontario*. Toronto: Joint Centre of Excellence for Research on
   Immigration and Settlement (CERIS), 2001. http://www.ceris.metropolis.
   net/Virtual%20Library/other/kilbride2.html (accessed October 9, 2007).
Anisef, Paul, Kenise M. Kilbride, Joanna Ochocka, and Rich Janzen. *Par-
   enting Issues of Newcomer Families in Ontario*. Kitchener: Centre for
   Research and Education in Human Services and Centre of Excellence
   for Research on Immigration and Settlement, 2001.
Anthias, Floya, and Nira Yuval-Davis, eds. *Woman-Nation-State*. New
   York: St Martin's Press, 1989.
Ashenburg, Katherine. "A Loyalist Legacy in Fredericton." *New York
   Times*. November 30 1997.
Averett, Susan, Daniel I. Rees, and Laura M. Argys. "The Impact of Gov-
   ernment Policies and Neighbourhood Characteristics on Teenage Sexual
   Activity and Contraceptive Use. *American Journal of Public Health* 92,
   no. 11 (2002): 1773–8.

Baaba Folson, Rose, and Hijin Park. Introduction to *Calculated Kindness: Global Restructuring, Immigration and Settlement in Canada*. Edited by Rose Baaba Folson, 11–20. Halifax: Fernwood Publishing, 2004.

Bahbahani, Kamilla. *The Changing Face of Kelowna: Best Practices for Creating a Welcoming Community*. Kelowna: The Intercultural Society of the Central Okanagan, 2008. http://www.interculturalkelowna.com/docs/best-practices.doc (accessed November 17, 2010).

Bach, Robert L. *Changing Relations: Newcomers and Established Residents in US Communities*. National Board of the Changing Relations Project. New York: Ford. Foundation, 1993. http://www.fordfound.org/elibrary/documents/0133/008.cfm (accessed October 10, 2007).

Baker, Cynthia, Manju Varma-Joshi, and Connie Tanaka. "Sticks and Stones. Racism as Experienced by Adolescents in New Brunswick." *Canadian Journal of Nursing Research* 33, no. 3 (2001, republished 2009): 87–105.

Baldacchino, Godfrey. *Coming to, and Settling on, Prince Edward Island: Stories and Voices: A Report on Recent Immigrants to PEI, Canada*. Charlottetown: University of Prince Edward Island with the Support of the Prince Edward Island Population Secretariat, 2006.

Baldacchino, Godfrey, Lisa Chilton, Shine-Ji Youn Chung, and Mathew Mathiang. *The Host Program and Immigrant Retention on Prince Edward Island*. Charlottetown: University of Prince Edward Island and the Prince Edward Island Association for Newcomers to Canada, 2009.

Bankston, Carl L. III. "Social Capital, Cultural Values, Immigration, and Academic Achievement: The Host Country Context and Contradictory Consequences." *Sociology of Education* 77, no. 2 (2004): 176–9.

Bankston, Carl L. III, and Min Zhou. "Social Capital and Immigrant Children's Achievement." In *Schooling and Social Capital in Diverse Cultures, Volume 13*. Edited by Bruce Fuller and Emily Hannum, 13–39. Amsterdam: JAI, 2002.

Barker, Martin. *The New Racism*. London: Junction Books, 1981.

Baron, Stephan, John Field, and Tom Schuller, eds. *Social Capital: Critical Perspectives*. Oxford: Oxford University Press, 2000.

Baumer, Eric P., and Scott J. South. "Community Effects on Youth Sexual Activity." *Journal of Marriage and Family* 63 (2001): 540–54.

Bazeley, Patricia Ann. *Qualitative Data Analysis with NVivo*. Thousand Oaks: Sage, 2007.

Beiser Morton, Robert Armstrong, Linda Ogilvie, Jacqueline Oxman-Martinez, and Joanna Anneke Rummens. "The New Canadian Children and Youth Study: Research to Fill a Gap in Canada's Children's

Agenda." *Canadian Issues/Themes Canadiens, Special Issue on Immigration and Intersections of Diversity.*

Beiser, Morton, Feng Hou, Ilene Hyman, and Michel Tousignant. "Poverty and Mental Health Among Immigrant and Non-immigrant Children." *American Journal of Public Health* 92, no. 2 (2002): 220–7.

Beiser, Morton, Angela Shik, and Monica Curyk. *New Canadian Children and Youth Study: Literature Review.* Toronto: Joint Centre of Excellence for Research on Immigration and Settlement (CERIS), 1999. http://ceris.metropolis.net/Virtual%20Library/RFPReports/BeiserMRI1998.pdf (accessed November 6, 2010).

Bell, Avril. "Being 'At Home' in the Nation: Hospitality and Sovereignty in Talk About Immigration." *Ethnicities* 10 (2010): 236–56.

Benson, Peter L. *All Kids Are Our Kids: What Communities Must Do To Raise Caring and Responsible Children and Adolescents.* San Francisco: Jossey Bass, 1997.

– "Developmental Assets and Asset-building Community: Conceptual and Empirical Foundations." In *Developmental Assets and Asset-Building Communities: Implications for Research, Policy, and Practice.* Edited by Richard M. Lerner and Peter L. Benson, 19–43. New York: Kluwer Academic/Plenum Publishers, 2003.

Benson, Peter L., Nancy Leffert, Peter C. Scales, and Dale A. Blyth. "Beyond the 'Village' Rhetoric: Creating Healthy Communities for Children and Adolescents." *Applied Developmental Science* 2, no. 3 (1998): 138–59.

Berkes, Fikret, and Carl Folke. *Linking Social and Ecological Systems.* Cambridge: Cambridge University Press, 1998.

Berg, Bruce L. *Qualitative Research Methods for the Social Sciences.* Boston: Allyn and Bacon, 2001.

Berry, John W. "Immigration, Acculturation, and Adaptation." *Applied Psychology: An International Review* 46 (1997): 5–34.

– "Acculturation: Living Successfully in Two Cultures." *International Journal of Intercultural Relations* 29 (2005): 697–712.

Berry, John W., Uicho Kim, Thomas Minde, and Doris Mok. "Comparative Studies of Acculturative Stress." *International Migration Review* 21 (1987): 491–511.

Berry, John W., Jean S. Phinney, David L. Sam, and Paul Vedder. *Immigrant Youth in Cultural Transition: Acculturation, Identity, and Adaptation Across National Contexts.* Mahwah: Lawrence Erlbaum and Associates, Inc, 2006.

Berry, John W., and David L. Sam. "Acculturation and Adaptation." In *Handbook of Cross-Cultural Psychology: Social Behaviour and Appli-*

cations, Volume 3. Edited by John W. Berry, Marshall H. Segall, and Cigdem Kagitcibasi, 291–326. Boston: Allyn & Bacon, 1997.

Bevan, Karen. "Young People, Culture, Migration and Mental Health: A Review of the Literature." In *Deeper Dimensions – Culture, Youth and Mental Health.* Edited by Marie Bashir and David L. Bennett, 1–63. Sydney: Transcultural Mental Health Centre, 2000.

Bloemraad, Irene. "The Limits of de Tocqueville: How Government Facilitates Organizational Capacity in Newcomer Communities." *Journal of Ethnic and Migration Studies* 31, no. 5 (2005): 865–87.

Blyth, Dale A., and Nancy Leffert. "Communities as Contexts for Adolescent Development." *Journal of Adolescent Research* 10 (1995): 64–87.

Bogenschneider, Karen. "An Ecological Risk/Protective Theory for Building Prevention Programs, Policies, and Community Capacity to Support Youth." *Family Relations* 45, no. 2 (1996): 127–38.

Boissevain, Jeremy. *Friends of Friends: Networks, Manipulators and Coalitions.* Oxford: Basil Blackwell, 1974.

Borjas, George. "Immigrants, Minorities, and Labor Market Competition." *Industrial and Labor Relations Review* 40 (1987): 382–92.

Bourdieu, Pierre. "The Social Space and the Genesis of Groups." *Theory and Society* 14, no. 6 (1985): 723–44.

– "The Forms of Capital." In *Handbook for Theory and Research for the Sociology of Education.* Edited by John G. Richardson, 241–58. New York: Greenwood Press, 1986.

Bourhis, Richard Y., Genevieve Barrette, Shaha El-Geledi, and Ronald Schmidt, Sr. "Acculturation Orientations and Social Relations Between Immigrant and Host Community Members in California." *Journal of Cross-Cultural Psychology* 40, no. 3 (2009): 443–67.

Bowles, Roy T., ed. *Little Communities and Big Industries.* Toronto: Butterworth, 1982.

Boyd, Monica. "Educational Attainments of Immigrant Offspring: Success or Segmented Assimilation?" *International Migration Review* 36, no. 4 (2002): 1037–60.

Boyle, Michael H., and Ellen Lipman. *Do Places Matter? A Multilevel Analysis of Geographic Variations in Child Behaviour in Canada.* W–98–16E. Applied Research Branch, Strategic Policy, Human Resources Development Canada, 1998. http://www.hrsdc.gc.ca/eng/cs/sp/sdc/pkrf/publications/research/1998–002608/page04.shtml (accessed November 6, 2010).

Brennan, Mark A. "Conceptualizing Resiliency: An Interactional Perspective for Community and Youth Development." Special Issue of *Child*

Care in Practice Building – Resilience in Children, Families, and Communities 14, no. 1 (2008): 55–64.

Brettell, Caroline B. "Voluntary Organizations, Social Capital, and the Social Incorporation of Asian Indian Immigrants in the Dallas-Fortworth Metroplex." *Anthropological Quarterly* 78, no. 4 (2005): 853–83.

Bronfenbrenner, Urie. *The Ecology of Human Development: Experiments by Nature and Design.* Cambridge: Harvard University Press, 1979.

– *Making Human Beings Human: Bioecological Perspectives on Human Development.* Thousand Oaks: Sage, 2005.

Brooks-Gunn, Jeanne, Greg J. Duncan, Pamela K. Klebanov, and Naomi Sealand. "Do Neighborhoods Influence Child and Adolescent Development?" *American Journal of Sociology* 99, no. 2 (1993): 353–95.

Bruce, David. "The Challenges of Immigration as a Rural Repopulation Strategy in Maritime Canada." *Our Diverse Cities* 3 (2007): 90–6.

Bryk, Anthony S., and Barbara L. Schneider. *Trust in Schools: A Core Resource for Improvement.* New York: Russell Sage Foundation, 2002.

Byrne, Donn. *The Attraction Paradigm.* New York: Academic Press, 1971.

Buriel, Raymond, William Perez, Terri L. DeMent, David V. Chavez, and Virginia R. Moran. "The Relationship of Language Brokering to Academic Performance, Biculturalism, and Self-efficacy Among Latino Adolescents." *Hispanic Journal of Behavioral Sciences* 20 (1998): 283–97.

Burns, Peter, and James G. Gimpel. "Economic Insecurity, Prejudicial Stereotypes, and Public Opinion on Immigration Policy." *Political Science Quarterly* 115 (Summer, 2000): 201–25.

Canada. Citizenship and Immigration Canada. *Immigration Statistics to Canada by Intended Occupation and by Province of Destination, 1946–1956.* Ottawa: Citizenship and Immigration Canada, 1956.

Canada. Citizenship and Immigration Canada/ Library and Archives Canada. *Immigration Statistics (Ottawa, 1972–1996).* 1997. http://epe.lac-bac.gc.ca/100/202/301/immigration_statistics-ef/index.html (accessed December 11, 2007).

Canada. Citizenship and Immigration Canada Integration Branch. *Immigrant Integration in Canada: Policy Objectives, Program Delivery and Challenges.* Discussion Paper. 2001. http://atwork.settlement.org/downloads/atwork/Immigrant_Integration_in_Canada_discussion_paper_Hauck_May01.pdf (accessed August 28, 2007).

Canada. Citizenship and Immigration Canada. *Facts and Figures 2006: Immigration Overview, Permanent Residents by Province or Territory.*

2007. http://www.cic.gc.ca/english/resources/statistics/facts2006/permanent/17.asp (accessed September 14, 2007).

– *Facts and Figures 2007: Immigration Overview, Permanent Residents by Province or Territory.* Catalogue No. C & 1–955–12–08. Ottawa: Minister of Public Works and Government Services Canada, 2008.

– Immigrating to Canada. 2009. http://www.cic.gc.ca/english/immigrate/ index.asp (accessed June 20, 2010)

– *Facts and Figures 2008, 2009: Immigration Overview, Permanent Residents by Province or Territory.* 2010. http://www.cic.gc.ca/english/ resources/statistics/facts2008/permanent/02.asp (accessed April 3, 2009).

– *Preliminary Tables – Permanent and Temporary Residents 2010.* 2011. http://www.cic.gc.ca/english/resources/statistics/facts2010-preliminary/ 02.asp (accessed February 15, 2011).

Canada. *Statistics Canada. General Social Survey on Social Engagement, Cycle 17: An Overview of Findings.* Ottawa: Statistics Canada, 2003.

– *Longitudinal Survey of Immigrants to Canada: Process, Progress and Prospects.* Catalogue No. 89–611-XIE. Ottawa: Special Surveys Division Statistics Canada, 2003.

– *Immigration in Canada: A Portrait of the Foreign-born Population, 2006 census.* Catalogue No. 97–557-XIE. Ottawa: Minister of Industry Canada, 2007. http://www12.statcan.ca/english/census06/analysis/ immcit/pdf/97–557-XIE2006001.pdf (accessed December 4, 2008).

– *Community Profiles Fredericton, New Brunswick (city), Fredericton, New Brunswick (census agglomeration).* 2007. http://www12.statcan. ca/census-recensement/2006/dp-pd/prof/92–591/search-recherche/frm_ res.cfm?Lang=E (accessed April 12, 2009).

– *Fredericton 2006 Census.* Presentation made by Statistics Canada. April 21 2009.

– *Village of Florenceville 2006 Census.* Presentation made by Statistics Canada. April 21 2009.

Canadian Council on Social Development. *Immigrant Youth in Canada.* Ottawa: 2000.

Caplan, Nathan, Marcella H. Choy, and John K. Whitmore. *Children of the Boat People: A Study of Educational Success.* Ann Arbor: University of Michigan Press, 1991.

Chaskin, Robert J. "Building Community Capacity for Children, Youth, and Families." *Children Australia* 34, no. 1 (2009): 31–9.

Chaskin, Robert J., Prudence Brown, Sudhir Venkatesh, and Avis Vidal. *Building Community Capacity.* Hathorne: Aldine de Gruyter, 2001.

Chavez, Leo R. "The Power of the Imagined Community: The Settlement of Undocumented Mexicans and Central Americans in the United States." *American Anthropologist* 96, no. 1 (1994): 52–73.

Chavis, David M., and Abraham Wandersman. "Sense of Community in the Urban Environment: A Catalyst for Participation and Community Development." *American Journal of Community Psychology* 18 (1990): 55–81.

Chipuer, Heather M. "Dyadic Attachments and Community Connectedness: Links with Youth's Loneliness Experiences." *Journal of Community Psychology* 29, no. 4 (2001): 429–46.

Chiswick, Barry R., ed. *Immigration, Language, and Ethnicity: Canada and the United States*. Washington: The AEI Press, 1992.

– "Are Immigrants Favorably Self-selected: An Economic Analysis." In *Migration Theory: Talking Across Disciplines*. Edited by Caroline D. Brettell and James F. Hollifield, 61–76. New York: Routledge, 2000.

Chow, H.P.H. "The Effects of Ethnic Capital and Family Background on School Performance: A Case Study of Chinese-Canadian Adolescents in Calgary." *The Alberta Journal of Education* 50, no. 3 (2004): 321–26.

Clément, Richard, and Robert C. Gardner. "Second Language Mastery." In *The New Handbook of Language and Social Psychology*. Edited by W. Peter Robinson and Howard Giles, 489–504. London: Wiley, 2001.

Clews, Rosemary. "Diversity, Immigration and Rural Communities: New Brunswick- A Case Study." Paper Presented at the Fifth International Metropolis Conference November 13–17, 2000, Vancouver. 2000.

– "Changing the Same Old Story: Mounting a Challenge to Metanarratives About Racism by Exploring Stories in Rural Communities." Paper Presented at the International Rural Human Services Conference, Halifax, 2003.

– "Exploring and Overcoming Barriers to Immigration in New Brunswick." In *Rendez-vous immigration 2004: Enjeux et défis de l'immigration au Nouveau-Brunswick /Immigration in New Brunswick Issues and Challenges*. Edited by Hélène Destrempes and Joe Ruggeri, 263–92. Fredericton: Policy Studies Centre, University of New Brunswick, 2005.

Cohen, Anthony. *The Symbolic Construction of Community*. London: Routledge, 1985.

Coleman, James S. *Report of the Panel on Youth of the President's Science Advisory Committee*. Chicago: University of Chicago Press, 1974.

– "Social Capital in the Creation of Human Capital." *American Journal of Sociology* 94 (1988) Supplement: s95-s–120.

– *Foundations of Social Theory*. Cambridge: Harvard University Press, 1990, 1994.
– "Some Points on Choice in Education." *Sociology of Education* 65, no. 4 (1992): 260–2.
Conrad, Margaret. "The 1950s: The Decade of Development." In *The Atlantic Provinces in Confederation*. Edited by E.R. Forbes and Delphin A. Muise, 382–420. Toronto: University of Toronto Press, 1993, reprinted in 1997.
– "They Come and They Go: New Brunswick's Immigration Policy." *Telegraph Journal*. 21 March 2006.
Conrad, Margaret, and Heather Steel. "They Come and They Go: Four Centuries of Immigration to New Brunswick." In *Rendez-vous immigration 2004: Enjeux et défis de l'immigration au Nouveau-Brunswick /Immigration in New Brunswick Issues and Challenges*. Edited by Hélène Destrempes and Joe Ruggeri, 43–77. Fredericton: Policy Studies Centre, University of New Brunswick, 2005.
Constant, Amelie, and Douglas S. Massey. "Self-selection, Earnings, and Out-migration: A Longitudinal Study of Migrants to Germany." *Journal of Population Economics* 16, no. 4 (2003): 631–53.
Cook, Stuart W. "Experimenting on Social Issues: The Case of School Desegregation." *American Psychologist* 40 (1985): 452–60.
Corak, Miles. "Are the Kids All Right: Intergenerational Mobility and Child Well-being in Canada." In *Review of Economic Performance and Social Progress*. Edited by Keith Banting, Andrew Sharpe, and France St-Hilaire, 273–92. Montreal and Ottawa: Institute for Research on Public Policy and Centre for the Study of Living Standards, 2001.
Corbett, Michael. *Learning to Leave: The Irony of Schooling in a Coastal Community*. Blackpoint: Fernwood Publishing, 2007.
Crane, Jonathan. "The Epidemic Theory of Ghettos and Neighborhood Effects on Dropping Out and Teenage Childbearing." *American Journal of Sociology* 96 (1991): 1226–59.
Croniger, Robert G., and Valirie E. Lee. "Social Capital and Dropping Out of High School: Benefits to At-risk Students of Teachers: Support and Guidance." *Teachers College Record* 103, no. 4 (2001): 548–81.
Cummins, Jim. "Cognitive/Academic Language Proficiency, Linguistic Interdependence, the Optimum Age Question and Some Other Matters." *Working Papers on Bilingualism* No. 19 (1979), 197–205.
– "Age on Arrival and Immigrant Second Language Learning in Canada. A Reassessment." *Applied Linguistics* 2 (1981): 132–49.

- "Language and Literacy Acquisition in Bilingual Contexts." *Journal of Multilingual and Multicultural Education* 10 (1989): 17–31.

Davidson, William B., Patrick Cotter, and James Stovall. "Social Predispositions for the Development of Sense of Community." *Psychological Reports* 68 (1991): 817–18.

Dei, George J. Sefa, Josephine Mazzuca, Elizabeth McIsaac, and Jasmin Zine. *Reconstructing "Drop-out": A Critical Ethnography of the Dynamics of Black Students' Disengagement from School.* Toronto: University of Toronto Press, 1997.

Destrempes, Hélène, and Joe Ruggeri, eds. *Rendez-vous immigration 2004: Enjeux et défis de l'immigration au Nouveau-Brunswick/Immigration in New Brunswick Issues and Challenges.* Fredericton: Policy Studies Centre, University of New Brunswick, 2005.

Diaz, Joseph D. "School Attachment Among Latino Youth in Rural Minnesota." *Hispanic Journal of Behavioral Sciences* 27 (2005): 302–18.

Dinh, Khanh T., and Meg A. Bond. "Introduction to Special Section the Other Side of Acculturation: Changes Among Host Individuals and Communities in their Adaption to Immigrant Populations." *American Journal of Community Psychology* 42, no. 3–4 (2008): 283–5.

Dinovitzer, Ronit, John Hagan, and Patricia Parker. "Choice and Circumstance: Social Capital and Planful Competence in the Attainments of Immigrant Youth." *Canadian Journal of Sociology* 28 (2003): 463–88.

Donoghue, Ellen M., and Victoria Sturtevant. "Social Science Constructs in Ecosystem Assessments: Revisiting Community Capacity and Community Resiliency." *Society and Natural Resources* 20 (2007): 899–912.

Domínguez, Silvia, and Isidro Maya-Jariego. "Acculturation of Host Individuals: Immigrants and Personal Networks." *American Journal of Community Psychology* 42, no. 3–4 (2008): 309–27.

Duncan, Greg J., and Stephen W. Raudenbush. "Neighborhoods and Adolescent Development: How Can We Determine the Links?" In *Does it Take a Village? Community Effects on Children, Adolescents, and Families.* Edited by Alan Booth and Nan Crouter, 105–36. State College: Pennsylvania State University Press, 2001.

Eagly, Alice H., and Shelly Chaiken. *The Psychology of Attitudes.* Fort Worth: Harcourt Brace Jovanovich College Publishers, 1993.

Ebaugh, Helen Rose. "Religion and the New Immigrants." In *Handbook of the Sociology of Religion.* Edited by Michele Dillon, 225–39. Cambridge: Cambridge University Press, 2003.

Eccles, Jacquelynne S, and Bonnie L. Barber. "Student Council, Volunteering, Basketball, or Marching Band: What Kind of Extracurricular

Involvement Matters?" *Journal of Adolescent Research* 14 (1999): 10–43.

Eley, Geoffrey, and Ronald Grigor-Suny, eds. *Becoming National*. New York: Oxford University Press, 1996.

Epps, Edgar G. "Race, Class, and Educational Opportunity: Trends in the Sociology of Education." *Sociological Forum* 10, no. 4 (1995): 593–608.

Esses, Victoria M., Leah K. Hamilton, Caroline Bennett- AbuAyyash, and Meyer Burstein. *Characteristics of a Welcoming Community*. Citizenship and Immigration Canada. 2010.

Etzioni, Amitai. "The Responsive Community: A Communitarian Perspective." *American Sociological Review* 61 (1996): 1–11.

Faist, Thomas. *The Volume and Dynamics of International Migration*. New York: Oxford University Press, 2000.

Farr, James. "Social Capital a Conceptual History." *Political Theory* 32, no. 1 (2004): 6–33.

Farrell, Susan, Tim Aubry, and Daniel Coulombe. "Neighborhoods and Neighbors: Do They Contribute to Well-being." *Journal of Community Psychology* 32, no. 1 (2004): 9–25.

Fleras, Augie, and Jean Leonard Elliot. *The Challenge of Diversity, Multiculturalism in Canada*. Toronto: Nelson Canada, 1992.

Flora, Cornelia Butler, and Jan L. Flora. "Entrepreneurial Social Infrastructures: A Necessary Ingredient." *The Annals of the American Academy of Political and Social Science* 529 (1993): 48–58.

Flora, Cornelia Butler, and Jan L. Flora, with Susan Fey. *Rural Communities: Legacy and Change*, 2nd ed. Boulder: Westview Press, 2004.

Flora, Jan L., Cornelia Butler Flora, Gary P. Green, and Frederick E. Schmidt. "Rural Economic Development Through Local Self-development Strategies." *Agriculture and Human Values* 8, no. 3 (1991): 19–24.

Flora, Jan L., Gary P. Green, Edward A. Gale, Frederick E. Schmidt, and Cornelia Butler Flora. "Self Development: A Viable Rural Development Option?" *Policy Studies Journal* 20 (1992): 276–88.

Florida, Richard. *The Rise of the Creative Class: And How it's Transforming Work, Leisure, Community and Everyday Life*. New York: Basic Books, 2002.

Florida, Richard. *The Flight of the Creative Class: The New Global Competition for Talent*. New York: Harper Collins, 2005.

Foley, Michael W., and Dean R. Hoge. *Religion and the New Immigrants: How Faith Communities Form Our Newest Citizens*. Oxford: Oxford University Press, 2007.

Fredericks Jennifer A., Phyllis C. Blumenfeld, and Alison H. Paris. "School Engagement: Potential of the Concept, State of the Evidence." *Review of Educational Research* 74 (2004): 59–109.

Fuligni, Andrew J. "The Academic Achievement of Adolescents from Immigrant Families the Roles of Family Background, Attitudes, and Behavior." *Child Development* 68, no. 2 (1997): 351–63.

– "The Adjustment of Children from Immigrant Families." *Current Directions in Psychological Science* 7 (1998): 99–103.

– "Family Obligation and the Academic Motivation of Adolescents from Asian and Latin American, and European Backgrounds." In *Family Obligation and Assistance During Adolescence: Contextual Variations and Developmental Implications*. Edited by Andrew J. Fuligni, 61–76. San Francisco: Jossey-Bass, 2001.

Fuligni, Andrew J., and Krista Perreira. "Immigration and Adaptation." In *Handbook of U.S. Latino Psychology, Developmental and Community-Based Perspectives*. Edited by Francisco A. Villaruel, Gustavo Carlo, Josefina M. Grau, Margarita Azmita, Natasha J. Cabrera, and T. Jaime Chahin, 99–113. Thousand Oaks: Sage Publications, 2009.

Fuligni, Andrew J., and Melissa Witkow. "The Postsecondary Educational Progress of Youth from Immigrant Families." *Journal of Research on Adolescence* 14, no. 2 (2004): 159–83.

Furnham, Adrian, and Stephen Bochner. *Culture Shock: Psychological Reactions to Unfamiliar Environments*. London: Methuen, 1986.

Furrer, Carrie, and Ellen Skinner. "Sense of Relatedness as a Factor in Children's Academic Engagement and Performance." *Journal of Educational Psychology* 95 (2003): 148–62.

Furstenberg, Frank F., and Mary Elizabeth Hughes. "Social Capital and Successful Development Among At-risk Youth." *Journal of Marriage and the Family* 57 (1995): 580–92.

Gabarino, James. *Children and Families in the Social Environment*, 2nd ed. New York: Walter de Gruyter., Inc, 1992.

Galabuzi, Grace-Edward. *Canada's Economic Apartheid: The Social Exclusion of Racialized Groups in the New Century*. Toronto: Canadian Scholars' Press, 2006.

García Coll, Cynthia. "Cuando se Convierte la Cultura en un Factor de Riesgo Contextual?" En *Factores de riesgo en psicopatología del desarrollo*. Edited by E.L. Ezpeleta. Barcelona: Masson, 2005.

Garner, Catherine L., and Stephen W. Raudenbush. "Neighbourhood Effects on Educational Attainment: A Multilevel Analysis." *Sociology of Education* 64, no. 4 (1991): 251–62.

Ghuman, Paul A. Singh. *Double Loyalties: South Asian Adolescents in the West*. Cardiff: University of Wales Press, 2003.

Gibson, Margaret. *Accommodation Without Assimilation: Punjabi Sikh Immigrants in an American High School*. Ithaca: Cornell University Press, 1988.

Gibson, Margaret A., Patricia C. Gándara, and Jill Peterson Koyama. "The Role of Peers in the Schooling of U.S. Mexican Youth." In *School Connections: U.S. Mexican Youth, Peers, and School Achievement*. Edited by Margaret A. Gibson, Patricia C. Gándara, and Jill Peterson Koyama, 1–17. New York: Teachers College Press, 2004.

Gilroy, Paul. *There Ain't no Black in the Union Jack*. London: Routledge, 1987.

Gimpel, James C., and James R. Edwards, Jr. *The Congressional Politics of Immigration Reform*. Boston: Allyn & Bacon, 1999.

Gimpel, James G., and J. Celeste Lay. "Political Socialization and Reactions to Immigration-related Diversity in Rural America." *Rural Sociology* 73, no. 2 (2008): 180–204.

Gittel, Ross J., and Avis Vidal. *Community Organizing: Building Social Capital as a Development Strategy*. Thousand Oaks: Sage, 1998.

Glick Schiller, Nina, Linda Basch, and Christina Blanc Szanton. *Towards a Transnational Perspective on Migration: Race, Class, Ethnicity and Nationalism Reconsidered*. New York: New York Academy of Sciences, 1992.

Gold, Steven J. *From the Worker's State to the Golden State: Jews from the Former Soviet Union in California*. Boston: Allyn & Bacon, 1995.

Goldring, Luin. "The Power of Status in Transnational Social Fields." In *Transnationalism From Below*. Edited by Michael Peter Smith and Luis Eduardo Guarnizo, 165–95. London: Transactions Publishers, 1998.

Goodenow, Carol, and Kathleen E. Grady. "The Relationship of School Belonging and Friends' Values to Academic Motivation Among Urban Adolescent Students." *The Journal of Experimental Education* 62 (1993): 60–71.

Gozdziak, Elzbieta N., and Micah Bump. "Poultry, Apples, and New Immigrants in the Rural Communities of the Shenandoah Valley: An Ethnographic Case Study." *International Migration* 42, no. 1 (2004): 149–64.

Granovetter, Mark S. "The Strength of Weak Ties." *American Journal of Sociology* 78 (1973): 1360–80.

Guimond, Serge, Douglas L. Palmer, and Guy Bégin. "Education, Academic Program and Intergroup Attitudes." *Review of Sociology and Anthropology* 26, no. 2 (1989): 193–216.

Hagan, John, Ross MacMillan, and Blair Wheaton. "The Life Course Effects of Family Migration on Children." *American Sociological Review* 61, no. 3 (1996): 368–85.

Hakuta, Kenji, Yuko Goto Butler, and Daria Witt. *How Long Does It Take English Learners to Attain Proficiency?* University of California Linguistic Minority Research Institute Policy Report 2000–1. 2000.

Halseth, Greg R., and Laura Ryser. *Service Provision in Rural and Small Town Places: A Report for Mackenzie, British Columbia.* Montreal: Initiative on the New Economy, Project of the Canadian Rural Revitalization Foundation, Concordia University, 2006.

Han, Gil-Soo, and John S. Humphreys. "Overseas-trained Doctors in Australia: Community Integration and Their Intention to Stay in a Rural Community." *Australian Journal of Rural Health* 13, no. 4 (2005): 236–41.

Harker, Kathryn. "Immigrant Generation, Assimilation, and Adolescent Psychological Well-being: The Importance of Mediating Factors." *Social Forces* 79, no. 3 (2001): 969–1004.

Harwood, Jake. "Alienation: American Attitudes Towards Immigrants." *Public Opinion* 6 (1983): 49–51.

Hatton, Timothy J., and Andrew Leigh. *Immigrants Assimilate as Communities, Not Just as Individuals.* CEPR Discussion Papers 547. London: Centre for Economic Policy Research, 2007.

Hayes-Bautista, David E. *La Nueva California : Latinos in the Golden State.* Berkeley: University of California Press, 2004.

Hébert, Yvonne. "Transculturalism Among Canadian Youth: Focus on Strategic Competence and Social Capital." In *Belongings and Social Capital Among Youth in Comparative Perspective.* Edited by Dirk Hoerder, Yvonne Hébert, and Irina Schmitt, 103–28. Toronto: University of Toronto Press, 2005.

Hébert, Yvonne, Jennifer Wen-Shya Lee, Shirley Xiaohong Sun, and Chiara Berti. "Relational Citizenship as Social Networks: Immigrant Youth's Maps of their Friendships." *Encounters on Education* 4 (fall, 2003): 83–106.

Himelfarb, Alex. "The Social Characteristics of One-industry Towns in Canada." In *Little Communities and Big Industries.* Edited by Roy T. Bowles, 16–43. Toronto: Butterworth, 1982.

Horwitz, Elaine K., Michæl B. Horwitz, and Joann A. Cope. "Foreign Language Classroom Anxiety." *Modern Language Journal* 70 (1986): 125–32.

Houle, Rene. "Secondary Migration of New Immigrants to Canada." *Our Diverse Cities* 3 (2007): 16–24.

Howard, Rhoda E. "Being Canadian: Citizenship in Canada." *Canadian Studies* 2 (1998): 133–52.

Hsin-Chun Tsai, Jenny. "Xenophobia, Ethnic Community and Immigrant Youths' Friendship Network Formation. *Adolescence* 41, no. 162 (2006): 285–98.

Hum, Derek, and Wayne Simpson. "Closing the Wage Gap: Economic Assimilation of Canadian Immigrants Reconsidered." *Journal of International Migration and Integration* 1, no. 4 (2000): 427–41.

Hutchison, Bruce. *The Unknown Country: Canada and her People.* New York: Coward-McCann, Inc, 1942.

Hyman, James. "Exploring Social Capital and Civic Engagement to Create a Framework for Community Building." *Applied Developmental Science* 6, no. 4 (2002): 196–202.

Ighodaro, MacDonald E. *Migration, Exclusion, and Anti-Racist Practice.* Halifax: Fernwood, 2007.

Isajiw, Wsevolod. *Understanding Diversity: Ethnicity and Race in the Canadian Context.* Toronto: Thompson Educational Publishing, 1999.

Jencks, Christopher, and Susan E. Mayer. "The Social Consequences of Growing Up in a Poor Neighbourhood." In *Inner-City Poverty in the United States.* Edited by Laurence E. Lynn and Michael G. H. McGeary, 111–86. Washington: National Academy Press, 1990.

Jessor, Richard, and Shirley L. Jessor. *Problem Behavior and Psychosocial Development: A Longitudinal Study of Youth.* New York: Academic Press, 1977.

Jones, Curtis J., and Edison J. Trickett. "Immigrant Adolescents Behaving as Cultural Brokers: A Study of Families from the Former Soviet Union." *The Journal of Social Psychology* 145, no. 4 (2005): 405–27.

Kahane, Reuven. "Informal Agencies of Socialization and the Integration of Immigrant Youth into Society: An Example from Israel." *International Migration Review* 20, no. 1 (1986): 21–39.

Kalin, Rudy, and John W. Berry. "Ethnic and Multicultural Attitudes." In *Ethnicity and Culture in Canada: The Research Landscape.* Edited by John W. Berry and Jean Laponce, 293–321. Toronto: University of Toronto Press, 1994.

Kanu, Yatta. "Educational Needs and Barriers for African Refugee Students in Manitoba." *Canadian Journal of Education* 31, no. 4 (2008): 915–40.

Kao, Grace. "Social Capital and its Relevance to Minority and Immigrant Populations." *Sociology of Education* 77 (2004): 172–5.

Kao, Grace, and Jennifer Thompson. "Racial and Ethnic Stratification in Educational Achievement and Attainment." *Annual Review of Sociology* 29 (2003): 417–42.

Kao, Grace, and Marta Tienda. "Optimism and Achievement: The Educational Performance of Immigrant Youth." In *The New Immigration: An Interdisciplinary Reader*. Edited by Marcelo M. Suárez-Orozco, Carola Suárez-Orozco, and Desiree Qin-Hilliard, 331–4. New York: Taylor & Francis Group, 2005.

Kaplan, Kalman J. "On the Ambivalence-indifference Problem in Attitude Theory and Measurement: A Suggested Modification of the Semantic Differential Technique." *Psychological Bulletin* 77, no. 5 (1972): 361–72.

Katz, Irwin, and R. Glen Hass. "Racial Ambivalence and American Value Conflict: Correlational and Priming Studies of Dual Cognitive Structures." *Journal of Personality and Social Psychology* 55 (1988): 893–905.

Kazemipur, Abdolmohammad. "A Canadian Exceptionalism? Trust and Diversity in Canadian Cities." *Journal of International Migration and Integration* 7, no. 2 (2006): 219–40.

Kazemipur, Abdolmohammad, and Shiva S. Halli. "The Colour of Poverty: A Study of the Poverty of Ethnic and Immigrant Groups in Canada." *International Migration* 38, no. 1 (2000): 69–87.

– "Immigrants and New Poverty: The Case of Canada." *International Migration Review* 35, no. 4 (2001): 1129–56.

– "The Changing Colour of Poverty in Canada." *Canadian Review of Sociology and Anthropology* 38, no. 2 (2001): 217–38.

Kegler, Michelle Crozier, Roy F. Oman, Sarah K. Vesely, Kenneth R. McLeroy, Cheryl B. Aspy, Sharon Rodine, and LaDonna Marshall. "Relationships Among Youth Assets and Neighborhood and Community Resources." *Health Education and Behavior* 32 (2005): 380–97.

Kember, David, Kenneth Lee, and Natalia Li. "Cultivating a Sense of Belonging in Part-time Students." *International Journal of Lifelong Education* 20, no. 4 (2006): 326–41.

Kenyon, C. Elaine. "Immigrant Women: Journeying Towards Harmony." Master's Thesis, University of New Brunswick, 2000.

Kibria, Nazli. "Household Structure and Family Ideology: The Dynamics of Immigrant Economic Adaptation Among Vietnamese Refugees." *Social Problems* 41, no. 1 (1994): 81–96.

Kilbride, Kenise M. *A Review of the Literature on the Human, Social and Cultural Capital of Immigrant Children and their Families with Implications for Teacher Education.* 2000. http://ceris.metropolis.net/Virtual%20Library/education/WK%2013_Kilbride.pdf (accessed November 6, 2010).

Ko, Linda K., and Krista Perreira. "It Turned My World Upside Down: Latino Youths' Perspectives on Immigration." *Journal of Adolescent Research* 25 (2010): 465–93.

Koc, Mustafa, and Fernando Nunes. *Newcomer Youth at Risk in the School System.* Toronto: Joint Centre for Excellence for Research on Immigration and Settlement (CERIS) and Citizenship and Immigration Canada, 2001.

Kohen, Dafna, Clyde Hertzman, and Jeanne Brooks-Gunn. *Neighbourhood Influences on Children's School Readiness.* Ottawa: Strategic Policy. Applied Research Branch. Human Resources Development Canada. Working Paper. 1998. http://www.lanarkearlyyears.com/filesharing/files/93.pdf (accessed November 6, 2010).

Kouritzin, Sandra. "Immigrant Women Redefine Access to ESL Classes: Contradiction and Ambivalence." *Journal of Multilingual and Multicultural Development* 21, no. 1 (2000): 14–32.

Krahn, Harvey, Tracey Derwing, and Baha Abu-Laban. "The Retention of Newcomers in Second- and Third-tier Cities in Canada." Edmonton: Prairie Centre of Excellence for Research on Immigration and Integration, University of Alberta, 2003. Working Paper series no. WP01–03.

Krahn, Harvey, and Alison Taylor. "Resilient Teenagers: Explaining the High Educational Aspirations of Visible Minority Immigrant Youth in Canada." *Journal of International Migration and Integration* 6, no. 3–4 (2005): 405–34.

Kretzmann, John P., and John L. McKnight. *Building Communities from the Inside Out.* Evanston: Center for Urban Affairs and Policy Research, Northwestern University, 1993.

Kroger, Jane. *Identity Development: Adolescence Through Adulthood,* 2nd edition. Newbury Park: Sage Publications, 2007.

Kunz, Jean Lock. *Being Young and Visible: Labour Market Access Among Immigrant and Visible Minority Youth.* Ottawa: Human Resources and Skills Development Canada, SP–581–08–03E, 2003. http://www.hrsdc.gc.ca/eng/cs/sp/hrsd/prc/publications/research/2003-002376/page04.shtml (accessed November 17, 2010).

Kunz, Jean Lock, Anne Milan, and Sylvain Schetagne. *Unequal Access: A Canadian Profile of Racial Differences in Education, Employment and*

Income. Toronto: Canadian Race Relation Foundation, 2000. http://
atwork.settlement.org/downloads/Unequal_Access.pdf (accessed November 17, 2010).

Kymlicka, Will. "Well Done, Canada: Multiculturalism is Working." *Globe
and Mail*. 1 December 2007.

– *Finding our Way: Rethinking Ethnocultural Relations in Canada*. Don
Mills: Oxford University Press, 1998.

LaFromboise, Teresa, Hardin L. K. Coleman, and Jennifer Gerton. "Psychological Impact of Biculturalism: Evidence and Theory." *Psychological
Bulletin* 114, no. 33 (1993): 395–412.

Lalonde, Richard N., Janelle M. Jones, and Mirella L. Stroink. "Racial
Identity, Racial Attitudes, and Race Socialization Among Black Canadian Parents." *Canadian Journal of Behavioural Science* 40, no. 3
(2008): 129–39.

Lannegrand-Willems, Lyda, and Harke A. Bosma. "Identity Development-
in-context. The School as an Important Context for Identity Development." *Identity: An International Journal of Theory and Research* 6, no.
1 (2006): 85–113.

Lapinski, John S., Pia Peltola, Greg Shaw, and Alan Yang. "The Polls
Trends: Immigrants and Immigration." *Public Opinion Quarterly* 61
(1997): 556–85.

Lechner, Frank J. "Fundamentalism and Sociocultural Revitalization."
Sociological Analysis 46 (1985): 243–60.

Lee, Courtland C. "Culturally Responsive School Counselors and Programs: Addressing the Needs of All Students." *Professional School
Counseling* 4 (2001): 257–61.

Lerner, Richard M., and Peter L. Benson. *Developmental Assets and Asset-
Building Communities*. New York: Kluwer Academic/Plenum Publishers, 2003.

Leventhal, Tama, and Jeanne Brooks-Gunn. "The Neighborhoods They
Live: The Effects of Neighbourhood Residence on Child and Adolescent
Outcomes." *Psychological Bulletin* 126, no. 2 (2000): 309–37.

Levitt, Peggy. "Transnational Migration: Taking Stock and Future Directions." *Global Networks* 1, no. 3 (2001): 195–216.

Li, Peter S. *Destination Canada: Immigration Debates and Issues*. Oxford:
Oxford University Press, 2003.

– *Deconstructing Canada's Discourse of Immigrant Integration*. Metropolis Prairie Centre of Excellence Working Paper No. WP04–03, 2003.
http://pcerii.metropolis.net/WorkingPapers/WP04–03.pdf (accessed November 5, 2010).

Lin, Nan. *Social Capital, a Theory of Social Structure and Action*. New York: Cambridge University Press, 2001.

Long, Neyda H. "Conceptions of Political Participation Among Recent Latin-American Newcomers to Canada." In *Ruptures, Continuities, and Re-Learning: The Political Participation of Latin Americans in Canada*. Edited by Jorge Ginieniewicz and Daniel Schugurensky. Toronto: Transformative Learning Centre, OISE, 2006.

Long, Neyda H., and Benjamin Amaya. "'We'" and 'the Others:' Cultural Identity Among Latin Americans in Rural New Brunswick." *Our Diverse Cities* 3 (2007): 155–60.

Long, Neyda H., and Andrew Hughes. "The Political Integration of Newcomers of Latin American Origin to Canada: An Examination of the Role and Relevance of Prior Knowledge." *Encounters on Education* 4 (2003): 65–82.

Ma, Xin. "Sense of Belonging to School: Can Schools Make a Difference?" *The Journal of Educational Research* 96, no. 6 (2003): 340–49.

Mackey, Eva. *The House of Difference: Cultural Politics and National Identity in Canada*. Toronto: University of Toronto Press, 2002.

MacIntyre, Peter D., and Robert C. Gardner. "Methods and Results in the Study of Anxiety and Language Learning: A Review of the Literature." *Language Learning* 41, no. 1 (1991): 85–117.

Mahler, Sarah. "Constructing International Relations: The Role of Transnational Migrants and Other Non-state Actors." *Identities: Global Studies in Culture and Power* 7, no. 2 (2000): 197–232.

Maio, Gregory R., David W. Bell, and Victoria M. Esses. "Ambivalence and Persuasion: The Processing of Messages About Immigrant Groups." *Journal of Experimental Social Psychology* 32 (1996): 513–36.

Marcia, James E. "Identity in Adolescence." In *Handbook of Adolescent Psychology*. Edited by Joseph J. Adelson, 159–87. New York: Wiley, 1980.

Marks, Helen M. "Student Engagement in Instructional Activity: Patterns in the Elementary, Middle, and High School Years." *American Educational Research Journal* 37, no. 1 (2000): 153–84.

Martínez, M. Loreto, Maureen Black, and Raymond H. Starr. "Factorial Structure of the Perceived Neighbourhood Scale (OPNS): A Test of Longitudinal Variance." *Journal of Community Psychology* 30, no. 1 (2002): 23–43.

McGhee, Derek. "Getting 'Host' Communities on Board: Finding the Balance Between 'Managed Migration' and 'Managed Settlement' in Community Cohesion Strategies." *Journal of Ethnic and Migration Studies* 32, no. 1 (2006): 111–27.

McMillan, David W., and David M. Chavis. "Sense of Community: A Definition and Theory." *Journal of Community Psychology* 14 (1986): 6–23.

McQuillan, Jeffrey, and Lucy Tse. "Child Language Brokering in Linguistic Minority Communities: Effects on Cultural Interaction, Cognition, and Literacy." *Language and Education* 9 (1995): 195–215.

Merriam, Sharan B. *Case Study Research in Education: A Qualitative Approach*. San Francisco: Jossey-Bass, 1988.

Miedema, Baukje, and Nancy Nason-Clark. "Second-class Status: An Analysis of the Lived Experiences of Immigrant Women in Fredericton." *Canadian Ethnic Studies* 21, no. 2 (1989): 63–72.

Moran, Siobhan, Peter K. Smith, David Thompson, and Irene Whitney. "Ethnic Differences in Experiences of Bullying: Asian and White Children." *British Journal of Educational Psychology* 63 (1993): 431–40.

Muchnick, Arlene G., and David E. Wolfe. "Attitudes and Motivations of American Students of Spanish." *The Canadian Modern Language Review* 88 (1982): 254–61.

Mulder, Marlene, and Harvey Krahn. "Individual and Community-level Determinants of Support for Immigration and Cultural Diversity in Canada." *The Canadian Review of Sociology and Anthropology* 42, no. 4 (2005): 421–44.

Muñoz-Sandoval, Ana F., Jim Cummins, G. Alvarado, and Mary L. Ruef. *Bilingual Verbal Ability Tests*. Itasca: Riverside Publishing, 1998.

Murray, Deborah. "Spinning Their Own Webs: An Exploration of English Second Language Learning for Newcomers in New Brunswick." Master's Thesis, University of New Brunswick, 2006.

National Research Council. *Engaging Schools: Fostering High School Students' Motivation to Learn*. Washington: National Academies Press, 2004.

Nelson, William. "Addressing Rural Ethics Issues." *Healthcare Exec* 19 (2004): 36–37.

New Brunswick. "Be Our Future: New Brunswick's Population Growth Strategy." Government of New Brunswick Population Growth Secretariat, February 2008. http://www.gnb.ca/3100/Promos/PS/Strategy-e.pdf (accessed December 13, 2008).

Nguyen, Huong. "Acculturation in the United States." In *Cambridge Handbook of Acculturation Psychology*. Edited by David L. Sam and John W. Berry, 311–30. Cambridge: Cambridge University Press, 2006.

Noel, Julia. "Voices in Healthcare: Afro-Caribbean Women's Experiences."
Master's Thesis, Dalhousie University, 1996.

Noland, Carey M. "Auto-photography as Research Practice: Identity and
Self-esteem Research." *Journal of Research Practice* 2, no. 1 (2006):
1–19.

Nunes, Fernando. *Problems and Adjustments of the Portuguese Immigrant
Family in Canada*. Porto: Secretaria de Estado das Comunidades Portuguesas, 1986.

Nunes, Fernando. "Marginalisation, Social Reproduction, and Academic
Underachievement: The Case of the Portuguese Community in Can-
ada." In *The Education of Portuguese Children in Britain: Insights from
Research and Practice in England and Overseas*. Edited by Guida de
Abreu, Tony Cline, and Hannah Lambert, 122–58. Portugal: Ministry
of Education, 2003.

Obach, Brian K. "Demonstrating the Social Construction of Race." *Teaching Sociology* 27, no. 3 (1999): 252–7.

Ochocka, Joanna. *Pathways to Success: Immigrant Youth in High School*.
Kitchener: Centre for Research and Education in Human Services,
2006. http://www.communitybasedresearch.ca/resources/Pathways%20
to%20Success%20Immigrant%20Youth%20at%20School%20
Final%20Report.pdf (accessed November 4, 2010).

Olsen, Laurie. "Learning English and Learning America: Immigrants in the
Center of a Storm." *Theory into Practice* 39, no. 4 (2000): 196–202.

Olson, James M., and Mark P. Zanna. "Attitudes and Attitude Change."
Annual Review of Psychology 44 (1993): 117–54.

Omnifacts Bristol Research. *Bring 'em on Carefully: Excerpt from the
Inside Out Report* 3 (2006): 2.

Orum, Anthony M. "Circles of Influence and Chains of Command: The
Social Processes Whereby Ethnic Communities Influence Host Societies." *Social Forces* 84, no. 2 (2005): 921–39.

Osterman, Karen F. "Students' Need for Belonging in the School Community." *Review of Educational Research* 70, no. 3 (2000): 323–67.

Palmer, Douglas L. "Prejudice and Intolerance in Canada." In *New Faces
in the Crowd: Economic and Social Impacts of Immigration*. Edited by
the Economic Council of Canada, 103–19. Ottawa: Economic Council
of Canada, 1991.

Palmer, Howard. "Reluctant Hosts: Anglo-Canadian Views of Multiculturalism in the Twentieth Century." In *Immigration in Canada: Historical Perspectives*. Edited by Gerald Tulchinsky, 312–13. Toronto: Copp
Clark Longran, Ltd, 1994.

Park, Robert E. *Old World Traits Transplanted*. New York: Arno Press, 1969.

Parker, Patricia, John Hagan, and Ronit Dinovitzer. "Choice and Circumstance: Social Capital and Planful Competence in the Attainments of Immigrant Youth." *Canadian Journal of Sociology* 28, no. 4 (2003): 463–88.

Parra, Pilar A., and Max J. Pfeffer. "New Immigrants in Rural Communities: The Challenges of Integration." *Social Text* 24 (3 88, 2006): 81–98.

Partida, Jorge. "The Effects of Immigration on Children in the Mexican-American Community." *Child and Adolescent Social Work Journal* 13, no. 3 (1996): 241–54.

Pendakur, Krishna, and Ravi Pendakur. "The Colour of Money: Earnings Differentials Among Ethnic Groups in Canada." *Canadian Journal of Economics* 31, no. 3 (1998): 518–48.

Pepler, Debra J., Wendy Craig, and Jennifer A. Connolly. *School Experiences of Immigrant and Ethnic Minority Youth: Risk and Protective Factors in Coping with Bullying and Harassment*. CERIS Research Report. Toronto: Joint Centre for Excellence for Research on Immigration and Settlement (CERIS), 1999. http://ceris.metropolis.net/Virtual%20Library/education/pepler1/pepler1.html (accessed November 6, 2010).

Pettigrew, Thomas F. "The Inter-group Contact Hypothesis Revisited." In *Contact and Conflict in Inter-Group Encounters*, eds Miles Hewstone and Rupert J. Brown, 169–95. Oxford: Blackwell, 1986.

– "Generalized Inter-group Contact Effects on Prejudice." *Personality and Social Psychology Bulletin* 23, no. 2 (1997): 173–85.

Phan, Tan. "Life in School: Narratives of Resiliency Among Vietnamese-Canadian Youths." *Adolescence* 38 (2003): 555–66.

Phinney, Jean S. "Understanding Ethnic Diversity: The Role of Ethnic Identity." *American Behavioral Scientist* 40, no. 2 (1996): 143–52.

Phinney, Jean S., Gabriel Horenczyk, Karmela Liebkind, and Paul Vedder. "Ethnic Identity, Immigration, and Well-being: An Interactional Perspective." *Journal of Social Issues* 57, no. 3 (2001): 493–510.

Portes, Alejandro. "Immigration Theory for a New Century: Some Problems and Opportunities." *International Migration Review* 31, no. 4, Special Issue: Immigrant Adaptation and Native-Born Responses in the Making of Americans (1997): 799–825.

– "Social Capital: Its Origins and Applications in Modern Sociology." *Annual Review of Sociology* 24 (1998): 1–24.

– "An Enduring Vision: The Melting Pot That Did Happen." *International Migration Review* 34 (2000): 243–8.

Portes, Alejandro, and Rubén G. Rumbaut. *Immigrant America: A Portrait*. Berkeley: University of California Press, 1990.

Portes, Alejandro, and Richard Schauffler. "Language and the Second Generation: Bilingualism Yesterday and Today." *The International Migration Review* 28 (1994): 640–61.

Portes, Alejandro, and Min Zhou. "The New Second Generation: Segmented Assimilation and its Variants Among Post-1965 Immigrant Youth." *The Annals of the American Academy of Political and Social Science* 530, no. 1 (1993): 74–96.

Pretty, Grace M.H., Lisa Andrewes, and Chris Collett. "Exploring Adolescents' Sense of Community and its Relationship to Loneliness." *Journal of Community Psychology* 22 (1994): 346–58.

Pretty, Grace M.H., Colleen Conroy, Jason Dugay, Karen Fowler, and Diane Williams. "Sense of Community and its Relevance to Adolescents of All Ages." *Journal of Community Psychology* 24, no. 4 (1996): 365–79.

Prezza, Miretta P., Matilde Amici, Tizianna Roberti, and Gloria Tedeschi. "Sense of Community Referred to the Whole Town: Its Relations with Loneliness, Life Satisfaction and Area of Residence." *Journal of Community Psychology* 29, no. 1 (2001): 29–52.

Puig, Maria Elena. "The Adultification of Refugee Children: Implications for Cross-cultural Social Work Practice." *Journal of Human Behavior in the Social Environment* 5 (2002): 85–95.

Putnam, Robert D. "The Prosperous Community: Social Capital and Community Life." *The American Prospect* 1 (1993): 35–42.

– "Bowling Alone: America's Declining Social Capital." *The Journal of Democracy* 6, no. 1 (1995): 65–78.

– *Bowling Alone the Collapse and Revival of American Community*. New York: Simon & Schuster, 2000.

– "E Pluribus Unum: Diversity and Community in the Twenty-first Century. The 2006 Johan Skytte Prize Lecture." *Scandinavian Political Studies* 30, no. 2 (2007): 137–74.

Quaicoe, Lloydetta. "Canadian Heritage in the Atlantic Region: Engagement with the Multicultural Community – From Research to Practice: Immigrant and Refugee Children's Need to Belong." *Our Diverse Cities* 5 (2008): 45–9.

Raffo, Carlo and Michelle Reeves. "Youth Transitions and Social Exclusion: Developments in Social Capital Theory." *Journal of Youth Studies* 3, no. 2 (2000): 147–66.

Rajiva, Mythili. "Bridging the Generation Gap: Exploring the Differences Between Immigrant Parents and Their Canadian-born Children." *Canadian Issues* (Spring 2005): 25–8.

- "Brown Girls, White Worlds: Adolescence and the Making of Racialized Selves." *The Canadian Review of Sociology and Anthropology* 43, no. 2 (2006): 165–83.
Ramcharan, Subhas. *Racism: Non-Whites in Canada*. Toronto: Butterworths, 1982.
Rankin, Bruce H., and James M. Quane. "Social Contexts and Urban Adolescent Outcomes: The Interrelated Effects of Neighborhoods, Families, and Peers on African-American Youth." *Social Problems* 49, no. 1 (2002): 79–100.
Ream, Robert K. and, Gregory Palardy. "Re-examining Social Class Differences in the Availability and the Educational Utility of Parental Social Capital." *American Educational Research Journal* 45, no. 2 (2008): 238–73.
Reimer, Bill. "Immigration in the New Rural Economy." *Our Diverse Cities* 3 (2007): 3–8.
Reitz, Jeffrey G. *Warmth of the Welcome: The Social Causes of Economic Success in Different Nations*. Boulder: Westview Press, 1998.
- ed. *Host Societies and the Reception of Immigrants*. San Diego: Center for Comparative Immigration Research, 2003.
- "Tapping Immigrants' Skills: New Directions for Canadian Immigration Policy in the Knowledge Economy." *IRPP Choices* 11, no. 1 (2005): 1–18.
Reitz, Jeffrey G., and Rupa Banerjee. "Racial Inequality, Social Cohesion, and Policy Issues in Canada." In *Belonging? Diversity, Recognition and Shared Citizenship in Canada*. Edited by Keith Banting, Thomas J. Courchene, and F. Leslie, 489–545. Montreal: Institute for Research on Public Policy, 2007.
Rhodes, Jean, Jean B. Grossman, and Jennifer Roffman. "The Rhetoric and Reality of Youth Mentoring." *New Directions for Youth Development* 93 (Spring 2002): 9–20.
Richards, Lyn. *Handling Qualitative Data: a Practical Guide*. London: Sage, 2005.
Rieger, Jon H., and J. Allen Beegle. "The Integration of Rural Migrants in New Settings." *Rural Sociology* 29, no. 1 (1974): 42–55.
Roth, Jodie L., and Jeanne Brooks-Gunn. "Youth Development Programs: Risk, Prevention and Policy." *Journal of Adolescent Health* 32 (2003): 170–82.
- "Youth Development Programs and Healthy Development: A Review and Next Steps." In *Reducing Adolescent Risk: Toward an Integrated*

Approach. Edited by Daniel Romer, 355–65. Thousand Oaks: Sage Publications, 2003.

Ruddick, Elizabeth. "Immigrant Economic Performance." *Canadian Issues* 5 (2003): 16–17.

Rumbaut, Ruben G., and Alejandro Portes. *Ethnicities: Children of Immigrants in America*. Berkeley: University of California Press and Russell Sage, 2001.

Ryabov, Igor. "The Role of Peer Social Capital in Educational Assimilation of Immigrant Youths." *Sociological Inquiry* 79, no. 4 (2009): 453–80.

Sampson, Robert J. "How do Communities Undergird or Undermine Human Development? Relevant Contexts and Social Mechanisms." In *Does It Take a Village? Community Effects on Children, Adolescents, and Families*. Edited by Alan Booth and Nan Crouter, 3–30. Mahwah: Lawrence Erlbaum Associates, Publishers, 2001.

Sampson, Robert J., Jeffrey D. Morenoff, and Felton Earls. "Beyond Social Capital: Spatial Dynamics of Collective Efficiency for Children." *American Sociological Review* 64, no. 5 (1999): 633–60.

Sampson, Robert J., Jeffrey D. Morenoff, and Thomas Gannon-Rowley. "Assessing Neighborhood Effects: Social Processes and New Directions in Research." *Annual Review of Sociology* 28 (2002): 443–78.

Sampson, Robert J., Stephen Raudenbush, and Felton Earls. "Neighborhoods and Violent Crime: A Multilevel Study of Collective Efficacy." *Science* 277 (1997): 918–24.

Samuel, John. "Barriers to Attracting and Retaining Immigrants in Atlantic Canada." In *Rendez-vous immigration 2004: Enjeux et défis de l'immigration au Nouveau-Brunswick / Immigration in New Brunswick Issues and Challenges*. Edited by Hélène Destrempes and Joe Ruggeri, 185–244. Fredericton: Policy Studies Centre, University of New Brunswick, 2005.

Sarason, Seymour B. *Work, Aging, and Social Change: Professionals and the One-Life One Career Imperative*. New York: Free Press, 1977.

Sassen, Saskia. "America's Immigration Problem." *World Policy*, 6 (Fall 1989): 811–32.

Savoie, D.J. *Visiting Grandchildren: Economic Development in the Maritimes*. Toronto: University of Toronto Press, 2006.

Scales, Peter C., Peter L. Benson, Nancy Leffert, and Dale A. Blyth. "Contribution of Developmental Assets to the Prediction of Thriving Among Adolescents." *Applied Developmental Science* 4, no. 1 (2000): 27–46.

Scales, Peter C., and Nancy Leffert. *Developmental Assets*. Minneapolis:
     Search Institute, 1999.
Scales, Peter C., Nancy Lefert, and Renee Vraa. "The Relation of Com-
     munity Developmental Attentiveness to Adolescent Health." *American
     Journal of Health Behavior* 27 (Suppl. 1 2003): S22-S34.
Glick Schiller, Nina, Linda Basch, and Cristina Blanc Szanton. "From
     Immigrant to Transmigrant: Theorizing Transnational Migration."
     Anthropological Quarterly 68, no. 1, (1995): 48–63.
Simard, Myriam. "Immigrant Integration Outside Montreal." *Our Diverse
     Cities* 3 (2007): 109–14.
Simon, Rita J., and Susan H. Alexander. *The Ambivalent Welcome: Print
     Media, Public Opinion, and Immigration*. Westport: Praeger, 1993.
Smith, Susan. "Immigration and Nation-building in Canada and the
     United Kingdom." In *Construction of Race, Place, and Nation*. Edited
     by Peter Jackson and Jan Penrose, 50–77. Minneapolis: University of
     Minnesota Press, 1993.
Solomon, Daniel, Victor Battisch, Marilyn Watson, Eric Schaps, and Cath-
     erine Lewis. "A Six-district Study of Educational Change: Direct and
     Mediated Effects on Child Development." *Social Psychology of Educa-
     tion* 4 (2000): 3–51.
Sonn, Christopher C. "Immigrant Adaptation. Understanding the Process
     Through Sense of Community." In *Psychological Sense of Commun-
     ity: Research, Applications and Implications*. Edited by Adrian T. Fisher,
     Christopher C. Sonn, and Brian J. Bishop, 205–22. New York: Plenum
     Publishers, 2002.
Stanton-Salazar, Ricardo. "A Social Capital Framework for Understand-
     ing the Socialisation of Racial Minority Children and Youths." *Harvard
     Educational Review* 67 (1997): 1–40.
– "Social Capital Among Working-class Minority Students." In *School
     Connections: U.S. Mexican Youth, Peers, and School Achievement*.
     Edited by Margaret A. Gibson, Patricia Gándara, and Jill Peterson
     Koyama, 18–38. New York: Teachers College Press, Columbia Univer-
     sity, 2004.
Stanton-Salazar, Ricardo, and Sanford M. Dornbusch. "Social Capital and
     the Reproduction of Inequality: Information Networks Among Mex-
     ican-origin High School Students. *Sociology of Education* 68 (1995):
     116–35.
Stanton-Salazar, Ricardo, and Stephanie Urso Spina. "Adolescent Peer Net-
     works as a Context for Social and Emotional Support." *Youth and Soci-
     ety* 36 (2005): 379–417.

Steel, Heather. "Immigration to New Brunswick, 1945–1971: A Study of Provincial Policy." Master's Thesis, University of New Brunswick, 2004.

– "Where's the Policy? Immigration to New Brunswick, 1945–1971." *Acadiensis* 35, no. 2 (2006): 85–104.

Steinhausen, Cristoph, Cinzia Bearth-Carrari, and Christa Winkler Metzke. "Psychosocial Adaptation of Adolescent Migrants in a Swiss Community Survey." *Social Psychiatry and Psychiatric Epidemiology* 44, no. 4 (2008): 308–16.

Stephan, Walter G., and Cookie White Stephan. "An Integrated Threat Theory of Prejudice." In *Claremont Symposium on Applied Social Psychology*. Edited by Stuart Oskamp, 23–46. Hillsdale: Erlbaum, 2000.

Stephan, Walter G., Oscar Ybama, Carmen Martínez, Joseph Schwartz-wald, and Michal Tur-Kaspa. "Prejudice Toward Immigrants: An Integrated Threat Theory." *Journal of Applied Social Psychology* 29 (1998): 2221–37.

Stephan, Walter G., and John C. Brigham. "Intergroup Contact: Introduction." *Journal of Social Issues* 41, no. 3 (1985): 1–8.

Suárez-Orozco, Carola, Hee Jin Bang, Erin O'Connor, Francisco X. Gaytán, Juliana Pakes, and Jean Rhodes. "Academic Trajectories of Newcomer Immigrant Youth." *Developmental Psychology* 46, no. 3 (2010): 602–18.

Suárez-Orozco, Carola, Marcelo Suárez-Orozco, and Irina Todorova. *Learning a New Land: Immigrant Students in American Society.* Cambridge: Belknap Press of Harvard University Press, 2008.

Suarez-Orozco, Marcelo M. "Globalisation, Immigration and Education: The Research Agenda." *Harvard Educational Review* 71 (2001): 345–66.

Suárez-Orozco, Marcelo M., Carola Suárez-Orozco, and Irina Todorova. "Moving Stories: Immigrant Youth Adapt to Change." *Du Bois Review* 4 (2007): 251–9.

Super, Donald E. "Vocational Development in Adolescence and Early Adulthood: Tasks and Behaviors." In *Career Development: Self-Concept Theory*. Edited by Donald E. Super, 79–95. New York: College Entrance Examination Board, 1963.

Swanson, Louis. "Rural Social Infrastructure." In *Foundations of Rural Development Policy*. Edited by J. Norman Reid, David Sears, Glenn Nelson, Thomas J. Rowley, and Mervin Yetley, 103–22. Boulder: Westview Press, 1992.

Tajfel, Henri, ed. *Differentiation Between Social Groups: Studies in the Social Psychology of Intergroup Relations*. London: Academic Press, 1978.

Tajfel, Henri, and John. C. Turner. "An Integrative Theory of Intergroup Conflict." In *Psychology of Intergroup Relations*. Edited by Stephan Worchel, and W.G. Austin, 2–24. Chicago: Nelson-Hall, 1986.

Taylor, J. Edward, Philip L. Martin, and Michael Fix. *Poverty Amid Prosperity: Immigration and the Changing Face of Rural California*. Washington: The Urban Institute Press, 1996.

Tennent, Lee, Collette Tayler, Ann Farrell, and Carla M. Patterson. "Social Capital and Sense of Community: What Do They Mean for Young Children's Success at School?" In *Proceedings Australian Association for Research in Education (AARE) International Education Research Conference, Sydney Australia*. 2005. www.aare.edu.au/05pap/ten05115.pdf (accessed July 18, 2009).

Thomas, Wayne P., and Virginia P. Collier. *School Effectiveness for Language Minority Students*. National Clearinghouse for English Language Acquisition (NCELA) Resource Collection Series, No. 9, December 1997.

Thompson, Franklin T. "Student Achievement, Selected Environmental Characteristics, and Neighborhood Type." *Urban Review*, 34, no. 3 (2002): 277–92.

Thompson, Megan M., Mark P. Zanna, and Dale W. Griffin. "The Conflicted Individual – Personality-based and Domain-specific Antecedents of Ambivalent Social Attitudes." *Journal of Personality* 63 (1995): 259–88.

Thompson, Nora E., and Andrea G. Gurney. "'He is everything:' Religion's Role in the Lives of Immigrant Youth." *New Directions for Youth Development* 100 (2003): 75–90.

Thornton, Patricia. "The Problem of Out-migration from Atlantic Canada, 1871–1921: A New Look." *Acadiensis* 15, no. 1 (1985): 3–34.

Tocqueville, Alexis de. *Democracy in America*. New York: Everyman's Library, 1835 (republished 1994).

Tramonte, Lucia, and Jon Douglas Willms. "Cultural Capital and its Effects on Education Outcomes." *Economics of Education Review* 29, no. 2 (2010): 200–13.

Tse, Lucy. "Language Brokering in Linguistic Minority Communities: The Case of Chinese- and Vietnamese-American Students." *The Bilingual Research Journal* 20 (1996): 485–98.

Turley, Ruth N. López. "When Do Neighbourhoods Matter? The Role of Race and Neighbourhood Peers." *Social Science Research* 32 (2003): 61–79.

Tyyskä, Vappu. "Parents and Teens in Immigrant Families: Cultural Influences and Material Pressures." *Canadian Diversité Canadienne* 6, no. 2 (2008): 79–83.

Uslaner, Eric M. *The Moral Foundations of Trust.* Cambridge: Cambridge University Press, 2002.

Valenzuela, Angela, and Sanford M. Dornbush. "Familism and Social Capital in the Academic Achievement of Mexican Origin and Anglo Adolescents." *Social Science Quarterly* 75 (1994): 18–36.

Van Ngo, Hieu and Barbara Schleifer. "Immigrant Children and Youth in Focus." *Canadian Issues,* (Spring 2005): 29–33.

Van Oudenhoven, Jan Pieter, Colleen Ward, and Anne-Marie Masgoret. "Patterns of Relations Between Immigrants and Host Societies." *International Journal of Intercultural Relations* 30, no. 6 (2006): 637–51.

Vartanian, Thomas P., and Philip M.Gleason. "Do Neighborhood Conditions Affect High School Dropout and College Graduation Rates?" *Journal of Socio-Economics* 28, no. 1 (1999): 21–42.

Verkuyten, Maykel, and Jochem Thijs. "Multiculturalism Among Minority and Majority Adolescents in the Netherlands." *International Journal of Intercultural Relations* 26 (2002): 91–108.

Vertovec, Steven. "Conceiving and Researching Transnationalism." *Ethnic and Racial Studies* 22, no. 2 (1999): 447–462.

Walker, Barrington. *The History of Immigration and Racism to Canada: Essential Readings.* Toronto: Canadian Scholars' Press, Inc, 2008.

Walters, David, Kelli Phythian, and Paul Anisef. "The Acculturation of Canadian Immigrants: Determinants of Ethnic Identification with the Host Society." *Canadian Review of Sociology* 44, no. 1 (2007): 37–64.

Walton-Roberts, Margaret. "Regional Immigration and Dispersal: Lessons from Small- and Medium-sized Urban Centres in British Columbia." *Our Diverse Cities* 2 (2006): 158–61.

Warren, Mark E. *Democracy and Association.* Princeton: Princeton University Press, 2001.

Watt, David, and Hetty Roessingh. "The Dynamics of ESL Drop-out: Plus Ça Change ..." *Canadian Modern Language Review* 58, no. 2 (2001): 203–23.

Weinfeld, Morton, and Lori Wilkinson. "Immigration, Diversity and Minority Communities." In *Race and Ethnicity in Canada.* Edited by Peter S. Li, 55–87. Toronto: Oxford University Press, 1999.

Weiss Roberts, Laura, John Battaglia, and Richard S. Epstein. "Frontier Ethics: Mental Healthcare Needs and Ethical Dilemmas in Rural Communities." *Psychiatric Services,* 50 (1999): 497–503.

Weisskirch, Robert S., and Sylvia Alatorre Alva. "Language Brokering and the Acculturation of Latino Children." *Hispanic Journal of Behavioral Sciences* 24 (2002): 369–78.

Willms, Jon Douglas. *Monitoring School Performance: A Guide for Educators*. London: Falmer Press, 1992.

– *Student Engagement at School: A Sense of Belonging and Participation*. Paris: Organization for Economic Cooperation and Development, 2003.

Wright-Mills, C. *The Sociological Imagination*. New York: Oxford University Press, 1959.

Youniss, James, Jeffrey A. McLellan, Yang Su, and Miranda Yates. "The Role of Community Service in Identity Development: Normative, Unconventional, and Deviant Orientations." *Journal of Adolescent Research* 14 (1999): 248–61.

Youniss, James, Jeffrey A. McLellan, and Barbara Mazer. "Voluntary Service, Peer Group Orientation, and Civic Engagement." *Journal of Adolescent Research* 16, no. 5 (2001): 456–68.

Zhou, Min. "Growing Up American: The Challenge Confronting Immigrant Children and Children of Immigrants." *Annual Review of Sociology* 23 (1997): 63–95.

Zhou, Min, and Carl L. Bankston III. "Social Capital and the Adaptation of the Second Generation: The Case of Vietnamese Youth in New Orleans." *International Migration Review* 28 (1994): 821–45.

– *Growing up American: How Vietnamese Children Adapt to Life in the United States*. New York: Russell Sage Foundation, 1998.

Index